Fame Without Fortune
Motown Records
—The Al Cleveland Story

Brick Tower Press
Habent Sua Fata Libelli

Brick Tower Press

1230 Park Avenue
New York, New York 10128
Tel: 212-427-7139
bricktower@aol.com • www.BrickTowerPress.com

Library of Congress Cataloging-in-Publication Data
Cleveland, Daryl
Lucido, Burt
Soucy, Glenn
Fame Without Fortune, The Al Cleveland Story
ISBN 978-1-883283-84-1

1. Biography, Songwriters 2. Performing Arts—United States
3. Biography—Business Leaders 4. Motown Records

First Printing, June 2013

Fame Without Fortune Motown Records
—The Al Cleveland Story

Concept by Daryl Cleveland
Original Story by Burt Lucido

Written by Glenn Soucy and Ron Sheffey

Dedication

This book is dedicated to
the memory of Alfred W. Cleveland, Mrs. Ella M. Cleveland,
Ms. Dorothy Danze Cleveland; my children, Mrs. Brittney Cabrea
Cleveland, Daryl R. Cleveland,
Richard J. Frempong and all my grandkids;
and to Ms. Shawna Carter Cleveland

Acknowledgements

A big thank you to Mr. William Smokey Robinson (my Godfather); Mr Berry Gordy Jr.; Ms. Claudette Robinson (my Godmother); Mr. Lawrence H. Williams and family; Mr. Kenny Johnson, brother and friend; Mr. Ted Mills (brother), I love you; Mr. Ron Tyson, Mr. Otis Williams, The late Melvin Franklin—The Temptations; Mr. Renoldo Obie Benson—Four Tops, Uncle Obie; The Jackson Family J5; Mr. Donald McChearn; Mr. Daryl Brown; Mr. Daryl Fitch, brother and friend; Mr. Claude J. Jones Jr.; Alton Williams; Mr. Jimmy Morris; Big Bubba; Easey; Ms. Shawna Carter Cleveland; Mr. Leroy Miles, uncle; The Funk Brothers; Mr. John T. Colby Jr. and family, not only my publisher, but a good friend; Mr. Berry Rothman; The late Frankie Gaye; Mr. Mikito Soto; the late Tie Lee Truitt; Mrs. Janie Bradford-Hobbs; Ms. Sylvia Smith; Ms. Michelle Fitch; Rev. Dr. Geo. A. Fitch and Mrs. Carry Fitch; Mr. James White; Mr. Jeff Everett (Smooth); Ms. Gladys Knight and brother Bubba Night; Mr. Joey Diggs, friend and brother; Uncle Marvin Gaye and Ron Sheffey; Ms. Remedios Marpicio. Thank you. I love you all—Daryl Cleveland

For my father

"Al jumps in the car with Smokey. He pinches the bridge of his nose in an attempt to get himself to calm down and to collect his thoughts. He can't believe it; he is going to meet Berry Gordy, the head of Motown Records. The record company has only been in business for seven years, but it is already clear that it is headed for phenomenal success in the music business. The owner seems to know the ins and outs of it, and is considered a genius by many in the music world."

—Fame Without Fortune, The Al Cleveland Story

Broadcast Music Industry (BMI) presents the 1967 Citation of Achievement for the song "I Second That Emotion," in recognition of popularity in the R & B field.

(pictured l-r) Al Cleveland, Songwriter, George Gordy, A& R Motown Records, Berry Gordy, President of Motown Records, Smokey Robinson, Recording Artist and Songwriter presented by Edward M. Cramer, President of BMI.

(pictured l-r) Tom Ross (friend), Melvin Franklin, Al Cleveland, Otis Williams, and Ron Tyson

Al Cleveland having a meeting at his Motown office. (pictured l-r)
Bobbie Taylor, Al Cleveland, and Lawrence Payton (The Four Tops)

Daryl Cleveland and Smokey Robinson

CHAPTER 1

Pittsburgh, Pennsylvania 1959

The downtown area is crowded with shoppers and pedestrians going home after a long day's work. They are all bundled up in warm wool jackets and thick clothes as the cold wind pushes fallen leaves and a few snowflakes around. The early-setting sun begins to lose its glow against the advancing night, as holiday shoppers struggle to carry all their packages.

Through the crowd walks a tall man wearing a long wool overcoat, with a simple brown suitcase tightly grasped in his hand. His name is Al Cleveland, and standing at six foot three, he is a gentle giant. His skin is the color of caffe latte, and his eyes usually have a special twinkle in them, a sense of adventure and stardom hidden inside. But not this time—butterflies fill his stomach as he thinks about his destiny, and what he must do to get there.

Al weaves his way through all the people and stops in front of the Greyhound bus depot. He stops and looks in through the large picture window. There are only a few people in line to buy tickets—nothing really to stop him, or to change his mind. His eyes focus on his own reflection. He quickly dusts off his jacket and straightens out his clothes before going in.

"You can do this, Al, you can do this," he whispers to himself.

He walks inside the bus depot. The warm air inside the office feels good but does little to settle the butterflies that seem to have launched an assault on his stomach walls. He patiently waits in line to buy a ticket.

"Can I help you?" a young man asks from the desk window, which is protected by brass bars, like a bank window.

Al stares off into the distance, his mind a million miles away.

"Next," the man says a little louder.

Al snaps to and walks up to the ticket window. *This is it. Either go home and admit defeat, or move on.* He reaches into his back pocket and pulls out his wallet. He does his best to keep steady.

"A one-way ticket to New York City, please."

A few minutes later he is watching his suitcase being tossed into the luggage section under the bus. There is no turning around now, nothing left to stop him. He climbs onto the bus and takes a seat near the back. His mind is a whirlwind of emotions as he watches the bus fill up halfway before the driver climbs on board and takes his seat. *Remember that this is your dream, your life, you don't owe anything to anyone,* he thinks to himself.

His eyes widen slightly as the doors close, sealing off his only escape route. He sits up straight and becomes restless as he listens to the sound of the engine while it pulls away from the bus depot. They drive through the city and onto the highway. Al closes his eyes as the city lights fade and darkness slowly encases the bus. The decisions that he made are still fresh on his mind.

* * *

He remembers standing near the doorway of his apartment. The home is decorated nicely for a middle-class family, and it was done through his blood, sweat, and tears, but he cannot take it any longer. There is an unquenchable thirst that will never go away as long as he is there.

His wife Ella is standing just a few feet away, crying. Her stomach is wrenching with emotional pain as the tears roll down. She is wearing a blue bathrobe and slippers, and is about to go to bed. Her eyes are focused on the brown suitcase behind him; she had just found out that he was leaving. Two boys—Daryl, Al's own, who is only four and a half, and eight-year-old Ted, Al's stepson—stare wide-eyed, and wonder what is happening. They run over to Al and hold onto his legs. Hoping everything will be all right, they begin to play tag with one another.

"Come on, baby, don't do this to me," Al says to his wife. "You know this is hard for me too. I don't want to leave you and the boys behind." He pauses and raises his hands from his sides. "I don't have a job there in New York or a place to live. Where would you and the boys stay?"

Ella re-ties her bathrobe and wipes away several tears as they continue to fall. Her lower lip trembles as her eyes dart from her husband to the suitcase.

"You had a job here," she whispers softly. Ella swallows and attempts to make her voice louder. "You had a job here. You had security and love, and now you are going to throw it all away and leave us behind."

She completely breaks down. Al stares at her as his heart pounds. The open road is calling him and he wants to leave now, but he can't just yet.

"Baby, don't do this. You know I hated that job at the steel mill. Every day was putting me closer to my grave. Every second I spent in there ate at my soul. I am a music man; that's what I enjoy doing."

Ella shakes her head. She can't bear to look at him any longer. "You had your music on the weekends. Wasn't that enough?"

"No it wasn't," he replies softly. "It's like drinking water from a thimble—sure, you're getting water, but it really never does anything for you."

Ella turns and slowly walks away. It crushes Al. There is no hug or kiss, not even a simple good-bye. He wishes she would support him more with his dream. His attention is drawn to his two kids, who are still holding onto his legs. With his large hands he gently scoots them in front of him so he can kneel down. Ted doesn't appear too concerned over the situation, but Daryl is visibly shaken.

"Are you leaving us, Daddy?" Daryl asks.

Al slowly nods. "Yeah, son, for now." He suddenly perks up. "But soon we will all live in New York together, all right?"

Daryl's head bounces up and down. He reaches over and hugs his father tightly. He holds on and doesn't want to let go.

"I'm going to miss you, Daddy."

"I'm going to miss you too."

Al feels one of Daryl's tears touch his cheek.

* * *

Suddenly Al sits up in the bus and opens his eyes, which are welled up with tears. He quickly looks around to see if any of the other passengers are watching him. He tilts his head back and bats his eyes as he tries to maintain his composure.

* * *

It is midmorning as the bus enters the massive concrete jungle of New York City. The huge skyline seems to be calling the passengers as they begin to wake up. Al smiles as he stares at the tall buildings; he can feel the energy emanating from them, calling him to his destiny. The bus begins to slow down as it passes through the crowded streets, until it reaches the bus depot and stops.

"Welcome to New York City," the bus driver says.

Al can't wait to get started, he feels so young and alive as he gets his suitcase from the storage compartment. It is early in the morning, so he is not worried about finding a place to stay, not yet—first he has to head over to Times Square. He has to at least see it. He walks for several blocks. The weather is the same as at home, cold and icy. As he draws closer, he decides to ask for locations of any music companies. The streets are full of people, so he feels this shouldn't be a problem.

"Excuse me, sir—"

The person keeps on walking.

"Ma'am, could I—" He looks at the next person. "Sir, would you please—"

The people keep passing by as if he is invisible. He spots a black man approaching and walks over toward him.

"Excuse me."

The man stops and looks at him. "Can I help you?"

"Yes," Al replies with a big smile. "Could you direct me to the nearest music company?"

"Sure, it would be the Russ Building, about two blocks from the heart of the city," the man replies, pointing down the street.

"Thank you."

Al picks up his stride, still holding tightly onto his suitcase. As he passes the center of the city, his eyes begin to search the buildings for a building with a sign that bears the name "Russ" on it. He finally sees the large, square building, and walks right in through the front doors.

The lobby is simple, and filled with people coming and going. A directory by an old, iron-cage elevator catches his eye. He walks over to it and sees that most of the fourth floor is made up of music studios and offices. He stares at all the names and wonders whom to contact first.

The elevator reaches the first floor and the iron cage is pushed open. A young black man rushes out and begins to walk around the lobby in a nervous fashion. Al is still looking at the directory; he can feel the weight of this person's stare. Al looks to his left, and the man is standing there, looking him up and down. He is about five foot eight, with a medium build. He is dressed very nicely, and doesn't have a hair out of place.

"Can I help you?" Al asks.

"Maybe. Can you sing?"

He feels a little funny about this, but smiles, nonetheless. "Yeah, I can sing."

The man sticks his right hand out. "I'm Arthur Crier, talent scout. And you are . . ."

He shakes his hand. Disbelief is still in his head. "Ah . . . Al Cleveland."

"That's great, Al, come with me."

Arthur grabs Al by the arm and quickly escorts him onto the elevator. The old door is closed, and the elevator gives a slow, slightly jerky ride to the fourth floor. Arthur sticks his hands in his pockets and looks over Al one more time.

"Yeah, you'll do fine. Have you ever heard of Bobby Vinton?"

"Of course I have. Who hasn't?"

"My point exactly, my man. I am his producer. We're recording right now and—"

The elevator reaches its destination and stops. Arthur pushes the iron gate to the side. He takes hold of Al's arms again, and escorts him off with a rapid pace. He continues as they walk down the hall to a recording studio.

"—right now one of the backup singers is absent, so we need a fill-in. In case you're wondering, the man for the job is Al Cleveland."

Arthur pushes open a door, and together they walk into the studio. Al stops and looks at all the equipment and instruments. He feels right at home, and envisions himself to be the second black artist to be on the cover of *Life* magazine. It would only be right, after all. The first was Billy Eckstein, and he was from Pittsburgh, Pennsylvania, as well.

Bobby Vinton is standing over by his drummer, and turns around to see who came in. His arms fly up from his sides.

"Arthur, who is this?" he asks, motioning towards Al.

Arthur helps Al take off his jacket, and hands him some sheet music. "Oh, this person? This is one of your backup singers—Al."

Bobby places his hands on his hips and glances at Al, and then looks right back at Arthur.

"Stevie is my backup singer."

"Do you see Stevie?" Arthur asks. He doesn't get a response. "All right, then—meet Al, your backup singer."

"Well, let's at least hear the man."

Arthur quickly walks him over to the rest of the backup singers. "Do you see which lines are yours?"

"Sure do, no problem," Al replies with total confidence.

Bobby holds up his hand, and his band members take their places. "All right, I want to hear "Roses Are Red" on three. Ready, one, two, three."

The music begins, and Al fits right in. He doesn't miss a beat, and even begins to do the same dance moves as the other backup singers. The song is halfway over when Bobby raises his hand again.

"Stop, stop, stop," Bobby quickly says, with a huge smile on his face. The band stops.

"Arthur, where did you find this guy?"

Arthur can already see that Bobby is very pleased.

"By the elevator."

"By the elevator?"

"Yup, just standing there."

"I suppose he was just waiting for you."

"You see, that is exactly what I thought too. I am so good at finding talent that talent comes looking for *me*."

Bobby laughs hard and looks towards Al. "You've got some rhythm. How would you like to hear your voice on a record?"

Goose bumps rise all over Al. He hasn't even been in New York for an hour yet, and he is already recording an album.

"I'd love it, Bobby."

"Well then, let's do it."

They record the song "Roses Are Red (My Love)," and everything goes smoothly. Afterwards the studio is empty except for Al and Arthur, who are closing everything down. Al is still on a natural high, and feels that this was a sign that he is going all the way to the top. Arthur notices Al's suitcase.

"You must be new in town. Do you have a place to stay?" he asks.

Al shakes his head. "I just got here when I met you."

"Well, I have a apartment. It's nothing real fancy, but you're welcome to stay there, if you'd like to."

Al smiles; this man is being so generous it is hard to believe. "Yeah, that would be great; thanks, Arthur."

Later that evening, Al is at Arthur's modest apartment. It doesn't have a lot of furnishings, but it will do. Arthur is a single man, so there is not much to eat. The two decide to order out. Arthur explains how he finds talent and acts as producer for several artists. He has been working in New York for several months, and is ready to get back on the road again.

"So, I was thinking of gathering up all my artists and hitting the Chitlin' Circuit again. Would you like to go?" Arthur asks.

The Chitlin' Circuit was a string of small and large nightclubs and juke joints throughout the South and Eastern Seaboard. They were places where black artists could perform for black customers. Most of these places were tiny, smoke-filled rooms that actually served chitlings, fried chicken, fish, and ham hocks—soul food. Al wasn't too crazy about the idea. He hated the fact that he was being treated like a second-class citizen just because he wasn't white. But nonetheless, he wanted to get his name out there, and that would be a way to do it. Maybe he could be like Fats Domino or Smokey Robinson or even The Blue Belles; they had already attained their success, and they all started off the same way.

And if it worked out for him, he could go the number-one spot, the Apollo in New York. Of course, there was always Hollywood and TV. His mind rambled on with the thoughts of stardom.

"All right, I'll do it."

Arthur gives him a huge smile and pats him on the back. His voice suddenly shoots out with excitement, "We're going to have some fun, I can feel it already."

"When do we leave?"

"Two days," Arthur replies, holding up two fingers.

Al's eyes grow big. He didn't think they would be leaving that soon; he figured a month or two. "Do you have a phone I can use?"

"Yeah, there is one in the back. Help yourself."

Al goes to the back of the apartment and picks up the phone. His mind is already racing with images of Ella; he misses her dearly. He calls home. The phone rings several times, and no one answers.

"Come on, Ella, pick up the phone," he whispers.

"Hello?"

"Hey, baby, it's me. I made it."

"I was getting worried. Where are you?"

"Here in New York in someone's apartment. His name is Arthur and he is a talent scout. Hey, you're not going to believe this, but today I was a backup singer for Bobby Vinton, and we recorded a song!"

Ella struggles to show enthusiasm. "That's great, Al. Are you looking for an apartment for the boys and I?"

"Well, that's the problem, sweetie, we leave in two days for the Chitlin' Circuit. Just think, it will only be a few months, and it will be a great way to get my name out there, right?"

Silence greets him. He listens to the static. Ella takes several deep breaths, and slowly sits down as she envisions raising the children alone. Then he can hear her start to cry.

"Come on Ella, don't do this."

"How am I supposed to feed our boys and pay the bills?" she asks tearfully.

"I'll send you money, I promise. Trust me, the big time is just around the corner."

Her mood suddenly changes, as does her tone. "Fine, Al, you do what you gotta do," she says softly, and slowly hangs up the phone.

CHAPTER 2

Late the following afternoon, Arthur and Al bundle up in warm clothes and go downtown to rent three station wagons. As they walk down the street, Al begins to wonder how the two of them are going to drive three vehicles.

"Say, Arthur, who is going to help us?" he asks.

His friend changes direction slightly and begins heading towards a building. "She is, right there."

There, standing at the corner of a building, is a black woman, and to Al's eyes she appears to be an angel. She is slender and rather tall. Her face is beautiful, with light-brown skin and green eyes that demanded attention. She's wearing a long, dark overcoat and a white knitted hat that lets her hair peek out.

"Wow, she's beautiful," he mumbles.

Arthur walks right up to the woman, who is standing there waiting for them.

"Oh, there you are," she replies, with a smile that was so warm it could melt an iceberg.

Her name Is Natalie; she was bom in Memphis, and in her early years she performed on the streets. She exudes confidence, and a tough act with which she could brush off anyone that she felt wasn't kind. But when she first laid eyes on Al, she knew he had a kind heart, and he would never see the tough act.

"Al, I would like you to meet Natalie Rose Jenkins, the star of my show. She's a fantastic singer and a wonderful dancer," Arthur explains.

Al smiles at her and sticks out his right hand. "It's very nice to meet you." She returns the smile, slips off her glove, and shakes his hand. Her grip seems so small compared to his, but her hand is so warm and soft. Their eyes lock onto one another's.

"It's nice to meet you too, Al. I hope you're joining us on the road."

Man, is her voice sweet. "Oh, I am. I'll be right there next to you."

She smiles at him and holds back from being too flirtatious as her pulse begins to rise. Gently she withdraws her hand and places it back in its glove. Arthur starts walking down the street again, and the two of them follow in silence. They pick up the three station wagons and bring them over to the studio, where they are loaded up with equipment, supplies, and instruments. After they finish, Natalie puts on her jacket again, and prepares to leave.

"Hey, Arthur, I have to get going," she says.

"OK, thanks for your help."

Al walks over to her to say good-bye. "I'll see you tomorrow, right?"

She looks up at him, and he swears he can see heaven in her large green eyes. Her pulse begins to rise again; her palms turn sweaty. "Yes, Mister Al Cleveland, first thing in the morning."

His heart gives several loud thumps as he squeezes his left hand in his jacket pocket. He can feel his wedding ring press up tightly against his fingers. Guilty feelings swoosh over him. *Stay out of trouble, Al. Ella is a good woman.*

* * *

Arthur wakes up early the next morning and stirs Al out of bed. It is a wonderful, clear day, and the air is crisp without being too cold. They are the first ones down to the station wagons. A few minutes later another singer walks up. Arthur introduces her as Lorraine Roberts. Al still feels a little guilty for flirting the way he did with Natalie, so he doesn't comment on how pretty she is. She has slightly lighter skin than Natalie, and is just as tall. She is West Indian, with an extremely soft complexion. Lorraine is an intelligent woman and a registered nurse, so she doubles as the group's medic. Al looks past her and sees a face that he easily recognizes.

"Ron? Ron Jolley?"

"Hey, Al. Don't tell me that you teamed up with the old conniver Arthur."

The two embrace each other. Ron is a comic who has opened for many of Al's acts back in Pittsburgh. They have known each other for years. Ron is an average-sized man, and slightly chubby. His face is round, and seems to be on the verge of smiling at all times. As the two talk, huge plumes of steam exit their mouths from the cold air.

"How long have you been in town?" Ron asks.

"Just three days, my man," Al replies with an upbeat tone, excited about doing some shows.

"Dang. You just got here and now you're leaving again. Where's Ella and the boys, in your suitcase?"

"No." He stops and chuckles. They're still in PA. I plan to send for them after we get back from our tour."

Arthur claps his hands. "All right, performers, let's get aboard and get going!"

* * *

The next month is hard. Performances and rehearsals go on day after day. The hours are long and the quarters are cramped, but it is what they live for and what they love. As the days go by, Al and Natalie continue to bond, but they both know that their careers are the most important thing to them.

One night the three station wagons are cruising down a lonesome stretch of highway. Arthur and Ron are in the front seat; Natalie, Al, and Lorraine are in the back. Al is in the middle, and both of the pretty women are asleep with their heads on his shoulders. Al nods off and on. Half asleep, he smiles at the two beauties. *Man, Al, you are the luckiest guy in the world right now. You've got a beauty on your right and a beauty on your left; what more could you ask for?* His eyes close again. Natalie moans and moves her hand; it lands in the middle of his thigh. Suddenly his head shoots up and his eyes open wide. Her warm hand feels so good, so tempting. Fantasies begin to swirl in his head. *Relax, she's just sleeping. She didn't mean to do that.* He debates whether or not to move her hand off of him. His temperature rises as her hand slowly slides up and down his leg. It feels good—soft and caring. Temptation is calling him. She picks her head up. Her eyes are half shut and her hair is just slightly messed up, but those green eyes are sending messages of love.

"I am so glad you came with us," she whispers in his ear, and then kisses him on the cheek.

Caught completely off guard, Al can barely get his voice to work. "Glad to be here."

She rubs his leg a few more times, and snuggles up to him again. Al's heart jumps into his throat. Once again he attempts to touch the wedding ring on his left hand, but he took it off three days ago, and hadn't put it back on yet. He knows it is in his suitcase, but he has no idea where his suitcase is.

As the sun rises, the caravan stops at a small diner just outside of Louisville, Kentucky. They are just a few miles from a very important stop for them, the "Across the Tracks Club," a big one for the Chitlin' Circuit. Al goes over to a pay phone and calls home as Natalie goes inside for coffee.

"Hello?" A small voice answers; the nose sounds stopped up.

Al smiles; he loves that little voice. "Hey, Daryl, it's Daddy."

"Hey, Daddy!" he replies happily. "Where are you?"

"I'm in Kentucky, son. Is your mama there?"

"Noooooo," he says, dragging the word out. "She's at work."

Al's eyebrows scrunch together. "Work? She got a job?"

"Yeah. She said she needed more money to pay the damn bills."

Al's eyes open wide; obviously Ella is upset. Daryl rambles on about something that happened at school. Al listens wholeheartedly, but then his thoughts turn elsewhere as he spots Natalie walking out of the coffee shop. His heart races as he watches her slender hips sway in her tight, dark-green slacks. *My God, she is beautiful.* She walks over, carrying coffee in a styrofoam cup for him.

"Here you go, sweetie," she says, and hands him the coffee.

Daryl stops mid-sentence. "Who was that girl, Daddy?"

Al spins around, his eyes open wide. It was as if Daryl could read his mind. "That . . . that was . . . ah, just another singer, son."

Sensing it must be a private phone call, Natalie backs up. Al turns back around and looks her up and down; his heart fills with lust.

"Why did the girl call you sweetie?"

Al's eyes dart to the floor of the phone booth; there was nothing like being snapped back to reality by a stopped-up five-year-old.

"All the singers are real friendly, son; that's all, Daryl, nothing else. Listen, tell your mom that I called, and that I sent some money, and it should be there in a couple of days."

"All right, Daddy. I wish I could see you in a couple days too."

"I wish that too, son. I'll call you later."

"Bye-bye," Daryl says, and hangs up the phone.

Al comes out of the phone booth and drinks his steaming coffee. He tries to act casual while thinking about what to tell Natalie. He never told her he was married, and wonders if he should. But much to his surprise, she doesn't ask whom he was talking to.

"Ready for the big show tonight?" she asks, her eyelashes batting at him.

"Oh yeah. Arthur said it should be a sellout crowd. Hopefully we can get noticed in there."

* * *

As the day passes, the group rehearses their act several times; they all want it to be perfect. The "Across the Tracks Club" is by far one of the nicest places they have visited. It is large and nicely decorated. Al and Natalie are both surprised to hear that even white people came to the club on occasion.

Arthur comes out with his hands up to get everyone's attention. His voice is filled with excitement. "Excellent job, everybody! We are going to be hot tonight, I can just feel it. Take a three-hour break, and be back here at six sharp. Then we are going to rock the house."

The performers begin to walk off in different directions. Natalie walks over to Al as he straightens out his microphone. She smiles at him, and purposely flirts with her eyes again. "Do you want to see what everyone else is doing?" she asks.

"No," he quickly replies, with a smile. She sticks her hands in her pockets and shrugs, while turning away and looking innocent. He can't help but look her up and down again. His blood pressure rises. Fantasies flood his mind once more as he thinks about holding her and caressing her on a moonlit night.

"Well, Mister Cleveland, what do you want to do?"

"Get away. Just us, no one else. Some place simple, so we can talk."

The two walk down the street, looking for a quiet dinner spot. As they stroll, they casually bump into one another, as if the wide sidewalk isn't big enough for both of them. With each touch, Natalie's skin tingles with excitement. They travel for two blocks, then stop in a small place where the group is not likely to find them. They had to find a smaller restaurant, one that would serve blacks. They purposely take a back booth in the small, dark place.

Moments later they are eating and smiling at each other. One candle lights their little area. Their eyes keep locking onto one another's, as the moment unfolds. There is something about her that Al cannot put a finger on, something that seems to steal all his thoughts.

"Do you have any family?" Al asks. Her face is blank as she ponders his question. She has been on her own for over two years now, and she hasn't seen any of her family in a long time.

"Yeah. One sister, a brother, a couple aunts and uncles in Memphis."

"No parents?"

"Nope," she replies softly.

There was more to it, but Al figured it might be bad news and could ruin the moment, so he quickly changes the subject.

"So, Natalie Rose, how old are you?"

She smiles sheepishly, and stirs her drink with her straw.

"Ninety."

They both laugh out loud. It feels good for Natalie to do this. It is the first time in a long time that she has let her guard down for any man. But deep inside she feels that Al is so much different than any other man.

"You are one hot mama for ninety."

"Actually, I am twenty-five. And what about you, Al? I hear you left your wife and two kids back in Pittsburgh."

Images of his family flood his mind as he closes his eyes. *Damn, she knows. But maybe this will be all right; I mean, the truth is already out, and she is still here with me.* He opens his eyes as he does his best to push any feelings of guilt out of his heart.

"Yeah, you have it right. I had to get out of there. I had to get on the road and go after my dream. I was dying a slow death."

He says it more for himself than for her. But nonetheless he feels better, and is surprised to see her nod.

"I know exactly how you feel. I went through the same thing. I had to get away and show my talent."

"Finally, someone who understands me," he replies with a smile.

The had finished their meals quite a while back, but neither of them are in a hurry to leave. If it weren't for the show, they probably would have spent several more hours talking. Al pays for the dinner, and they walk out together. Together they slowly stroll back to the club, hand in hand.

That night they do their show to the largest crowd yet; there are people standing outside who desperately want to come in, but there isn't enough room inside the club. For Arthur it is a dream come true— his group is starting to get the recognition that he wants. Now other clubs are calling him and asking them to perform.

After the show, they all have to leave the club through the back door. Right out front there are two black-and-white police cars, their single red lights twirling. Four white cops stood by their cars, their nightsticks out and ready. They say they are just there to keep the peace, but the group knows better; the racial tension is high. Even white patrons of the club have to sneak out, some with their jackets over their heads, in fear of being persecuted for seeing black performers.

The gang all travels down the road to the shady part of town, to the nearest "black" hotel. It is a simple, six-story brick building that was built in the 1920s. It is nothing special to look at, but it will do. To celebrate their success, they throw a wild party. Everyone is laughing, drinking, and enjoying themselves. Al socializes, but he keeps his eyes on Natalie. He has made up his mind; he wants her, and he is going to have her. She is doing the same thing to him, and they keep exchanging glances throughout the evening. A passion for one another begins to build.

They are all still wearing gowns and tuxedos. The guys have their bow ties undone and the tops of their shirts unbuttoned. A couple of hours pass, and he walks over to her.

"How are you doing?"

She smiles, slightly tipsy from too much wine.

"Wonderful, Mister Al Cleveland."

"What do you say that you and I get out of here?"

"And do what?" she asks, as if she didn't know already.

He smiles with a devilish grin. "You'll see."

They sneak out of the room and walk down the hall, arm in arm. Arthur has already reserved rooms for the group, but to save money, they are always shared by four or five people, so Al had rented his own room on the fifth floor. Like a couple of kids, they laugh and giggle along the way. They open the door and enter the small room. There by the bed is a bottle of champagne on ice.

"What's this about?" she asks, playing innocent again, something that drives him crazy.

"I thought we could drink to our success."

He walks over, pours her a glass, and hands it to her. But before she can drink it, he takes her head and holds it. Slowly he draws himself closer, and then kisses her passionately. Natalie can feel her heart pounding as she practically melts in his hands. They break apart, their breaths long and heavy. She stands there almost trembling as he plants kisses along her cheek and down her neck. She slips out of her high-heeled shoes and moans.

"Ow," she says softly.

Al backs away and looks at her. "Did I do something wrong?"

"No," she whispers as she tries to catch her breath. She snuggles up against him. "I had to take my shoes off; my feet are killing me."

Al rubs his hands up and down her back as he holds her close. He finds the zipper at the top of her beautiful dress. Her hands explore underneath his jacket, feeling his warm skin.

"I know what we could do."

"What?" she whispers.

He begins to unzip her dress. Her eyes open wide, and then she closes them as she holds him tighter. She does nothing to stop him.

"We could light a few candles and take a hot bubble bath together. Then I'll massage your feet for you."

Her eyes are half shut and her heart is filled with passion as she slowly unbuttons his shirt, exposing his chest.

"Why, Mister Cleveland, if we were in the bathtub together, neither of us would have any clothes on," she whispers.

Ever so gently she kisses his chest, and unbuttons his shirt further. Each time her soft lips touch his skin, it feels like electricity shooting through him.

"I promise not to look," he whispers in her ear, as her dress falls to the floor.

* * *

The next morning the gang is all sitting down eating breakfast at a corner restaurant. Al and Natalie climb out of bed, smiling at each other and slightly embarrassed. She stands and wraps herself in the bedsheet. Al lays there and watches her, mesmerized by her beauty.

"You were wonderful last night," he says.

She holds onto the sheet and bends over to kiss him.

"So were you. I'm sure the others are beginning to wonder where we are, so I had better hurry up and get ready."

She runs off to the shower. Al knows she is right, so he stands and stretches. He smiles as he hears the water turn on and Natalie beginning to sing. *You are the man; damn, that was one good night.* Still groggy and slightly hung over, he strolls over to his suitcase and opens it up. There, right on top of his clothes, is his wedding ring. It seems to shine where it sits—dead center in the small, brown suitcase. It is the perfect reminder of what he left at home. Guilt bombards him; it rams its way into his heart as his mind fills with vivid pictures of his wife and children. *What am I doing? I have a wonderful wife and two great kids.* He plops back down on the bed and twirls the gold ring with his fingers. Al so desires to place the ring back on his finger, but he feels too guilty. Suddenly the water to the shower shuts off. His eyes widen as they shoot towards the bathroom and then back at the ring. He quickly places the wedding band back in his suitcase, burying it deep down inside.

"Are you going to take a shower, sweetie?" Natalie asks.

"Yeah, I'm on my way," he blurts out.

Al quickly grabs some clothes and heads for the bathroom. Natalie walks out, wearing nothing but a small towel. The color of her skin stands out against the white towel, magnifying her slender build.

Her shoulders and smooth legs are still covered with tiny droplets of water. Al's mouth falls open.

"I don't know what you did with your wings, but you are definitely an angel."

She smiles at him and gives him another kiss. "Thank you, Mister Cleveland. Now, hurry up and get ready," she says, as she pushes him towards the shower.

* * *

Twenty minutes later the two try to act as casual as possible as they enter the restaurant, which has a row of long windows facing the parking lot. All eyes are upon them as they walk up, side by side, to one of the booths. Arthur, nearly done eating, stands up and lets Natalie sit down beside him. Al sits across from them.

"Some party last night, huh?" Arthur asks.

"Yeah, yeah, it was," Al says, his eyes on Natalie.

"Where did you two end up?"

"Somewhere over the rainbow," they both reply at the same time, and laugh.

Arthur's raises his eyebrows and smiles, looking away. Al reaches across the table and takes Natalie's hand as he stares deep into her eyes.

Arthur clears his throat. "The club liked us so much that they want us to stay for another week. It's good money and real good exposure."

"That's great!" Al replies with a big smile.

"That is nice news," Natalie says in a softer tone. "Excuse me, please; I have to use the ladies' room."

Al taps his hands on the table, looking forward to more performances. "While you're gone, I'll go find out where our waitress is."

Al gets up and leaves. Natalie waits for Arthur to move, but he doesn't; he just sits there, playing with a paper napkin. He slowly pushes his plate away.

"Arthur, please let me out."

Arthur is only slightly older than they are, but he has always been a father figure to the group—or at least the one with the most common sense.

"Do you know how hard it is for a black person with any type of talent to get recognized?" Arthur asks.

She wonders where he is going with this, and quickly replies, "Yes, I do; I am working very hard at it right now."

"Then you would surely know that it would take an act of *God* for a married black man to get a black woman pregnant out of wedlock, then have either of them get noticed by anyone."

Natalie is completely silent; the words hit her like a ton of bricks. The worst thing is, he's right.

"I don't want to butt into your personal business, Natalie. But I would hate to see you throw it all away over an affair."

Arthur is being truthful; he is concerned about her well-being and her future. But he is also worried about himself; after all, she is the star of the show, and without her it would not be the same.

Al comes rushing back over. "OK, I found our waitress, and she's on the way."

Arthur stands and lets Natalie out to use the restroom. She seems rather distraught.

"What's wrong?" Al asks Arthur, as his new girl leaves.

"Just watching out for my star," he says, squeezing Al's shoulder as he walks away. "Oh, practice is at noon; don't be late."

"You can count on it."

Moments later, Natalie returns to the table. She seems nervous and uncomfortable, but says nothing about Arthur's warning. Lorraine watches the couple from a few tables away as she sits with the guitar players and Ron Jolley. She stares at Al, her eyes full of affection. A jealous seed sprouts in her heart as she watches him smile and laugh. She wishes she could be with him, but his eyes are set on Natalie.

* * *

The group performs at the club for another week, and it goes extremely well. They all feel they are becoming a success. Al tries to call home several times, but each time there is no answer. Arthur's warning to Natalie sticks in her head, but she and Al continue to make love on a nightly basis. The bond between them grows as their love develops.

The hard but satisfying week of work and sellout crowds passes quickly. The group loads up the station wagons once more. Unfortunately, however, their time at the big club is done, and they are headed to the smaller ones again. Al decides to try and call home one more time. He listens patiently as the phone rings.

Ella answers. "Hello?"

"Hey, you're there! How are you doing, honey?" Al asks.

There is silence on the phone, and then Ella speaks again, but she doesn't sound too enthusiastic. "I'm all right. Working at my job, trying to keep the house going, and feeding the kids. So how's everything down there? Are you a star yet? Are your little 'sweetie' singers taking care of you?"

He looks across the parking lot towards Natalie, who is still helping load up the car. His heart pounds an his mind fills with confusion as he thinks about both women at the same time. He knows that Daryl must have snitched on him, however innocently. He also knows he is falling in love with Natalie, but deep down he loves his wife as well. He closes his eyes as he attempts to gather his thoughts.

"Ella, it isn't anything like that. You know—"

She cuts him off. "I know how you are, Al. You go with the flow." She lets out a heavy, emotion-filled sigh. "I just hope . . . I just hope that you will be back in New York soon, so we can be a family again."

Al tries to stay upbeat. "Me too, Ella. I sure do miss you and the boys."

"Good-bye, Al," she whispers, and softly hangs up the phone.

Al stands in the phone booth for a few seconds as he gathers the emotions that seem to have spilled on the floor. His ear is pressed up against the receiver; he wants to hear more from his wife. *I'm going to lose everything if I am not careful. But I know when I go back to New York I can pass it off, and everything will be fine,* he thinks to himself. He steps out of the phone booth. To his left he can hear someone running. He turns and sees Arthur heading towards the group. He seems very happy as he jumps into the air, waving papers at everyone. Al hurries over to see what all the commotion is about.

"Change of plans!" he yells out. Arthur is filled with energy and excitement as he shows them the papers. "Club Handy in Memphis wants us! It's a premier club on the Chitlin' Circuit, and it's a big one! This could mean the big time awaits all of us. And Natalie Rose, this is your homecoming; you're the queen. So let's load up, because Beale Street, here we come!"

They all cheer, quickly pile into the cars, and take off. All of them are excited about the news. They know the opportunities are endless in Memphis. Rumors have long circulated that movie and music agents hang out there, looking for talent.

CHAPTER 3

It is early on Friday morning when the small caravan pulls up to Club Handy. At one time the old, run-down club stood by itself on a dirt lot. But it has done so well that the owner fixed it up, and other businesses popped up around it, adding even more to its customer base.

The sky is filled with thick, dark clouds, and rain. But it doesn't damper the group's mood; they can feel the energy in the air and the excitement in their hearts. All of them seem rather speechless as they climb out of the station wagons and stare at the large, barn-like, red building with white trim. The names flashes on a huge neon sign.

"I feel different about this one," Natalie whispers to Al. "Like good things are going to happen for me here."

Al puts his arm around her and gives her a passionate, deep kiss.

"Well, don't hog all those good vibes, baby. You have to share them."

They both laugh as they walk inside. Once they enter through the thick double doors, they stop. The club is by far the best one yet. It can hold a lot of people, and has a very large stage that sits chest high to the floor. They can't wait to perform on it, to show off their talents for everyone to see.

The last club was long rumored to have a mixed crowd of black and white patrons; here it was no rumor, it was the truth.

"Finally a club worthy of all your talent," Arthur says out loud as he walks in. "I have faith in all of you that you will reach stardom right here."

It doesn't take much to get them fired up again. Soon the stage is filled with their equipment and instruments. They run through two rehearsals, then take a much-needed break. Al plops down in a chair as Lorraine massages the back of his neck with a tender touch of hidden affection. Her soft hands rub his tired muscles as she wishes he would hold her the way he holds Natalie. She stops as soon as she sees Natalie coming out of the restroom. Calmly she backs away. Al is so emotionally wrapped up with his new love that he doesn't even notice Lorraine.

He watches Nataline stroll over to the stage, smiling, her green eyes calling him again.

Arthur, who had been on the phone for quite some time, suddenly comes out and looks at his gang.

"Good news for all you top-notch performers—we've got four shows right here at the best club on the Chitlin' Circuit." They all clap their hands. "And some good news for all you homesick lost souls—after our four shows, we're heading back home."

Although none of them clapped, every one of them was kind of glad to hear the news.

They had been on the road for over two and a half months, and home was beckoning. Arthur doesn't reveal why he has suddenly cut the trip short by almost three weeks; something in New York must be calling him. He glances at his watch.

"Relax for another thirty minutes, and then start getting dressed."

The night comes quickly as darkness overtakes the light. The clouds release a tidal wave of rain that would have driven away almost any customer from any other club. But Arthur's group has a style and performance that is unmatched, so the parking lot is lined with cars as patrons begin to drive up. The club starts to fill early with a mixed crowd as the group prepares themselves in their dressing rooms.

"The club is already packed, and it's thirty minutes until showtime!" one of the drummers says as he jogs past Al.

Al gives a happy-to-be-here smile, and struts over to Natalie's dressing room. He raises his hand to knock on the door, but then realizes it is ajar. Then his heart skips a beat as he hears an unfamiliar man's voice in her room. He hesitates to push the door open. *She's yours, you can't let some little punk take her!* Then he pushes hard on the door.

It swings open and hits a chair without making much noise. Natalie, sitting in front of her vanity and still in her robe, spins around and looks at him. There is a white man with slicked-back, light-brown hair standing next to her. He is tall and heavyset, with a nice suit on that is covered with tiny raindrops—he obviously hasn't been inside that long.

"Hey, sweetie," Nataline says to Al, in an extremely cheerful tone.

She seems to be glowing as she puts down a pen and hands the man several pieces of paper. The man smiles at her and carefully folds the papers, then places them inside his jacket pocket.

"Thank you, Miss Natalie Rose; I'm looking forward to seeing you in a few days," the man says.

He nods at Al, and then walks out of the dressing room. Natalie leaps from her seat and lands in front of Al. Immediately she wraps her arms around him and begins giving him rapid kisses all over his face. Al laughs at her good mood.

"What was that all about?" he asks.

"That was a movie agent that came all the way from Hollywood! I just signed up with him. He said that he could get me some big-time exposure, and into some movies."

She claps her hands and jumps up and down with excitement. Quickly she goes over to her evening gown and begins to put it on. Al is happy for her, even though deep down he was hoping she would come to New York with him.

"He signed you up without seeing you perform?" Al asks.

"No," she replies, wiggling into her beautiful, shiny, red dress with a low-cut neckline.

The form-fitting outfit is lined around the neck with black fur. "Zip me up, please," she says, turning her back to Al. "That guy saw us at the 'Across the Tracks Club.' He said he tried several times to talk to me." She stops and giggles. "Guess every time he tried I was gone, sneaking off with you."

Her back still faces Al; he reaches around her and holds her tight, swaying back and forth. "I'm real proud of you. You are going all the way."

He pauses and slowly nibbles along her bare neck and earlobe. It sends shock waves through her body. Her knees begin to tremble as she feels herself heat up.

"I have to get ready," she moans, not really telling him to stop.

Al stops, and stands there holding her. It takes a moment for both of them to regain their composure.

There is no mention of the fact that they will be departing in just a few days. They both try with all they have to keep the good-byes as distant as possible. For now they just want to enjoy every minute they have.

Suddenly someone knocks on the door. They turn around and look; it is Arthur.

"Hey lovebirds, ten minutes until showtime."

They stand there holding each other as they listen to Arthur knock on Lorraine's door and tell her the same thing. Natalie taps Al's hands for him to let go. She rushes over and puts on her red pumps, which match her dress perfectly.

"You're a beautiful woman."

She smiles at him and gives him a kiss.

"And you are a handsome man, Mister Cleveland. What do you say that tomorrow we get away for a while?"

"And do what?"

"Show you my old home; meet some of my family."

Al smiles and nods. "Just you and I, huh? That sounds nice."

They stare deeply into each other's eyes. They can feel their love for one another.

Slowly their heads come closer as their hands slide over their bodies. They are just inches apart when they hear Arthur yell, "Let's get ready to take places, everyone!"

Natalie chuckles and breaks away; her head hits Al's chest. She quickly moves, then puts on black, feathered earrings.

"Arthur has impeccable timing," Al says, as he sticks his hands in his pockets.

"Yes," she replies with a giggle. "But you really must admire his will to keep the show going."

That night they put on their best show yet. Al is not in the beginning act, so he ventures out into the audience to see it from a patron's point of view. He walks out into the club and quickly notices how the crowd is divided into two groups, whites on one side and blacks on another. It bothers him to see that. He stares at the thick rope that divides the two groups, and slowly sits down.

Natalie spots him almost immediately, and keeps an eye on him as she sings and does a dance routine with Lorraine. The first song finishes, and the room, which is filled to capacity, goes crazy with applause and cheers. The audience quiets down as they wait for Natalie to speak.

"Thank you so much for braving the storm to come see us perform," she says with an ear-to-ear grin.

Lorraine suddenly joins in. "You never realize it until you do a show, but there are a lot of people that don't get the proper spotlight they deserve."

"So we would like to change that tonight," Natalie says. She winks at Al and points to him. "Sitting right over there is a man named Al Cleveland. Al, would you please stand up and join us for a moment?"

Al doesn't know what his love is doing, but he stands up and climbs the stairs. The crowd is still silent as he positions himself between the two beauties. The bright spotlight beams on the three of them.

"Today is Al's birthday," Lorraine says.

"Happy birthday, Al!" some of the crowd yell from the back.

Al smiles and looks towards the floor. He thought no one knew.

Natalie speaks again. "And Al is a very talented songwriter. So for his birthday I would like to sing him one of my favorites that he wrote, 'Yester Love.' "

Lorraine begins the song, then she and Natalie exchange the verses as they take turns giving him attention—as if they both were his. The song comes to an end, and the applause is long and wonderful. Al is on cloud nine; things couldn't be better. He remains onstage performing for the rest of the concert, and loves every minute of it.

The next morning he awakens with Natalie's naked body half draped over him. He rubs his hand along her silky-soft skin as she stirs herself to consciousness. Thoughts of making love to her in the morning come to mind. She smiles at him.

"Did you enjoy your birthday present?"

He chuckles and kisses her. "It was the best one yet. Thanks for singing my song last night too."

She holds him tight and snuggles her body against his. "I love singing your songs. You write beautiful ones."

She slowly gets up on top of him and begins to grind her body into his. The happy couple makes love again, and then get ready together for their day's plans.

The storm from the night before left the ground wet and the air smelling fresh. All the trees have lost their fall-colored leaves, bare branches are left behind. But the air is still warm—at least warm compared to what Al is used to in Pittsburgh. They walk arm in arm along the river's edge. The huge, muddy river drifts slowly past them as a silent witness to their love while they walk on an old sidewalk that is cracked and warped due to huge tree roots underneath.

"Our time is coming to an end," Natalie says softly.

The subject that they both have been ignoring is now out in the open, ready for discussion. It seems to hang there for a moment as they both think about it. No matter how much they wished it, the day of a major decision was coming.

"I know," Al replies with a distant voice. "I keep putting it off, but I know it is coming, and it will be here a lot sooner than I want it to be."

Natalie stops and looks at Al. She takes her hands and gently rubs them over his cheeks and neck as she stares deep into his eyes. Her heart pounds for him as she dreams of them being married one day.

"It doesn't have to be like this, you know? You can come with me to Hollywood. Just think, Al, you and I could be together forever."

The thought of spending the rest of his life with her sounds great, but he would be giving up on his dream, and that is why he left Ella. He looks at the river as if it would give him the right words to say at a time like this.

"I would love to be with you, but then I would be living under your shadow, Natalie. I can't have that."

"But . . . there are music companies out there," she pleads in a soft, baby-like voice.

Don't do this to me baby, please. Flashbacks of him leaving Ella come to him in vivid color.

"You and I both know that all the best ones are in the eastern part of the country."

She breaks away from his embrace. "And you know that all the good movie studios are in the western part of the country."

They both stand there, staring at each other in silence. What seems like an eternity passes. A flock of small birds flies by, and somehow they take away some of the tension. Al finds the courage to smile.

"And what do you find so funny, Mister Cleveland?"

His smile grows. "You *make* me fall in love with you, and this is the thanks I get."

She laughs. "I *made* you? You *made* me fall in love with you," she replies, poking him in the chest with her index finger."

They return to each other's arms, and stand there holding and kissing each other. For the time being the tension of departing is on the back burner—put away, but not out of sight.

"I don't want to stand in the way of your career, Natalie. I think it is great that you're going to Hollywood."

"Thank you, and I don't want to stand in the way of yours either, because I know you'll do well in New York."

They walk upstream, holding hands in total silence. Several large barges slowly go by as they make it to their destination. After walking for two or three blocks, Natalie stops and stares at an old house that needs a paint job. It is a rather simple building, one that many would pass by, never giving it a second glance.

"That's it," she says, nudging him.

Al looks at the little house that has seen better days. The lawn was mostly brown, except for the thriving weeds growing around it in a cluttered mess.

"That's what?"

"The place I was born."

He looks back at her, then at the house. "You're kidding me, right?"

She laughs. "No, I'm not. Come on up the street; I want you to meet my sister."

"First you have to let me hold you and kiss you for a while."

Al and Natalie spend the whole afternoon together. He meets some of her family, and figures that she stole all the good looks from the gene pool. They have a wonderful time, and then both head back to the club to get ready for another night's performance.

The two of them walk into the motel, and Arthur comes running up to them. He is out of breath, and seems rather scared.

"Where have you guys been?" he asks as he tries to catch his breath.

Natalie smiles and tries not to laugh. "Were you worried that we left without finishing the last three shows?"

He wipes the sweat off of his forehead. "Well . . . yeah, I was. You are staying, right?"

Al pats Arthur on the back as he walks by. "Of course we are; you have nothing to worry about."

"I knew that. I knew it all along," Arthur replies.

Unfortunately for the couple, the following days seem to fly by at a rapid rate.

The next morning, for the first time in a while, Al wakes up alone. Natalie had left for Hollywood right after last night's final show. Al's heart aches as he stares out the window of the small motel room and watches a few cars pass by. He wonders if he should have gone with her. *Well, she's gone, and there is nothing I can do about it. Maybe now I can get things squared away with Ella and the kids. Yeah, that would be best.* Al gets dressed and joins everyone else; they are already in the motel's restaurant, eating breakfast.

With a slow, lonely pace, he walks over and plops down next to Ron Jolley and Arthur. He stares at the menu lying in front of him, but doesn't pick it up.

"Oh, the sound of a broken heart hitting the floor," Ron says as he slides the newspaper over to him. "Hey, do you know this girl?"

Ron taps the paper, pointing to an article. Al smiles as he sees a picture of Natalie; it must have been taken during one of the shows at "Club Handy." It shows her onstage in her red evening gown, singing away. The caption below the picture reads, "It's a leap up the ladder of stardom." *They better have said something good about my girl.* He leans forward and reads the article. It is a small story about her going to Hollywood, and it wishes the hometown girl good luck.

"Man, it's like someone just kicked your dog or something," Ron says with a tight smile, his round, chubby face ready to explode with a larger grin. "Cheer up already."

Al stares at the picture. "Hush up, I'm hurting inside."

Ron leans back and puts his arm around Al. "Oh yeah, I feel your pain. Poor Al, poor, poor Al. Out here on the road, singing and making good money, and on top of that, getting laid on a nightly basis." Ron's head falls back as if he is dying. He places his hand over his heart and moans as he takes several deep breaths. "Oh, I feel your pain, your own living hell that only Jesus can take you out of."

Al chuckles and picks up the menu. "You wouldn't understand."

"How could I? I haven't touched a pair of panties in a long time. How about you, Arthur, you been getting any lately?"

Arthur was always more modest and reserved when it came to that topic. "I have no comment for you, Ron."

Ron has a huge smile on his face. "Oh yeah, you ain't getting any either. I can tell. Matter of fact, I heard that the only time you touch a pair of panties is when you do Lorraine's laundry."

"No one better be touching my panties," Lorraine says in a high-pitched voice from the table next to them.

Arthur raises his hands and looks at her. He tries to be serious, but is on the verge of laughing. "I assure you that no one is touching your undergarments."

"That just means that Al hasn't been over there yet," Ron whispers.

"I heard that," Lorraine says.

Ron stares at Al as the man tries to read the menu. Finally Al smiles again and asks, "What now, Ron?"

"So, what was it like?"

Al plays innocent. 'What was what like?"

"You know what I am talking about, man, Natalie Rose. Did you get up all in there or what?"

Al laughs again and puts down the menu. "It's none of your business. Where's our waitress?"

"Oh no," Ron quickly blurts out loudly. "Don't tell me you're pulling on the waitress's panties too." He looks at Arthur with wide eyes and grabs his hand. "My heavens, can you think about how many waitresses we have had over the last few months? I think Al has been with all of them, even that fat one in Mississippi. We could have an epidemic on our hands."

The entire group is laughing, as other tables begin to look over to see what is going on.

Al shakes his head. 'There is no epidemic, and I was not with the fat waitress either."

Ron puts his index fingers together to make a cross. He makes his voice sound like a preacher's. "Back Satan, you fill Al's mouth with lots of lies." Ron sits up and looks at Al as if he is not really there. "Al, if you can hear me, I am going to put my hands on your head and cast out those foul demons in the name of Jesus Christ."

He starts to raise his hands when Arthur grabs his arm and gently pulls it back down. The entire restaurant is watching them.

"That's it," Arthur says, "no more coffee for you."

In the blink of an eye, Ron's face turns from one of laughter to one that is dead serious. "But it keeps me regular. Man, if you take away my java juice, in three days' time my butt will explode!"

"I heard enough. I'm out of here," Lorraine says as she gets up and walks away.

Again, Arthur tries to maintain his composure. "See, you offended the lady."

Ron's eyebrows cross as if there was no way that it could be true. "I did? I did? Al told me that if you washed her panties, I mean *undergarments*, correctly, that she wouldn't be so uptight."

The gang breaks up laughing again. Even Lorraine, who is walking out the door, laughs and shakes her head in disbelief. That is a gift Ron has. Always lively and full of energy, he can turn any situation into a comical one

After they are done eating, they load up the station wagons for the last time and head for the long road back to New York. Deep down Al is still heartbroken; Natalie is constantly on his mind. As the long, lonesome miles pass, he just stays in the backseat and stares out the window at the ground passing by.

CHAPTER 4

The streets of New York seem colder than before, but Al is still on fire from the tour. As soon as they are back, he hits the streets and quickly lines up several gigs. Things are looking good, and the money seems to be coming in a rather steady fashion.

Arthur is only there for a matter of hours before he leaves for Canada to look for different talent. Al soon hears he is doing shows up in Toronto and Montreal. In fact, all of the gang seems to have split up and gone their own way. Al calls Natalie now and then, but she is real busy; other than that, the only person he has contact with is Lorraine. Like always, she is warm and friendly to him. She keeps her feelings towards him a secret, but it is getting harder each time she sees him.

A good month passes, but Al is having a hard time getting hold of Ella or his kids. He has to move out of Arthur's apartment, but can't afford one that will fit his whole family. He has to settle for a small one in a run-down neighborhood. The sounds of gunshots and yelling are constant. He sits on the edge of his bed and dials the well-remembered phone number one more time. *Come on sweetie; answer just this once for me.*

"Hello?" Ella says as Al finally gets through.

Yes, you're there! "Hey, your home! How are you doing, sweetie?"

She doesn't sound that excited to hear from him. "I'm all right."

Al does his best to keep up a happy tone. "Did you and the boys get the Christmas presents that I sent just for you?"

Her tone is plain and flat, as if she is talking to an annoying car salesman. "Yes, we did, thank you."

"What's the matter, Ella? You don't sound very happy to hear from me."

There is dead silence on the phone; he listens to the static. She finally speaks again.

"You must be heartbroken after Natalie Rose left you and went to Hollywood."

Al's mouth falls open and his stomach ties itself into several tight and painful knots. "How . . . who?"

Her voice becomes upset; she has had a long time to think about this. The has run the statement she is about to give through her head a million times. "You guys were so busy walking down the riverbank and looking at her birth house that you didn't even notice the person taking pictures of you two kissing. The person who took your picture was a reporter for the Pittsburgh press, so I got to be the laughingstock with all my friends as the newspaper did an article on . . . on that . . . woman," she finishes her sentence with gritted teeth.

Al is completely caught off guard. Every thought that had been rambling through his head evaporates in the blink of an eye. A dark void fills his mind instead, as his heart pounds in lonely desperation.

Say something, stupid! "Baby, it wasn't like that," he whispers.

She quickly responds in a harsh, betrayed tone. "Don't 'baby' me, mister. I have had enough of your crap!"

"All right, Ella, all right; please calm down." His eyes flash around his dark room, as if someone would be there with an answer to his problem. "It wasn't all that; things must have just looked bad in the one picture."

She is silent for a moment. Ella doesn't believe him, but Al is still her husband. She closes her eyes and takes a deep breath as she tries to keep herself in control. "Are you coming back home?"

Al jumps up and begins to walk around while carrying the phone. "What? No. You know this is where I want to be."

"Then do you have enough room for the boys and I?"

He quickly looks around; the tiny apartment seems ten times smaller than it just did a minute ago. "Hey . . . now, you know—"

"Al."

"—I'm crowded and—"

"Al."

"—if you just give me a little longer."

"It's over, Al, it's all over."

The words register in his ears loud and clear. His knees buckle and he falls on the worn-out bed. Had he been gone that long? Ella was much stronger than he remembered. How could she change so quickly?

"Ella," he says softly, emotionally. "Please don't throw our marriage away. We've been together for years."

She is standing strong, not budging. She grips the phone tighter as her voice grows louder. "You threw the marriage away the day *you* walked out on us, Al. Don't you dare put the blame on me!"

His mouth falls open as tears begin to roll down his cheeks. He envisions a life alone, without his wife—worse, without his children. The kids matter to him. They are his world. "Please don't take the boys away from me. Please let me see my boys."

Deep down she wants to tell him to take a flying leap off the nearest cliff. But she knows it isn't the boys' fault, and it would only hurt them. She turns and stares at the two of them watching TV as they sit on the floor. They are watching cartoons, totally oblivious to the marital problems that are tearing their parents apart. Biologically, Ted isn't even Al's, but he has always treated him as if he were his, and Ella has nothing but respect for that.

"I won't stop you from seeing the boys."

"You know I love them."

"I know you do, Al."

"And I love you too."

She pauses and lets out a long, shaky sigh. Her tough exterior has melted away.

"Good-bye, Al," she whispers tearfully.

Al wants to talk more and try to work things out. but she hangs up the phone. The soft click seems as loud as thunder. It feels as if his world has suddenly become a lot smaller, lonelier, and darker. He stands, then ventures down to the nearest bar to drown his sorrows in a bottle of booze.

* * *

Long, muggy summer months pass, and fall begins to approach once again. Al has resorted to smoking marijuana as a form of escape. The habit has become a strong one that takes up his time and money.

He no longer has the amount of gigs that he used to. With each passing day, he struggles to pay the bills, to survive. Even his run-down apartment is becoming too expensive. He has not heard from Natalie or any of the gang in a long time. Only one of them is in town that he knows of—Lorraine. In the past they have only talked on the phone, so this time he decides to pay her a visit.

Late on a Wednesday evening, he knocks on her door. She opens it a crack, and looks at him with the chain lock still in the way. He is nicely dressed, and that is nothing new. It doesn't matter where Al is going; he always tries to look his best.

"Hey, Lorraine," he says, with a warm smile and sadness in his eyes.

She knows something is wrong. It might as well be written all over his face. His eyes look so sad and filled with emotion. His once-happy cheeks seem to droop.

"Al? I haven't seen you in a while. Just a minute. Let me unlock the door."

She closes the door, undoes the chain lock, and immediately opens the door again. He barely has a chance to come in when she reaches up and gives him a warm, caring embrace. For both of them, it feels so good to be held again. Her subdued emotions for him come flooding back as her heart flutters.

"Sorry it's so late," he says, and then backs away from the hug. He looks her up and down, and then he notices what she is wearing. "Hey, you have a nurse's uniform on. Did you go back to work?"

She straightens out her uniform and nods. "Yeah, the singing and all was a lot of fun, but I needed a regular paycheck. Why don't you come in and take a seat?"

She can smell booze on him, and knows that he is high, but she'll brush those things aside and look for the goodness in him. He takes a seat on the edge of the couch. He doesn't want to seem overly comfortable. She ventures into the kitchen. He can hear cabinets open and close, and dishes being moved.

"Would you like a cup of coffee?" she asks from around the corner, hoping he will have one; it will sober him up.

"Love one. So, have you heard from anyone in the gang?"

She walks out, carrying a tray with two cups and a pot of steaming coffee. With a small frown on her face, she shakes her head.

"Heard from Ron Jolley a couple times, but that was it."

Al grins, thoughts of Ron running through his head. Lorraine sits down next to him, not too far or too close, and pours the coffee. She knows she will maintain her morals, so sex is out of the question. But she also doesn't want to appear frigid.

Al takes a moment to look around her apartment. It is done mostly in white and bright colors. The couches are white leather, the coffee tables and end tables iron and glass. Candles of different sizes, with burnt wicks and melted wax, lay on the tables, pleasantly located. Al quickly notices how much larger her place is than his, and wonders how it looks by candlelight.

"You have a wonderful place here; you must be doing well."

"I'm making it. Where does the mighty Al Cleveland live?" she asks, sniffing her coffee, then taking a sip of it.

"Over by the Kent building," he replies softly.

She almost chokes on the hot beverage. "That's a horrible part of town. I wouldn't go over there even if I had an army to protect me."

He smiles at her. "It's not that bad. Most of the gunshots aren't near me." He picks up his coffee and warms his hands on the hot cup. "Besides, it's all I can afford right now."

She puts her coffee down and taps his thigh. "Listen, Al, my roommate just moved out, so I have a spare room. Why don't you move in here with me?"

"That's sweet of you, but I can't afford this."

"Yes you can, and I insist."

"You know you're beautiful when you're forceful. I like that in a woman."

She laughs lightly, but then her face turns serious as he places his hand on her knee. He leaves it there for a couple of seconds. He can feel the heat coming through her white panty hose. He squeezes his hand, and retracts it. He doesn't want it there long enough for her to reject him.

As always in the past, his simple touch causes her pulse to rise. She's not sure if she would have left his hand there, or let it slide up further. She clears her throat and quickly grabs her coffee to keep her mind on the subject.

"I sure did miss you, Lorraine."

"I missed you too, Al Cleveland. So, is it a deal?"

"I would love to live with you."

* * *

A few weeks pass. Al is totally moved in, and the two have grown very close. Lorraine is footing most of the bills. Al desperately wants to keep writing and singing, but he can't stand to see her work so hard to support him. Reluctantly he gets a job as a mailman to help out with the bills, and hopes his break will come soon.

Lorraine is working late one day, and comes home tired. She opens the door to find the apartment totally clean and spotless. The dining-room table is set with hot food fresh out of the oven. All the candles in the apartment are lit, and the soft, bobbing lights give it a peaceful and romantic glow. A smile appears on her face as she wonders where Al is.

"Where are you?" she asks softly, expecting him to jump out at any moment.

He walks out from the kitchen wearing one of his nicest suits. He is clean-shaven, and doesn't have a hair out of place.

"I'm glad that you came home."

Her eyes twinkle as she smiles. "I'm glad to be home. Were you expecting someone?"

He casually walks over to her, and takes her hand with his left one. His thumb rubs along the back of her hand as he looks deeply into her eyes. His eyes are filled with love. Not only can she see it; she can feel it as well. She gives him her undivided attention as he prepares to speak.

"It's 1964. Five years ago I left my wife Ella in Pittsburgh. Now that I look back on it, I think it was a mistake, a big mistake, to let such a wonderful woman go. I don't want to make that mistake again, so I have something to ask you."

"Oh my," Lorraine says as she places her other hand over her pounding chest. Her eyes widen as her stomach fills with emotion.

Al slowly lowers himself onto one knee.

"Oh Lord," she says, as her breaths become short and choppy.

She wants to jump up and down and scream, but she can't. Her eyes follow his right hand as he pulls out a small, dark-blue, velvet-covered box. He opens it, exposing a gold engagement ring. It seems to sparkle in the candlelight. Lorraine feels like she is going to pass out.

"Yes," she suddenly blurts out.

Al laughs. "I didn't ask you yet."

She moans and taps his hand for him to hurry up.

"Lorraine, will you marry me?"

"Yes! Yes, I will!"

Al stands, and she jumps into his arms. They enjoy their dinner and a night of making love. Neither one has a lot of money, nor do their families. So, two days later they have a simple wedding, and say their vows to one another.

* * *

It is early November; winter comes in, and Christmas is heading their way once again.

Ella keeps her promise and lets Ted and Daryl take a Greyhound bus to see their father. Al and Lorraine wait patiently at the bus depot. He is nervous, because it has been quite some time since he has seen his boys. *Daryl, how old is Daryl now? He is ten,* he remembers. *Wow, that means Ted is fourteen. All those years gone and I can't get them back. I'll just have to try and make up for lost time.*

Lorraine's stomach is filled with butterflies as she prays that the boys will accept her as Al's new wife. Bundled in their jackets and scarves, they both stand in total silence as the noisy bus pulls up to the depot and stops. The smell of diesel fumes drift by. It seems to take forever for the door to open. *Just relax, Al; they'll remember you—you're their father.* He squeezes Lorraine's hand, but she is too nervous to respond. The two boys climb off the bus, looking twice as big as they used too. Al rushes over to them as his wife stays still.

"Holy cow! Look how big you guys are!" he says happily as he hugs them both. It feels so good to hold his kids again. "How was the trip? Are you hungry?"

"The trip was OK, Dad," Daryl says.

"I'm hungry," Ted says; his voice has gotten deep over the years.

"You're always hungry," Daryl quickly replies.

Ted nudges him. "Am not."

Daryl hits him back. "Are too."

"Am not," Ted says louder.

"Hey," Al says, stopping it. "It's OK; we'll go get something to eat. But right now I would like you guys to meet someone very special to me."

Al stands up and motions for Lorraine to come over to them. She hesitates, and then walks over. She is extremely nervous, and feels like she is about to stand in front of two little judges who are going to sentence her for a crime she didn't commit.

Al clears his throat. "Boys, this is my new wife . . . your stepmom, Lorraine."

"She's not my mom," Ted mumbles under his breath.

"It's very nice to meet the both of you," Lorraine says with a steady voice.

The boys are silent and unsure of how they should deal with this. To them it is completely obvious that Lorraine is the reason why their dad left long ago. The whole reason their parents split up rests squarely on her shoulders, true or not.

Al gets their luggage and begins to escort them out of the depot.

"Now, let's get something to eat," he says.

"Yeah!" the boys cheer.

They all go out to eat, and then journey back to the apartment. Lorraine tries several times to talk to the boys, but they don't seem to have a lot to say to her. It bothers her to receive a cold shoulder, but she feels they might warm up later. Maybe much later. As soon as the boys walk in the apartment, their eyes light up at the silver Christmas tree in the corner. Two small rotating lights sit on the floor and shine different colors on it. It's not really the tree that the boys see, it's all the presents neatly wrapped underneath it.

"You already have your tree up and everything!" Daryl says loudly.

Al squeezes his shoulder. "That's right, and we'll be having an early Christmas just for you guys."

"Yeah!" the boys cheer, feeling as if they've found heaven on earth.

* * *

The next day Al and Lorraine both have to go to work. Al has an early shift, so he is already gone when Lorraine is in the kitchen drinking her coffee. She can hear the boys giggling out front, and figures they are snooping in the presents. She decides to stop them, and enters the main room to see them, but it is just as they are darting off to their bedroom.

"Maybe they weren't being bad after all," she mumbles.

Setting off to get ready for the day, she walks across the living room to the master bedroom.

Inside she heads for the bathroom so she can run her bath water. As soon as she opens the bathroom door, a cup full of water falls from the top of the door and splashes on her head. It stuns her as the plastic cup bounces on the tile floor. There is no doubt as to who did it. Her eyebrows cross, and she grinds her teeth. She is very mad, and has every right to be. But she still remains calm. She unclenches her fists, grabs a towel, and cleans up the mess with quick, harsh swipes at the floor.

She hangs the towel back up and pauses for a moment to calm down. She reminds herself that she is used to putting up with problem patients at the hospital. She decides to get her clothes out for the day. With steady steps she walks over to her dresser and opens the top drawer. Suddenly, two large tree frogs jump out at her.

"Ahh!" she shrieks at the two flashes of green.

The sounds of the boys laughing and running back to their room can be heard. Quickly she grabs an empty shoebox and places the two misplaced frogs in it. She leans on her dresser and stares at herself in the mirror. Her hair is all wet and messed up, and her face is void of any color from just being scared half to death.

"I've dealt with worse than this at work," she whispers. "Their father can deal with this when he comes home."

* * *

Later that evening she tells Al what the boys did, and he is none to pleased about it. He marches the two young men into their room, where he has a talk with them.

"But dad—" Ted says.

"Just be quiet and listen, boy. Whether you two like it or not, Lorraine is still my wife. Therefore I cannot have you guys doing as you please, like you did this morning."

Both of the boys sit on the edge of their bed with their heads hanging low. Ted can't believe that she snitched on them. He feels that it was all harmless games.

"I told her I was going to take my belt to the both of you." Their eyes widen, as they never thought about the punishment. "But she asked me just to have a talk with you instead. Do you realize that the Christmas tree and the early presents were her idea? If it was up to me, the only thing you would be looking forward to is some turkey and cranberry sauce. Do you understand what I am saying?"

Neither child answers. They just stare at the floor and nod every once in a while.

"Remember, half of those presents were bought with her money, not mine. She's not your mother, and she's not trying to be. All she wants to do is be your friend. Now come out here, apologize to her, and eat your dinner."

Lorraine stays in the kitchen as they sit down at the table. She feels horrible for telling on them. But she also knows it had to stop. After that, things quiet down for them. The boys stay for two more weeks, and they realize that Lorraine is just being nice to them, so they stop their assault of practical jokes.

CHAPTER 5

As the last of the winter's snow melts, Al gets a phone call from someone he hasn't heard from in a long time—Arthur. His old friend is back in town and wants to meet him at the recording studio tomorrow afternoon. Al is very excited about it, and can't wait to get back in the swing of things. He feels on fire, and alive all over again.

Al arrives at the studio and is ready to dive into things once again. He knows that Arthur has this certain magic or charisma to make any project come alive. They immediately begin to write and produce, in conjunction with the Halos, a hit called "Nag." The song takes off, and becomes a number-one hit. Al and Gene Pitney of the Halos hit the road for short engagements, promoting their new song. But no one there is prepared for the shock when the producers of Dick Clark's top-rated television show *American* Bandstand calls and asks them to appear on the show.

Just a few days later, they are onstage doing the live performance. Al's heart is racing as he watches the group sing the song from behind the curtain. He looks to his left and sees a white man standing there. He is wearing a nice suit, with his light-brown hair combed neatly. Al recognizes the man; it is Phil Spector, and he is a big producer and songwriter. He has done work for top groups like the Shirelles and Tina Turner. Al stands there and stares at the man, wondering what to say, or if to say anything at all.

"Are you Al Cleveland?" Phil asks.

"Yes, yes I am."

Phil sticks out his right hand. "I'm Phil Spector. Maybe you have heard of me before?"

Al shakes his hand. "Oh yes. I know who you are. You've done some wonderful work in the past."

"Thank you." He motions to the Halos, who are still singing "Nag." "It appears that you have done some wonderful work in the past as well. Are you under contract with anyone, Al?"

"No. For now I am a freelance songwriter."

"Good. What do you say you and I team up and do some work? I could really use a good songwriter like yourself."

Al smiles. He hopes his big chance about to happen. He almost has to gasp for air just to speak. "That sounds great, Phil. You have yourself a deal."

                              * * *

Two years go by. Al keeps contact with his children as they continue to visit for vacations. Daryl turns out to be quite talented, and helps to write his songs. Together they write the lyrics for a lot of music. But although Al's name is beginning to be recognized within the music industry, there is little money from that source. As much as he doesn't like it, he continues to work for the US Postal Service. His dream of being a successful songwriter is a bit battered, but not altogether shattered. He still writes, and waits for his day to come.

                              * * *

One day Al comes walking out of his room, wearing a black tuxedo. Lorraine is siting at the table, reading a magazine. She looks up at him. He holds out his arms and spins around once for her.

"How do I look?"

"You look wonderful." She stands, and straightens out his bow tie. "Is Phil going to meet you at the Apollo Theater?"

"Yeah. Smokey Robinson is the starring act tonight. I hope I get to see him backstage; it's been a while. Phil is hoping to get Curtis Mayfield and the Impressions to do some of our work."

She smiles and kisses him. "And what are you hoping for, Mister Cleveland?"

"My big break, so pray for me."

An hour later Al walks into the Apollo Theater in New York City. He stands in the lobby and looks at all the wonderful murals of

Redd Foxx, Moms Mabley, Ella Fitzgerald, and Billie Holiday. There was a lot more, and he knew them all by heart, many from his days on the Chitlin' Circuit. He turns and watches the crowd walk by. They are all dressed in their finest clothes, ready to enjoy an evening of fine entertainment.

"Oh, there you are," Phil says as he spots Al standing by the wall. "Ready to see the show?"

"Yes I am; ready to meet Curtis too."

The two sit near the back of the theater so they can leave early without disturbing too many people. The lights turn dim, and the audience falls silent. The curtain opens, and the show begins with a couple of opening acts. Soon Smokey Robinson comes out and does a wonderful job performing. Then Curtis Mayfield and the Impressions follow him. As soon as Curtis is done, Al and Phil quietly walk out and head backstage.

They travel through a series of narrow, dark hallways. The sound of the performing band is muffled by the concrete walls, but can still be heard. Al leads the way. Up front he can see some shadows of people moving towards him. As he comes closer, he recognizes the face.

"Hey Smokey," Al says.

"Hey, look who it is, big Al Cleveland. How are you doing? How's the family?"

"The boys are good. Ella and I got a divorce a few years back. But I remarried a little honey. Remember Lorraine?"

"Yes I do; you're a lucky man."

"How about you? How's your wife? Any kids yet?"

Smokey tries to hold onto his smile, but it fades slightly. There is pain in his eyes. "No, none yet. Still having problems."

A flood of memories come into Al's head from his days on the Chitlin' Circuit, and how he and Smokey first met.

* * *

It was just after one of their big shows; they had done everything according to the plan, and it went flawless. Every performer in Arthur's group was on cloud nine, and ready to party the night away. They all traveled to their boardinghouse and began to celebrate. The music was loud and continuous, as everyone drank, sang, danced, and drank some more. Then there came a knock on the door, and Al answered it.

"Can I help you?" he asked, opening the door wide.

"Yeah, I'm Smokey Robinson. I went onstage just before your group did."

At first Al thought he wanted to join the party. "You sure did. Man you got a hell of a voice."

"Thank you," Smokey replied in a softer tone.

Al could see the concern in his eyes. He was deeply worried about something. So Al stepped out into the hallway and closed the door so he could hear what Smokey wanted to say.

"Are you all right, man?" Al asked.

"I'm fine. It's my wife. Unfortunately we have the room directly below you, and you see, she is pregnant. She has already had two miscarriages, and she needs to rest and relax for a while. So could you guys please hold it down?"

Al opened the door again and looked at the room, which was packed full of rowdy people. They are growing louder by the minute. *What am I going to do? I can't tell them to quiet it down; in a few minutes they will be loud all over again.* With Smokey still standing in the doorway, Al walked into the room and didn't just turn the music down, he shut it off. Suddenly all eyes were on him.

"Hey, everybody," he said in a cheery tone. "I hear there is a bar across the street that isn't afraid to serve a few brothers and sisters. So what do you say we move the party over there so some of these people can get some rest?"

"Sounds good to me," some of them said.

In a moment they were laughing and singing as they filed out the door towards the bar across the street. Al is the last one out, and he locked his door. Smokey was still standing there; he knew without a shadow of a doubt that Al was a warmhearted person.

Al patted him on the shoulder. "There you go. Now you two can get some sleep, and I wish you the best of luck with your baby."

"Thank you. What's your name?"

Al shook his hand. "Al, Al Cleveland."

"Well, thank you, Al. I won't forget this act of kindness that you just showed me."

* * *

Claudette, however, ultimately miscarried that baby anyway. Al figures it would be best to leave that subject alone.

"So how are you doing?" Smokey asks. "Are you still singing and writing music?"

"Yes and no. I'm not singing anymore—at least not to anyone but me in the shower—but I am writing. Arthur and I did 'Nag,' which went right to the top. Got on *American Bandstand* and everything." He motions his head towards Phil, who is still walking down the hall. "Now Phil and I are doing some work and producing a few artists. But the money is slim. So honestly I am a mailman; that's my everyday job."

"Ain't nothing wrong with an honest day's pay. But if you're not happy here, you could come with me to Detroit. I work for Motown Records, and I am sure I could get you a job there."

Al can't believe it; could this be his big break? It takes just a second for him to get his head to stop swirling. "Are you pulling my leg?"

"No, I'm not pulling your leg. Do you want the job or not?"

"Yeah, of course I want the job!"

"Great. Give me your phone number, and I will arrange everything for you."

Al does his best to keep his hand steady as he writes down his number on a piece of scratch paper. Smokey looks at it and places it in his pocket.

"You'll be hearing from me in a couple of days, Al."

"I can't wait."

Al quickly jogs down the hall and meets up with Phil. He tells him the news. Although Phil will be sad to see him go, he knows that it is better for Al to be a producer of his own. That way Al can make his dream come true, and finally make a decent income.

* * *

Two days later Al hangs up the phone. Smokey had just called him from the Motown Records studio. He stares wide-eyed at the wall as Lorraine waits for some type of response to show that he is still alive.

"Well?" she asks; she can't wait any longer.

"It's all true," Al replies softly, his mind fills with ideas. Dreams of him making a living writing number-one songs begin to appear within reach. "We leave for Detroit in one week. Smokey's even paying for the plane tickets."

Lorraine sits on the couch. She can't believe this is happening. "This could be the dream you've been waiting for."

"I know, baby. See, I asked you to pray for me, and I guess you did—but wow, I wasn't expecting all this." He pauses and looks around the apartment. "I guess we should start packing! Because we're going to Detroit, baby, and I am going to be a producer!"

CHAPTER 6

The week passes by very quickly as Al and Lorraine sever their ties with New York City. Their belongings have been boxed up and put on a moving truck. The couple does one last walk-through in the empty apartment to make sure everything is gone.

"I can't believe I am finally leaving here," Lorraine says as she looks around the living room one last time. "I've been here since we came back from our tour."

Al comes over and starts to escort her out. "Well, believe it, sweetie, because we are heading for the big time now."

Like a couple of kids heading for summer camp, they rush out of the apartment, giggling as they go downstairs to get their taxicab. The taxi takes them through the busy city, and drops them off at the airport.

The plane is crowded but the flight is a short one, and soon they are landing in Detroit. They follow the long line of passengers walking off the plane. Just outside, they find Smokey and his wife Claudette waiting for them at the gate.

"Hey, look at these New Yorkers," Smokey says as he hugs Al. "How was the plane ride?"

"Short and sweet," Al replies. "I'm ready to get to work."

Smokey laughs. "Relax, we have something very important to do tomorrow."

"What's that?"

He smiles. "We have to play golf."

Smokey takes them to his house. It is a large, five-bedroom home that features a billiards room. Smokey and Claudette both like Chinese furnishings, so the home has a Chinese motif that is done to perfection. The new arrivals are shown to their room, where they do some unpacking.

The next day Smokey and Al do exactly what he said they were going to do, they play golf. In fact, they play every day for a week straight. Al thinks it is great, but he is beginning to wonder when this job proposal is going to come up. They are on the fifteenth hole. It's a perfect day, not too hot, and just a few small clouds dotting the blue sky. Smokey smacks a long drive right down the green.

"So, how do you like Detroit so far?" Smokey asks.

"So far it's fabulous. Hey, this beats the pants off delivering the mail."

Al takes his shot and nails his golf ball close to Smokey's. They are both silent as they watch it roll the last few yards.

"It looks like my wife and Lorraine are getting along well. How would you guys like to stay another week?"

Al smiles, dumbfounded at the man's generosity. "Well, Smokey, we'd love to . . . but—"

"But what?"

"But as much as I love being here with you and playing golf every day . . . well, let's face it, I ain't that good at it, and that explains why nobody's paying me to do it. I appreciate the vacation . . . but I was hoping to meet your boss soon."

Smokey puts his driver away, and calmly starts walking towards his ball.

"Berry is on vacation, just like you. But I made an appointment to see him after next week. What do you think—a nine iron should do it?"

Al stands there with his hands on his hips, smiling. "You son of a gun, you knew that all along, and kept me in the dark about it."

"I just wanted you and Lorraine to enjoy a vacation before the work started. So does that mean you'll be staying with us for another week?"

"Yes it does, and thank you, Mister Robinson."

"You're welcome, Mister Cleveland."

Another week passes; the women have been bonding and shopping. The men continue playing golf. First thing Monday morning Smokey calls Berry Gordy at Motown and arranges a time to meet on Tuesday. Smokey walks out to the living room and sits down on the couch with Al. The two watch TV for a moment.

"All right, you're going to meet with Berry tomorrow morning. That leaves you plenty of time to do what you have to do today," Smokey explains.

"What do I have to do?"

"Claudette and I rented you an apartment just around the corner. I figured you would like to check it out, and arrange for your furniture to arrive. If you take it, your old buddy Obie Benson will be living right below you."

Again Al is amazed; his friend is being so kind and giving. "I don't know what to say, Smokey. You and your wife have done so much for us, and I don't know how I can repay you."

Smokey chuckles and smacks him on the leg. "When you start to work for Motown, you just write me a few number-one songs like 'Nag,' and we'll call it even."

Al can feel his dreams coming to life once again. He envisions himself receiving awards for best songwriter. "You bet, you got yourself a deal."

* * *

Tuesday morning Al is getting dressed, and wants to make sure everything is perfect. He is nervous, and runs around his room trying to find his watch and his black socks. Lorraine sits on the bed and watches him run back and forth. He runs into the bathroom again. She tries not to laugh at him, but she's never seen him act this way.

"Honey, have you seen my watch?"

"It's on the nightstand where you left it."

He rushes over, grabs his watch, and darts back over to a tall dresser, where all his clothes are kept.

"Have you seen my black socks?"

Lorraine calmly looks at her nails. "I put them on the nightstand next to your watch. In fact, you moved them out of the way to get your watch," she says with a giggle.

He rushes back over and grabs them, mumbling something about being blind. Quickly he plops down next to her and puts his socks on. His nervous fingers fumble with his shoelaces as he attempts to tie them quickly.

"Would you calm down?" she asks.

"I will once I have the job."

"If the Lord wills it, you will have the job. Your worrying about it isn't going to make any difference."

"Thank you, dear." He bends over and kisses her. "That didn't really help any, but thank you anyway."

He turns and quickly walks out the door. His heavy footsteps begin to fade.

"Remember, I'll be at the new house by the time you get back."

"I'll remember," he shouts from down the hall.

Al jumps in the car with Smokey. He pinches the bridge of his nose in an attempt to get himself to calm down and to collect his thoughts. He can't believe it; he is going to meet Berry Gordy, the head of Motown Records. The record company has only been in business for seven years, but it is already clear that it is headed for phenomenal success in the music business. The owner seems to know the ins and outs of it, and is considered a genius by many in the music world.

Berry started to hit the big time with his first production, "Are You Lonesome Tonight?" It was a song by his songwriter friend, nineteen-year-old Smokey Robinson, who sang it with his group, the Miracles. It was an instant hit that sold over a million copies. After that, he rounded up bright young talent at an alarming rate, both songwriters and performers. He wanted to develop a new sound and style for soul music. He signed up Diana Ross and the Supremes right out of high school. Diana was already well known in Detroit church group circles, and had also been popular at weddings and other large social events. Along with Smokey and Diana, he has contracts with Marvin Gaye and the newest group, the Moonglows.

That is why Al is so excited; there is so much talent waiting for good songs to be written, songs he knows he can do. Songs he knows will be heard by millions of people.

They drive up and stop in front of Motown Music. Al's eyes fall upon a small storefront with a hand-painted sign on it that simply reads, "Motown Records." He is slightly disappointed; it seems so small, and somewhat run down. He hadn't been expecting a skyscraper, but at least a four-story building.

"Here we are," Smokey says. "I know it isn't much to look at, but remember, I made my first hit here."

Al does his best to keep his hopes up. "Yeah, you're right. I'm ready to meet him."

They get out of the car and walk in through the single glass door. The lobby is extremely small; it can barely hold the receptionist and two guests. The floor is covered in off-white tile that could use a sweeping, while light-brown paneling covers the walls. Al follows Smokey as they travel down the only hallway. Hanging on the wall are a few plaques and awards. Al attempts to read them as he passes by. Smokey stops at a closed door, and knocks twice.

"Come in," a man on the other side says.

They walk into the office. The room is a little bigger than the rest of the place. It has a large desk with a matching leather chair. Berry sits comfortably in his chair as he watches the two come in and close the door.

"Hey, Berry, this is the guy I told you about, Al Cleveland."

Berry stands and shakes his hand. "Al, it's nice to meet you."

"It's nice to meet you too."

Berry is a rather rugged-looking black man with a certain toughness that says he has been struggling for success all his life. He is not overly handsome, but has good-looking features. He stands about five foot nine, and loves golf and boxing. A nice, dark-blue suit that is obviously tailor-made covers his body. He quickly flips though some papers on his desk.

"Smokey has been telling me a lot about you, Al, so I did a little homework for myself. You used to work with Phil Spector, did you not?"

Al is surprised and flattered that he has been checking on his work. "Yes, I did."

"He does a lot of good work. Why did you leave him and come to me?"

"I want to be the producer and the songwriter, not just the songwriter. And besides, this was a chance to work for the powerful Berry Gordy," Al states, swaying his body with excitement.

Berry laughs. "That's good to hear." He pulls out a thick contract, places it on the desk, and turns it around so Al can see it. "After checking up on all the work you've done in the past, I knew I wanted you to work for me. So I took the liberty of drawing up a contract."

He hands Al a pen. Al's pulse instantly picks up as his palms begin to sweat. He glances at the first few pages of the ten-page contract, and then flips to the back page. He takes the pen and leans over to sign his name. The room falls silent; there is a buzzing sound in his ears. Suddenly he hesitates. He stands back up and thinks for a moment.

"If you don't mind, Mister Gordy, I would like to bring this home and go over it."

"We're family here, Al, so call me Berry. If you want to take it home and read it, that is fine with me. I'll give you twenty-four hours to think it over—fair enough?"

"Extremely fair . . . Berry; I will be back here in the morning."

Al turns to leave, and Smokey gives Berry a "thumbs up" as he walks out. They go back down the hall, and Smokey directs Al to the recording studio. Smokey watches Al as he looks around the small studio. Al is clearly surprised. The control room can barely fit four people.

There is an eight-track board with very few effects, and just one playback speaker. He is amazed that they are able to get any quality sound out of the small room.

"Not much to it," Al says as he looks around one more time, as if there was something he missed.

"No, there's not. But remember, this is where I made my first hit. Berry's engineering wizards can make a big sound in this room, and that means big money for you and me."

Al smiles and glances at the contract that he is holding; dollar signs begin to pop up before his eyes. "Now that's a good thing."

"What do you say we get out of here? Is there anything you wanted to do today?"

Al glances around the studio again, and begins to imagine himself producing top hits. "I should go and help Lorraine unpack." He begins to chuckle. "If I don't, I won't be able to find any of my things for months."

Smokey takes Al to their new apartment. It is a modest, two-story duplex. Al has the top floor, and living below him is his old friend and fellow musician Obie Benson. The movers are just bringing up the last few cardboard containers. Al walks up the stairs to find Lorraine chest high in boxes.

"Do we really have this much junk?" Al asks as he looks around. "There is stuff everywhere."

Lorraine pulls out several dishes and unwraps the brown paper off of them. "I'm beginning to think they brought over someone else's stuff as well."

"Well, if so, I hope they are rich people."

Al walks over to the kitchen, sets his contract on the counter, and begins to help her unpack the dishes.

"What's that?" she asks, looking over her shoulder.

"Berry gave me a contract to sign," he replies happily, with a smug look.

Lorraine walks over and looks at it. Slowly she begins to flip through the pages. "Wow, this is a lot of legal mumbo jumbo. We should have a lawyer look at it."

Al joins her by her side, and reads some of it. "I was kind of hoping you would understand it."

"I'm a nurse, not a lawyer," she replies evenly.

"Well, we can't afford a lawyer. Heck, if it wasn't for Smokey, we couldn't afford this place."

She flips through a few more pages. "I understand that, but how do you know this guy isn't going to rip you off?"

"Because he's a black man, a *brother*," Al says, tapping himself on the chest with the palm of his hand. "He knows what it is like to struggle in today's society; he's not going to let me down, I can feel it."

Lorraine's eyes shoot back to the contract. Her lips tighten. "I would still like to have a lawyer read it."

"That's because you're not black, honey." She gives him the eye. "You're a beautiful West Indian. Ow, a sexy West Indian." A soft jab from her elbow gets his mind back on track. "You saw my people's oppression in the South. Berry knows what that is all about."

Lorraine nods. She reaches over and hugs her husband. "I'm happy for you. I just hope you're right."

The very next day Al returns to Motown Music with the signed contract. Berry welcomes him to the music family. In the following weeks, Al and Smokey work on quite a few projects together. But the holidays are fast approaching, so the two friends take a day off and go downtown to do some early Christmas shopping in October.

They walk along the sidewalk, bundled up in their winter coats, as low-level, gray clouds hang over the city, dripping cold rain on them. They are about to enter a department store when they notice a beautiful young lady walking out. They each grab one of the double doors, then they hold them open for her.

"There you go," Al says.

Smokey smiles at her. "Merry Christmas," he says in a flirtatious tone.

"Merry Christmas to you too," she replies warmly, as she walks off, both the men watching her go.

Smokey shakes his head. "Wow, that was one incredible woman."

"I second that emotion," Al replies.

They stop and stare at each other; more people begin to pass by as they continue to hold the doors open. Their musically inclined minds begin to go to work at a rapid rate.

"That sounds like a song title," they both say at the same time.

Smokey and Al walk around the store and begin working on the song. Within a few minutes their few lyrics turn into entire verses. The whole song is completed an hour later. They quickly get back to their car, and head for the studio.

"Everyone has already gone home, so we should have the place to ourselves," Smokey says as he pulls up.

Excited, they rush inside and immediately begin their work. They have the enthusiasm of a couple of kids playing while their parents are out for the night. They record "I Second That Emotion" and two other tracks. Al's heart is pounding with excitement as he watches Smokey call Berry at home.

"Hey, boss, I know it's kind of late, but Al and I have been on fire, and we have some new tracks we just recorded. I was hoping you would like to hear them."

Berry is silent for just a few seconds. "If you already made them, just bring them by, and I'll be happy to listen to them."

Moments later they are driving up to Berry's large house. Al is shocked by the size of it, and wonders how he can afford such a mansion. The house is two stories, and he thinks it must be over four thousand square feet. It is painted gray, with white trim. Four huge columns guard the front entrance. The landscaping around it is perfect; it is extremely well manicured, with beautiful bushes and many different types of flowers.

They drive up on the circular driveway and stop in front of the ten-foot-tall double doors. Al glances at the huge golden chandelier hanging above the door. They get out of the car quickly and ring the doorbell. Berry answers it.

"Hey, there are my two hardworking producers. Come on in, let's hear this thing."

They enter, and Al looks around the large living room and foyer. The outside is a reflection of the inside; the house is like a palace fit for a king to live in. Al begins to wonder if he will ever get this lucky.

"Are you coming?" Smokey asks, as Berry leads them to the back.

They go to Berry's private office in the back of the large house, where Smokey plays the full recording for him. The boss sits in his large leather chair and gives the work his undivided attention while slowly rocking back and forth.

After they play it once, Berry seems to be trying to hide a smile. "Could you please play 'I Second That Emotion' one more time?"

"Sure thing."

Smokey plays it again, and Berry's hidden smile cannot stay hidden any longer. Suddenly he has an ear-to-ear grin. He claps his hands.

"Gentlemen, what we've got here is sure to be a number-one hit!" he says loudly, excited. "That is going all the way to the top, I guarantee it. Go back to the studio, cut the last verse off, and add a horn. And as soon as you are done with that, release that baby!"

Smokey and Al practically run out of the house and head back for the studio. They do exactly as Berry had instructed them to do, and much to Al's amazement, the song sounds even better. As far as he is concerned, Berry is a genius.

"I Second That Emotion" is released; it soars up the charts and becomes a million-seller.

Al's spirits soar as he watches it do so well. A few weeks later he is outside and sees the mailman coming. Al walks over and greets the man as he takes his mail. As he flips through the bills, he notices an envelope that was sent from Motown Records. His heart begins to pound. He knows what it is; it's his first royalty check. *This is it, Al, payment for your work. The dream you have been dreaming about is here.* He almost drops the other bills as he tears into the envelope.

"Let it be a nice one." he whispers.

Slowly he pulls out the check; it's much more than he expected, and he knows there are a lot more to follow. His eyes are as big as silver dollars as his mouth falls open. There are a few deductions listed, but plenty left over for him.

"Lorraine!" he suddenly yells. "Lorraine, you gotta see this!"

Like a wild bull, he charges up the stairs to his apartment, calling for his wife all the way. He thunders into the apartment.

"What's wrong?" she asks as she comes out of the bedroom.

"I just received my first royalty check. Take a look at this!" he blurts out.

With a trembling hand he holds out the check for her to see. She stares at it in disbelief, then her eyes grow bigger.

"Wow!"

"Do you know how long it would take me to earn this as a mailman?"

She hears the question but doesn't answer. "Oh, we should go out and celebrate with Smokey and Claudette."

"That sounds great, but first I have to call my boys." He is still nervous as he grabs the phone and starts dialing. "Man, is this going to be a good Christmas."

He listens patiently as the phone rings several times. His eyes stay on the check.

"Hello?"

"Ah? Daryl?"

"Yeah, Dad."

"Man, you sound older every day."

Daryl instantly becomes excited. "Hey, they're playing your song on the radio right now; it's so cool."

"That's right, son, I finally hit the big time. Lorraine and I want you and Ted to come out for Christmas and stay for a few weeks."

"Yeah, I'd like that. I'll get Mom to find out how much a bus ticket will cost."

Al's chest sticks out with pride. "No, son, this time you and your brother are flying out; no more buses for my boys. Understood?"

"OK," Daryl replies in a slightly nervous voice; he has never flown before.

* * *

In the weeks that pass, Al and Smokey stay on their hot streak. They quickly collaborate on other hits like "Baby, Baby, Don't Cry," "Here I Go Again," and an updated version of "Yester Love."

Al also writes a big hit for Bobby Taylor and the Vancouvers called "Melinda." Also, their small sound studio is stripped and redone. Now they are having no problem getting the bigger acts. Their old friend Ron Jolley has joined the team; he now works right with them, helping promote the new songs.

It is an early Monday morning, and Al is supposed to meet Berry and Smokey at Motown, but he is running late. As he is backing out of the driveway he spots the mailman putting mail in his mailbox. He has patiently been waiting for another royalty check to arrive; he hasn't seen another one since the first one. Quickly he puts the car in park and rushes over to the mailbox. There he finds one thing, a letter from the IRS.

"It's only December, guys, you have to wait until April 15, just like you make me wait."

He tosses the notice in the front seat of his car, and jets over to the studio. He makes it there in time, and they are able to record all the new tracks that they wanted to, but it is a long day. Later in the evening he returns home. He brings the letter from the IRS up to his apartment and tosses it on the counter. Lorraine is over by the stove, cooking dinner.

"Hey, honey, how was your day?" she asks.

He walks over and holds her from behind for a brief moment, and then kisses her on the top of her head.

"No good," he mumbles. He walks away and plops down on a chair. "We just couldn't get the right sound today, and the artists were not cooperating with us one bit."

She notices the letter and picks it up. "What this?"

"Huh? Oh, that's something I got in the mail today. I don't care what they want. It's not tax time. Yet."

"Well, you might want to." She opens it as he places his tired head on the table. Her eyebrows cross as she reads it. "They say that you're not paying in the right amount of taxes. You had better get this cleared up before it is tax time."

He picks up his head and stares at the wall for a moment. "Well, I don't know what the problem could be; Berry should be withholding enough taxes for me. But I'll check with him."

She returns to her cooking. "All right, but don't let it go too long."

Al's mind is already a million miles away. His kids are going to be there in just a few days, and he wants everything to be perfect for them. He is looking forward to writing more songs with Daryl again. It will be a great time to bond and to share experiences.

CHAPTER 7

It's December 21, 1968. Al and Lorraine climb into the car to drive to the airport. The temperature seems to be pegged at 33 degrees, with very little wind. They have joked about someone seeing a blue sky that they haven't seen in a long time. Once again it is covered with thick clouds instead. Large, fluffy, white snowflakes slowly drift down to the ground. The snowfall is just enough to seem magical, with Christmas so close.

At the airport they pick up the two young men, who seem to be growing by the minute. Ted is now seventeen and Daryl almost fourteen. Al can't believe how the years have gone by. He monkeys around with his boys as they get their luggage. He is so happy that they are together again. From there they head over to Smokey's house, where a small party is going to take place.

Smokey and Claudette still don't have any children, so the two teenagers are given the run of their large house. To them it is paradise. They are allowed to drink soda, eat ice cream, and play pool inside or football outside. Al is happy to see his children having fun. He joins Smokey out on the back patio as his friend gets a breath of fresh air. The two men watch the guys play football with some neighborhood kids and other band members.

"I don't know whether you know it or not, but you are a lucky man," Smokey says. Al knows how badly he wants children, but it just doesn't seem to be working out.

Al knows exactly what Smokey is talking about, and feels he would give anything if it would help Smokey and Claudette have children of their own. But he knows he can't interfere with God's will.

"Listen, Smoke, the other day I was talking to their mother, Ella, and she and I came to an agreement on something."

"What's that?"

"Well, I know this is real late in the game, but we were wondering if you and Claudette would be interested in being the kids' godparents."

Al's question sinks into Smokey's mind as he watches the kids play. Slowly he smiles and nods. "Yeah, yeah, I like that. Godparent, huh? I think that is nice, Al—you've got it."

* * *

Christmas comes and goes, and the boys receive a ton of presents. It is the early days of Motown Records, and all the recording artists feel and act like one big, happy family. So, Diana Ross and the Supremes, Marvin Gaye, Obie Benson, and many others all treat Al's kids as beloved nephews. The boys even have keys to their new godparents' house, just in case they feel like going over and playing pool.

With the holidays over, Lorraine and Al go back to work. Al has a lot of new material that Daryl had helped him write over the winter break. Daryl and Ted climb out of bed, and step over the new clothes and games they just received two weeks ago. Ted heads off to the bathroom to take a shower. Daryl's stomach is growling like crazy, so he heads straight for the kitchen and grabs a bowl of cereal. He knows the adults are gone, so there is no one to say anything to him about watching TV and eating in the living room. He reaches for the TV to turn it on.

Knock! Knock! Someone just hit the door hard, scaring him. He walks over and opens the door a few inches. There are three white men in suits standing there.

"Al Cleveland?" the one in the front asks.

Daryl doesn't like this; he knows something is wrong. Panic begins to set in. His voice trembles as he speaks. "That's my dad; he's at work."

The man gently pushes the door open all the way. His eyes search the room, as if Daryl is lying. He reaches into his jacket and pulls out his wallet. He flashes a badge in front of Daryl's face; the only word Daryl gets to see is "Internal." The man begins to walk in; Daryl backs up, frightened and confused. The next man follows him in with several papers, and hands them to the frightened boy.

"Internal Revenue Service. We are here to collect for you dad's back taxes."

The men come in, and are followed by others. Daryl backs up against the wall. With eyes wide, he watches them come in and begin to grab anything and everything.

"I don't have any money!" Daryl shouts, thinking he is being robbed.

Just a few miles away, Al is in the newly redone sound room at Motown Records. Smokey is singing one of the new songs that Al and his son had written just before Christmas. Suddenly one of the lights on the phone turns on, and the receptionist's voice can be heard.

"Al, line one is your son."

"This better be good," he mumbles as he reaches over and taps the button for line one. The kids know better than to disturb him when he is recording. "Yeah, son, what is it?"

Daryl's voice comes over the phone, small and filled with terror, "Dad?"

Al suddenly sits up as he pushes the phone into his ear. "Daryl, what's wrong?"

"They're here," he replies, almost in tears.

"Who's there?"

"Men—they're taking everything, our furniture, the TV . . . everything."

Adrenaline rushes into Al's veins. "Are we being robbed? I'll call the police!"

"The police are already here; they're watching."

Confusion fills Al's mind; he doesn't understand what is going on. For a very brief moment he listens to the men in the background talk as they move the furniture.

"Just hang on, son, I'm on my way."

Al jumps out of his seat and rushes out the door while the band he is helping record is still playing. Darting across the street, he makes it to his car and speeds to his place. His heart is racing frantically. *God, please let my children be all right.*

He stops his car in front of three parked police cars. All the cops are leaning on one car, watching, as the IRS agents remove the last belongings. Behind them is a large, plain, white moving van.

"Daryl! Ted!" Al calls out as he charges up the stairs to the apartment.

He finds his boys sitting on the kitchen counters. Almost all that is left in the house are the cereal bowls that they are eating out of. They both look frightened and confused. Al rushes over and hugs them both. Daryl almost breaks down, but he stays strong for his dad. Al looks around the apartment—just a few pieces of paper and discarded trash remain. The lead agent walks up to him.

"Are you Al Cleveland?"

Al does everything he can to hold back his anger. "Yes, I am," he replies through gritted teeth.

The agent holds out the court papers. "I am Agent Daniels of the Internal Revenue Service. This is a court order to pick up your belongings due to the back taxes that have not been paid."

Al takes the paper, mad as hell. "Back taxes? How much money could I possible owe?"

"One hundred thousand dollars, Mister Cleveland," Daniels replies calmly.

Al's knees become weak; he almost falls over. "One hundred thousand? A hundred thousand?" he repeats louder, as the veins in his head begin to surface. Suddenly he yells. "How could I possible owe that much? How much do you people think I make? Do I look like some millionaire?"

The police can hear the yelling, and in moments they enter the empty apartment to make sure no one gets hurt. Al calms down as the uniformed men walk in. He doesn't want to be arrested in front of his children.

"This is not a guessing game for us, Mister Cleveland. We are going off reports—reports submitted to us from your employer, Motown Records."

The room seems to spin as the agent and the police turn and leave. Lorraine comes running up the stairs, and stops in the doorway to the apartment. Her mouth falls open as she stares at the empty room. Everything they worked so hard for is gone. Suddenly she turns and watches the moving van drive away with all of their furniture. Al has a blank look on his face as he stares out the window, barely holding onto the court papers. He hopes to wake up and tell himself that it is all just a bad dream.

"What happened?" Lorraine asks.

"I don't know," Al's voice seems so small and distant as he tries to sort it all out. "They say that Motown is somehow reporting that I am making a lot more than what I do." He looks over and can see the worried look on his wife's face. "Don't worry, hon, as soon as the next royalty check comes in, I'll buy you a house full of new furniture."

"If we ever get one," she cries as she walks through the rest of the house to see what is missing.

Al resumes staring out the main picture window. He can see the mailman coming. *There you are. Please bring me my check; I need it more than ever.* Al walks downstairs and out onto the front lawn. He patiently waits as the mailman comes up to him.

"Morning," the mailman says.

"Morning. I hope you have something for me from Motown Records."

The mailman reaches into his bag and pulls out a small stack of letters. "Let's see here. Yup, sure do. Not one but two for you."

Al emits a big sigh of relief and smiles. "Thank you so much. I can't tell you how much that means to us."

Al already feels better; he knows things will turn around now. He hustles up the stairs as he tears into the first envelope. Suddenly, just a few feet from the door, he stops, pulls out a single sheet of paper, and flips it open; there is no check. Quickly he looks inside the envelope for the missing check, but it's not there. Slowly he walks into the apartment and opens the other envelope. It too has a single piece of paper with no check. He is angry to the bone as he stares at the two typed sheets. They are itemized reports on his pay. Each one has a long line of deductions listed; everything he would have earned was taken away.

"They took the pictures of my mother," Lorraine says as she comes around the corner, her eyes still wet with tears. "Why on earth would they take the pictures of my mother? It's all I have to remember her by."

Al's eyebrows cross with anger. At the top of both pages is the amount he should have been paid. But below that are minuses for speakers, microphones, and installation, along with a long line of other things he's never even heard of. It appears that Berry has been fixing up Motown Records with Al's money. What makes it worse is the fact that the IRS was told that Al received all the money, with no taxes taken out. Without a word to anyone, Al turns and starts walking out the door.

"Where are you going?" Lorraine asks.

"To go kill a black man!"

* * *

Moment's later Al comes barging into Berry's office. The heavy door slams against the wall. A secretary who was taking notes jumps to her feet. She can see the fire in Al's eyes, and quickly backs away from the desk.

"What the hell are you doing to me and my family!" Al yells with a red face. "You have been lying to the IRS at my expense!"

As Al comes closer, the secretary runs out of the office. Berry sits up in his large leather chair, and straightens out his clothes. He casually dusts off his pants, as if this were nothing new. Al comes closer. Berry reaches into his desk drawer and pulls out a small stack of papers. He points at them.

"You signed this contract," Berry says calmly. He flips to the back page. "Is this not your signature?"

Al barely gives the paper a glance as his two hands ball up into fists. "So what if it is?"

"Didn't you read it?"

Al doesn't answer, and Berry sighs, as if the whole thing would even be obvious to an entire class of second graders. He quickly flips through the pages. "Here it is, written in black and white, Mister Cleveland. On page 8, section 3, paragraph 18, line 9, the producer, which is you, shall be responsible for all upkeep, upgrades, and supplies that are deemed necessary for the studio by the owner, which is me."

Al's heart is pounding like crazy. "That is completely unfair and you know it!"

Berry is so calm it sickens him. "You signed the contract; you even initialed this page on the bottom. I don't know how to make it clearer to you people. It costs money to make money; you can't do one without the other."

Al's blood is now boiling. "The only one who is making money around here is you, Berry. The rest of us are left out in the cold to rot."

He turns and storms out of the office. He is almost out of the building when he passes Smokey.

"Al, what's wrong?" Smokey asks.

"We're being ripped off, that's what's wrong!" Al tosses over his shoulder as he makes his way outside.

Smokey follows him. "Al, come on. Please tell me what is wrong; maybe I can help."

Al stops at his car and turns around. He is somewhere in between screaming mad and crying. He stares at his friend and shakes his head. "They took everything," he says, in a soft tone that is muffled with anger.

"Who?"

"The IRS. Motown has been giving them reports showing that I am making a lot more money than I really am. That was my royalty money that fixed up the sound room."

"Man, that sucks," Smokey says as he glances back at the Motown Records building. It angers him too; after all, his employer is the same person. He feels sorry for Al, and tries to imagine what it would be like to have everything he owns taken from him. His heart hits his stomach. "What do you say we get out of here?" He motions his chin towards Motown, knowing full well that Al wants to leave. "You guys can stay with Claudette and I until we get you some furniture again."

"That's nice of you, Smokey, but furniture isn't going to solve all my problems. I need money to pay the bills too."

Smokey smiles. "I know an easy way of making some money that Berry can't touch."

Al's eyebrows rise, as if it were to good to be true. "How's that?"

"Concerts," Smokey replies with a devious grin. It is one of the ways he makes money on the side. "If you promote them for me and be a backup singer, I will make sure you get a nice piece of the pie. We can do some right here in Detroit, and all the money we make will be ours."

Al offers only a small smile; thoughts of the IRS raid are still very vivid. *But then again, it would be nice to be on tour and away from here.*

I've always liked being on the road, he thinks to himself. "That sounds good. I don't know what I would do without you."

They hug each other with a manly pat to each other's back. "And I don't know what I would do without you writing those songs for me," Smokey replies.

They get in their cars and leave the Motown lot. Al sends his boys back home, and immediately begins working on promoting Smokey's concerts. Smokey is a star, making Al's job that much easier.

Lorraine wants to fight Berry in court, but she and Al both know it would take a lot of money, and that is the one thing they don't have right now. It causes a lot of stress to the marriage; many arguments ensue because of what happened. But there is one thing Lorraine never does. She never states, "I told you so"—something that Al is grateful for.

CHAPTER 8

Several weeks pass, and news of the concert tour travels fast. Ron Jolley and Obie Benson join them, taking a much-needed break from Motown Records. Al teams up with Ron, and together they are able to line up a string of concerts all over the Eastern Seaboard. And this time it's not any Chitlin' Circuit they are on; they are heading for big halls that are capable of holding large crowds. Without giving a reason, Al makes Detroit their last stop, which will be in July.

"Are you all ready to go?" Smokey asks.

Al smiles and looks at the line of cars and moving trucks that hold all the equipment. It is a big step up from the old days and the three station wagons, and it feels great. He draws in a deep breath, filled with pride. "You bet I am. Lets go make some music."

The caravan pulls away and heads for the highway. They travel out of state, and do concert after concert. with other groups opening for them. The days are very long and the nights longer, but Al is able to make some good money, and recover some of what he has lost—namely his pride. But the few dollars he is making are nowhere near the amount that the IRS is asking for. It is merely a drop in the bucket. Somehow he still holds onto his dream of making the big time writing number-one songs. His love for music is too much for him to let go of.

* * *

The team rolls into Pittsburgh and completes three very successful shows, but for the last couple of nights Al has been very quiet. As they travel closer and closer to his old stomping grounds, he begins to feel nervous and unsettled. The pit of his stomach tells him what his problem is, but his heart doesn't want to listen.

Slowly he comes to the conclusion that he must go to Ella's apartment, their old home, so he can see the boys. He hates the thought of being in town and not seeing them. And it would be too rude to call and have them meet him on a street corner. After all, Ella didn't do anything wrong. Although he has talked to her numerous times on the phone, this will be the first real contact he has had with her in almost ten years. It's worse than a million blind dates wrapped up into one, he thinks.

It's a bright Saturday morning when he decides to go see his kids. He parks outside, and stares up at the old building. *It has hardly changed,* he thinks to himself. He can still remember charging up those concrete stairs into a home filled with the smell of dinner. And Ella could cook up a meal. He glances down the street and spots some kids playing ball. He is taken back to when he used to do that with the kids. He hopes it had some kind of impact on their lives.

With his nerves popping, he walks up to his old apartment and knocks on the door. He waits a few seconds, but it feels like an hour. He almost expects to hear the pitter-patter of small feet racing over to answer the door. But instead he hears loud thuds. Daryl opens the door. His eyebrows shoot up as his mouth falls open.

"Dad!" he shouts in his deep voice.

"Hey, son," Al says happily as they embrace.

Standing there holding his son, he knows the visit was worth the anxiety. The tension in his stomach doesn't fade, but his heart is on the road to recovery.

"What are you doing here?"

Al shrugs his shoulders. "Well, I was just passing though, and thought I would pop in."

Suddenly Ella's voice can be heard from around the corner. "Daryl, close that door; you're letting all the heat out."

Daryl looks over his shoulder and panics for a brief moment; he is not dressed to go outside, and he's not sure how his mom will react. Then Ella walks around the corner in her bathrobe to see why the front door is still open.

"Why is that door still—" She stops as her eyes lock with Al's. At first she stares at him as if he were a ghost. "Well, I'll be. Please tell me that you are here on business, and not running from the law."

Al is taken aback by that comment. "Now, that was uncalled for. I'm here on business and pleasure. I wanted to see the kids. Can I come in?"

It feels really strange, asking to enter the old apartment. But after all, he hasn't lived there in years.

"Daryl, let your dad on in out of the cold.'

"Mom, it ain't like dad's a criminal," Daryl says.

"Don't talk to your mom that way," Al quickly puts in before she can respond.

Ella stands there with her hands on her hips, and looks him up and down. Part of her wants to be nice, or at least civil. The other part wants to kick him in the groin, just to watch him keel over in pain. She decides to blend the two together and make the best of it. Al stands there and warms his bare hands by rubbing them together. Knowing that he is on her ball field, he decides to wait for her to make the first move.

"Would you like some coffee, Al?" she asks. Her tone isn't overly friendly, but it isn't as frigid as he expected.

"I would love some, thank you."

He takes off his jacket and hangs it up on the same hook that he used to hang it on all the time. He looks around as he walks out of the foyer and into the living room. Everything is basically the same— everything except his ex-wife. She is a steel fortress compared to the woman he left years ago—she has become a tower of strength in order to survive. His eyes fall on a paperback Bible resting on the coffee table. The pages of it are curled back, indicating that someone has spent a lot of time reading it.

"Mom and I go to church a lot now," Daryl explains, once he notices his dad staring at it.

"I'm glad to hear that, son, it's the best thing you can do. How's your brother? Did he move out?"

Daryl nods, and then suddenly claps his hands and shakes his hips. "Got the whole place to myself while Mom's at work."

Al's face turns serious as he remembers how he was at Daryl's age. "You just remember to do your schoolwork when you're here alone. Don't be wasting all your time chasing some hussy."

"He's chasing plenty of them already," Ella says, as she walks out carrying a tray with a pot of coffee on it and two cups.

"Aw, Mom. You know I've been doing good in school."

"Yes you have, dear. Why don't you get your report card and show it to your father?"

Daryl darts off to his room. Ella pours two cups of coffee, adding just a little bit of sugar and the right amount of cream—exactly the way Al likes it.

"You always did make a great cup of coffee," Al states, hoping to wash away some of the tension.

Ella sets the cup in front of him. She sits down on a chair, leans back with her cup, and crosses her legs. She is expressionless; Al can't tell how she feels. "How's Lorraine?"

The tension isn't washed away. They are only a few feet away, but there might as well be a ten-foot wall there.

"Oh, she's doing good . . . working hard."

"I heard about the IRS raid," she says, tight-lipped. She has to hold back a smile; Ella figures it was karma that caused the raid. "The boys thought it was quite the adventure."

"Yeah, that was pretty bad," he replies in a mumble, wishing it had never happened. The more he thinks about it, the more his stomach rumbles with anger.

"Are you two all right?" she asks in the old, soft voice that he used to hear all the time.

Man, do I miss that tone. It could warm me on the coldest of nights. "We'll make it."

Suddenly Daryl comes running out from his room. "Here it is, Dad!" he says as he plops down next to him. He shows him the report card.

"Wow, you are doing good. I'm real proud of you."

"So, what did you want to do today?" Daryl asks.

"Well, if it's all right with your mom, we could go see your brother's new place, and then I'll take you over to the theater, so you can see the gang."

Daryl loves music, and loves being around musicians. "OK, that sounds great. Is it OK, Mom?"

Ella looks at Al and makes a face that says *I don't care.* "Take him," she replies, as she shrugs her shoulders. "I could use a little break."

Daryl runs back to his room to get dressed. Al and Ella talk a little bit more, but mostly they sit in silence.

They visit Ted's apartment, and then spend the rest of the day together. Daryl is greeted with open arms at the theater. He helps his dad set up for the concert. Al keeps an eye on him, still in disbelief at how fast his sons are growing up.

* * *

Eventually Al has to say good-bye to his kids because the group is heading south, and after that they plan on heading westward, back home to Detroit. They have obtained celebrity status and have no trouble at all booking engagements. But although things are going very well, Al is rather quiet. He has not said why, but the Vietnam War has been deeply bothering him. He knows that his good friend Marvin Gaye's brother Frankie over there, and he prays nightly that he and all the others come home safely.

As the winter months fade away and the days become longer, the group finds itself back in Detroit—right in July, just like Al planned. He and Ron Jolley are sitting in the backseat of the car as they travel down the highway. Ron is reading the paper and suddenly chuckles.

"What?" Al asks.

"Now I know why you wanted to come back to Detroit so badly."

"And why would that be, Ron?"

Ron folds back the paper and shows him one of the pages. There in the center of the page, written in bold ink, is an advertisement that reads, "Live at the Fox Theater for a limited time, the legendary Natalie Rose Jenkins." Al looks away, not reading any more details.

"What do you know, both nights we're here, so is Natalie. You're going to see her, aren't yoooou?" Ron asks, as if he was a little kid.

Al continues his stare out the window as he watches the green trees pass by. "I thought I might check up on her."

Ron has a huge smile on his face. "Checking up on those panties is what you'll be checking up on."

"I didn't say anything like that," Al replies, squeezing his wedding ring. *I'm married, and I love Lorraine. But then again, I was married to Ella, and I loved her too.*

"Al and Natalie sitting in a tree, he's pulling her panties down to her knees," Ron sings out loud as he weaves his head back and forth.

The rest of the passengers laugh. Al remains quiet as he continues to gaze out the window. The trees seem to blend together as his mind drifts back in time to their good-bye. He hasn't seen her since, and has only talked to her a handful of times. Their conversations have always been warm, but not sexual. *Not this time, Ron. I want to be true to my wife.* Obie, who is sitting in the front seat, turns around and begins to talk to Ron about future projects. Al can hear them talk, but his thoughts are elsewhere. *I wonder how she will act when I see her? I wonder if I will be just an old friend . . . or more?*

When the group arrives in Detroit, they all call home. They are on the opposite side of the massive city, so they explain to their loved ones that they will be coming home right after they complete their last two shows. Both are at the same club, so there is more free time, because they can leave their equipment there until the next night.

Compared to the others, it's a small club. But that is the way Smokey prefers it. He enjoys more of a one-on-one crowd, especially in his hometown. He and the rest of the group are ready to do the shows and get them over with so they can go home.

As the group sets up, Al's thoughts drift more and more towards Natalie. He begins to fumble with the wires as he sets up the microphones. Feelings of guilt rush into him as he realizes he is dreaming about making love to her again. He quickly looks over his shoulder, as if one of the guys could read his mind. *Get your act together, Al, you guys are just friends now. You have nothing to be ashamed of.* He clears his thoughts and does his best to finish his job.

That night they put on an excellent concert, and the crowd loves it. But they are in the middle of a song when a fight breaks out between four men. Several bouncers come out and struggle to stop the brawl. The band continues to sing as things settle down once again. But someone has panicked and called the police.

After the song is finished, Smokey decides to address the crowd. "All right, everyone—just remember, we are all here to have a good time, so please take it easy."

They are about to start their next song when eight white police officers come barging into the nearly all-black club, with their nightsticks out. Suddenly the house lights come on, and everyone is blinded. A black man panics and runs for the door. Without warning, a blonde-haired. blue-eyed officer clubs the man to the floor with three hard blows.

What are you doing? Stop that, he's innocent! Unexpected anger begins to boil in Al's veins. But before he can move an inch, the man is handcuffed roughly and dragged outside. The man is wounded and barely conscious, but the policemen kick him as if the man is fighting them. The tension in the club is high, and a riot appears about to break out. Al stands there, tightly gripping his microphone stand. He desperately wants to rescue that man from the hands of injustice.

"Al, start the song," Smokey says, hoping the music will calm everyone down again.

Al begins to sing, starting the song. Once again the house lights come down, but it takes several songs for the crowd to get back into the groove of things again. The band members can all tell that something has changed in Detroit since they were last here. The easygoing spirit that was once in the clubs is no longer there. The tension and frustration in the air is so thick that one could cut it with a knife.

Due to the raid, the club closes early. The patrons are angry with the police; the owner of the club just wants to protect his property. Although the group is upset, it is no reflection on them. After everyone leaves, the members do some preparation for the next day's show. Al quickly walks over and grabs his things. Smokey notices what Al is doing, and walks over to him.

"Where are you headed?"

He glances at his watch. "Since it's an early night, I thought I would head over to the Fox Theater and check out Natalie's new show. Would you like to go?"

Smokey shakes his head. "No, I'm tired; we haven't had an early night in a long time, so I am going to take advantage of it and get some rest."

"Fair enough," Al states. "I guess I'll see you later."

"Just be good."

Al knows exactly what Smokey is talking about. "Hey, if I wasn't going to be good, I wouldn't have invited you along, right?"

"I guess. See you in the morning."

Smokey turns around, and Al quickly darts out the back door before Ron can hit him with any more wisecracks about seeing Natalie. But Al's actions bother Smokey; he doesn't believe in running around.

* * *

Al takes a yellow, checkered taxi to the large theater. He is happy for Natalie that she is doing so amazingly well in her career. Wearing a tuxedo, he walks through the lobby and heads in. Through the closed doors he can hear her soft, angelic voice carrying a tune.

He enters the dark theater and stands in the back. He can't help but smile at the sold-out crowd that is there to see her. Then his eyes focus on her. *My God, she is a beautiful woman.* Natalie has hardly changed over the years. Her body is just a shapely as it used to be. She is wearing a tight white dress that hugs her every curve. She has white feathers in her upswept hair. The talented lady is singing a Fats Domino song, "Blueberry Hill." She is doing it in the same style as Fats, and even puts on a black homburg hat in her imitation of Domino. A chubby piano player, a Fats Domino look-alike, plays the black grand piano onstage, accompanying Natalie as she sits on top of the shiny musical instrument. A circle of light beams down on them, and the two performers seem to be the only thing there; the stage appears to vanish into the black background.

Natalie finishes the song, and the audience comes alive with delight, cheering. Two male singers come out onto the stage. All falls silent; the only noise is the two new singers snapping their fingers. With a sultry walk, Natalie passes in between the two singers. They both stop and watch her go.

"Wow," the first singer says. "That is the finest, foxiest lady I've seen in a month of Sundays."

The second singer raises his microphone and says, "I Second That Emotion."

The audience cheers as Natalie returns to center stage and they sing "I Second That Emotion." Al has a huge smile on his face, and his chest puffs out with pride. *She's singing our song. Listen to how the crowd loves it.* Al stays and watches her give a great performance. The show comes to an end, and Al feels he has to see her once again.

He finds his way to the back of the theater, and travels down the dark corridors towards her dressing room. The other performers are happy as can be as they come down from the stage and enter their rooms. Al sees Natalie's dressing room. He smiles at her name on the door. *Finally, a black person can get some recognition around here.*

"Can I help you?" a deep voice asks.

Al stands at six foot three, and he has to look up to look her bodyguard in the eyes. The man stands there with his arms folded across his football-field–sized chest, waiting for Al to respond.

"I just wanted to see Natalie," Al explains, as he reaches for the doorknob.

The tall man puts his arm out, blocking Al from touching any part of the door. "She doesn't want any visitors right now. Maybe you could try later."

"Listen, could you please just tell her that Al Cleveland is here?"

The behemoth of a man shakes his head. "She's not looking for any visitors right now."

Al is doing his best to remain calm. "I know she isn't looking for any visitors *right now*, but if you would tell her that Al Cleveland is out here, she will change her mind."

Before the bodyguard can answer, the door opens. Al's heart skips a few beats as he stares into Natalie's green eyes—those wonderful eyes that can steal the soul of any man. As always she is stunning, and manages to capture every one of his thoughts. She stands there in disbelief. A smile forms on her face as she looks him up and down.

"Al?" She quickly looks at her bodyguard, who still stands in their way. "It's OK, he can come in."

She opens the door and Al walks in. His heart is pounding with excitement; she looks ten times better up close. He has always remembered her as beautiful. but she looks so much better than that. As soon as Natalie closes the door, she jumps into his arms. Al holds onto her once again, in a passionate manner. Thoughts rush through his head. *Remember, we're just friends.* Gently he backs away.

"How have you been?" she asks, in a happy-to-see-you tone.

"I'm good; everything is fine. I heard you sing my song."

She hits him, knowing that he is gloating about his achievement. "Nothing but the best for me. I was hoping you would come by and see me. Where's Lorraine?"

"We're just finishing our tour, so she's still at home."

Natalie's breaks into a devilish grin that causes Al's knees to tremble.

"That's nice to hear."

The young performer slowly walks behind a room divider and begins to undress. A lamp on a table shines on her, causing her shadow to fall on the far wall. Al watches her with his mouth slightly open as she unzips her dress and lets it drop to the floor. His pulse begins to pick up. He reminds himself: *we're just friends, no more.* He turns and looks at the door, wishing it were open—as if he wouldn't be strong enough to fight her off, and would need the assistance of the bodyguard.

"So, do you have plans tonight?" she asks.

"Huh?" Al asks, his voice sounding rather nervous.

She chuckles. "Do you have plans tonight?"

Quick, tell her yes. "No," he replies softly.

Al knows his answer will probably lead to trouble, but the temptation is quickly becoming too much. Natalie walks out from behind the room divider. She is wearing a nice pair of navy blue slacks and a white blouse. The clothes fit her to a tee; they seem to be tailor-made. His eyes slowly slide over her shapely curves. Man, she looks so good, so fit, he thinks. She sits down on a stool in front of her vanity, and changes her earrings.

"You are one beautiful woman," Al says, watching her reflection.

She spins around and smiles at him. "You know how to flatter a girl. You seem uptight; would you like a drink?"

"Yeah, that does sound good right about now. Do you have any Scotch?"

"Of course I do," she replies, opening a small refrigerator, which is loaded with different kinds of alcohol. She pours them each a glass. "Listen, the promoters of my concert are throwing me a party, and it would be kind of rude for me not to show up. I know there will be a lot of people there and if you aren't—"

"I would love to go," he says, and then takes a rather large sip of his Scotch, hoping it will make him feel more comfortable.

"Great! My driver will take us."

The word shocks Al. "Driver?"

"Yeah, the big fellow outside; he's also my driver."

"Dang," Al says, wiggling his head in a snooty fashion. He imitates her voice. "My driver will take us."

As he stands up, he finishes his drink. Natalie walks over and grabs him by the jacket collar, forcing him to bend over slightly. Without warning, she gives him a small kiss on the lips—a very small but very tender kiss that sends vibrations racing through him.

"You just better behave yourself, Mister Cleveland. Or my *driver* will take care of you."

He laughs as he stands up and pulls her in for another hug. They kiss once, and then again, each time with just a little more passion, igniting an old spark. It is as if they are both testing the waters before diving in.

"We had better get going," she whispers, burying her head in his chest.

They both leave, and a half hour later they arrive at the hotel where she is staying. Down on the main floor, a large party is being thrown for her in one of the banquet halls. The two enjoy themselves eating, drinking, and dancing. Al meets a lot of new people in the music industry, which he hopes will help later on. As the night progresses, they continue to drink, dance, and hold one another. Their hands tenderly rub each other in a manner that only lovers know. Later in the evening, a rather intoxicated Natalie motions with her index finger for Al to come closer.

"What is it?" he asks, slurring his words slightly as he bends over.

She brings her mouth close to his ear and nibbles on his earlobe. "Take me upstairs. I want to be yours again."

Al looks into her green eyes and holds her head. Gently he gives her a long kiss. Then they walk arm in arm out of the banquet hall and straight to the elevators. He brings her upstairs, where they make love once again. Late in the night the two fall asleep in each other's arms.

* * *

Al stands at a bar and watches a band that he cannot recognize. They are playing some song; the music is familiar, but he can't put his finger on it. Cigarette smoke drifts, and the smell of alcohol is in the air as the stage lights flash. The bar is filled with black people. Everyone around him is dancing and enjoying the music. He is just standing still and looking around. He can feel it; something is wrong, very wrong. The hairs on the back of his neck stand on end. His body changes gear, as if it is about to be involved in a fight, but he doesn't know against who, or why.

Suddenly, bam—a nightstick rams into his stomach. He keels over in pain as he struggle to breathe. His stomach wrenches with ripping pain. Looking to his side, he can see the blonde-haired, blue-eyed police officer standing there. It's the same one he saw before. He yells something at Al, but he can't understand it; the words are muffled. The officer raises the billy club again. Al sees it, and wants to stop it.

"I can take you," Al moans.

Bam—the nightstick hits him in the back, over an over. The repeated blows come from several different directions as other policemen join in.

"I can take you! I can take you!" he cries with each blow.

The beating continues. His legs give out, and he falls to the floor. For some unknown reason, he can't move his hands; they are stuck behind his back. He struggles and can feel cold metal around his wrists.

* * *

"Al, wake up. Wake up, Al," Natalie says, shaking him.

He shoots up in bed, a layer of sweat covering his skin. He looks around the room, confused, as he tries to sort out what is real and what was the dream. Slowly his mind dispenses with the fiction and lets reality come in. He relaxes, and gratefully lies back down.

"Are you all right?"

"Yeah, just had a nightmare. That was all. I have a feeling that something bad is about to happen."

Al tells her about the nightmare, and the policeman with the blonde hair, but it really doesn't make sense to either one of them. Slightly hung over, they climb out of bed, take a shower, and get ready.

An old friend of Al's lives on this side of town. His name is Doc Jacobs, and he is one of the original pioneers of the Chitlin' Circuit. The man is in his late fifties, and anyone who knows anything about the music industry knows him. And to Doc Jacobs, there is no such thing as a stranger. He is loved and adored by many. The gang has known him for years, and has always looked up to him.

Al picks up the phone and calls the hotel where Ron and Obie are staying.

"Hello?"

"Hey, Obie, it's me, Al."

"Man, Al, where have you been all night?"

"Just out."

Suddenly Ron's voice comes in from the background, *"With Natalie. K-I-S-S-I-N-G."*

He continues to sing his song as Al does his best to ignore him.

Obie begins to laugh. "Man, that guy is a goofball. So what's up?"

"Natalie and I are going to visit old Doc Jacobs. Would you like to go?"

"Yeah, that sounds great; I haven't seen him in a long time. Ron and I will meet you out front in forty-five minutes."

"All right, I'll see you then."

Al and Natalie go downstairs, grab a quick breakfast, and leave. They are within walking distance of where everyone else is staying, so they don't bother getting a taxicab. As soon as they reach the other hotel, they see Ron and Obie coming out.

"Hey, guys," Natalie says.

She hugs Obie, and is about to hug Ron when he suddenly curtsies and pulls away an imaginary dress.

"Greetings to the supreme ruler of Fox Theater," he says, with his round face bowing to her. "And how is your royal highness today?"

Natalie smiles at him and shakes her head. "It is good to be the queen."

Al flags down a cab. The taxi pulls over, and Al opens the door for Natalie. She climbs in, and Ron begins to go in after her.

"You're the man," he whispers to Al. "There are no safe women when Al is around."

"Just get in the cab."

Al gets in the front seat as the others sit in the back. He hands the driver Doc's address.

The driver stares at it for a moment, and then shrugs his shoulders.

"It's near the area of 12th and Clairmont Street."

The driver nods, and puts the cab into gear. Natalie is busy talking with Ron and Obie; they are catching up on each other's lives. Al watches the passing city through the windows. It is just beginning to wake up from its sleep. There is a low-hanging, overcast sky that seems to blanket the city with gloom.

As the taxi drives along, the buildings slowly become older and older. With each passing block, things look a little more run down. They are near Doc Jacobs' house when they round a corner and stop. Just a few feet away are two police cars, blocking the narrow road. Their single red lights flash from the center of their roofs. The street is lined with apartments and stores.

"What's going on here?" Al whispers.

Suddenly two white policemen came barging out of an after-hours bar, dragging a young black man who is handcuffed. With wide eyes Al stares at one of the cops. It is the same blonde-haired, blue-eyed one, the same one he saw in the bar, the same one in the dream. Using their nightsticks, they begin to beat the defenseless man. Al gets out of the cab. He and the blonde officer make eye contact.

"I can take you," Al whispers.

CHAPTER 9

Both policemen cease their assault. The young black man barely moves, blood spilling from his mouth and head. Time seems to stand still as the three of them stare at each other. Obie and Ron climb out of the cab. The blonde-haired policeman points his nightstick at them.

"You Negroes get back in that cab and get out of here!"

"I can take you," Al says a little louder, as both his hands ball up into fists.

Suddenly Natalie grabs Al's arm. "Let's get out of here. There is nothing we can do."

Al glares at the officer. "What did that man do to justify you beating him while he is handcuffed and defenseless?"

"Why don't you come over here and find out, boy?"

Natalie pulls on his arm again. "Please, Al, let's go."

"Hey, Whitey! You leave them alone!" a black man yells from an upstairs apartment.

"Yeah, why don't you beat up on your own kind?" another tenant yells.

Suddenly someone throws a beer bottle, and it shatters on the roof of the police car.

Everyone shields their faces from the flying shards of brown glass. The other officer yanks out his pistol and quickly fires two rounds at a high window. The noise is loud and echoes up the enclosed street. The taxi peels out and takes off down the road, leaving its former occupants standing there. Without warning, rocks and bottles begin to fly down at the policemen as several people from different apartments begin an attack. The back window on one of the cop cars shatters.

"Let's go!" Ron yells.

The four of them take off in the other direction. As they run, they can hear the policemen's pistols rattle off several shots as more debris is thrown down. Three blocks away, the foursome stops, gasping for air. Natalie places her hands on her knees and tries to catch her breath.

"I'm sure things will calm down now," she says.

Obie stares off in the direction from where they came. Slowly, he fixes his stare upward. "I don't think so."

They all turn and look as thick, black smoke plumes into the gloomy sky. Something is burning, and it's something big. For a brief second they all watch as it continues to grow. Distant sirens can be heard, bouncing off the walls and alleyways.

"This could be hell on earth. We had better get out of here," Al says. "Doc's house is just a block away."

With a quick step they make it to their friend's house, as a row of police cars zoom by with their lights and their sirens blaring. The group walks up onto the small front porch. Natalie nervously knocks on the door. They all wait, but there is no answer.

"This is great," Ron mumbles.

"Who is it?" Doc asks from behind the closed door.

"It's me. Natalie Rose and Al Cleveland. We're—"

She pauses as two more police cars speed down towards the disturbance. Doc opens the door; he is delighted to see them all. He is a slightly overweight black man in his sixties. A half circle of white hair covers the back part of his head, and he sports a short, white beard.

"Well, look who it is. I haven't seen you in years. I thought you were the police. I heard them go by," he says cheerfully. Doc always seems to be in a good mood.

"Yeah, there are a lot of them," Al states, anxious to take cover.

Doc leans out the door as he listens to someone yelling. Suddenly there is one loud gunshot, and the yelling turns into screams of pain. Natalie jumps, startled by the abrupt noise. The shot was not that far away.

"OK, I'm going in now," Ron blurts out as he darts past Doc and enters the house.

"Come in, come in," Doc says, watching the smoke rise into the air. "What are they doing over there?"

As soon as everyone is inside, he closes the door and locks it. He turns and looks at his younger friends standing there.

"Relax, everyone. I'm sure that disturbance is a long ways away."

"Yeah, yeah it is," Al states, reassuring everyone.

Doc goes into the kitchen to fix something for them to drink. Natalie follows him in to help. Al stands near the front window and watches as a black man runs down the street, carrying a TV that is still in the box. A person carrying an armful of clothes and two people taking a couch follow him. They were all taken from different stores. Whatever is going on up the road is getting out of hand.

"It's a riot," Al says.

"Here." Natalie passes him a glass of ice water.

They are both silent for a moment, as they watch smoke drift right by the front of the old house. More people begin to jog towards the disturbance rather than away from it. Neither says anything, but Al and Natalie know it is not a good sign. Doc comes over and stands next to them.

"Oh dear, look at the smoke. Fools will burn down our own houses to make a statement. I have a fire extinguisher; I'll get it and put it on the kitchen table."

"Do you own a gun?" Obie asks.

"Heavens, no," Doc says as he heads for the kitchen. "Don't believe in them," he says over his shoulder.

Al looks over at Ron, who is sitting on the couch with a nervous look on his face. "Ron, check the TV and see if they are saying anything about this."

He turns on the TV and flicks through the channels; there isn't a thing about it. Then one of the channels breaks in with a special announcement—a live shot of a newswoman standing just half a block from where the police officers were. One of the police cars has been turned upside down and set on fire. Scores of people are around it, dancing in victory. In the background, five other buildings are burning completely out of control. Flames that shoot over a hundred feet into the air send out massive heat waves. The fire department is held at bay; firefighters can't get near the emergency, as more rioters arrive by the minute. The street is filled, mostly with black people, but whites are beginning to join in.

The newswoman begins to speak. "As you can see by what is going on behind me, mayhem has taken over this part of town. It is rumored that this whole thing started when witnesses saw police beat a handcuffed Negro taken from a bar."

Suddenly a black man with a large Afro grabs the microphone and pushes her to the side. He is extremely upset. He points at the cameraman. "You had better keep that thing rolling!"

The cameraman's voice can be heard in the background. "It's rolling; say what you have to say."

"All right, let me tell you what is going on," he says in an angry voice. "We as a people are tired of being oppressed. The civil rights amendment passed in 1964, and that was years ago, but nothing has changed! Not one single thing! We are still being held down by the man, and today the man is going to pay!"

Boom! A large explosion rocks the street. A second later Al and the rest hear it as the shock wave passes them, rattling the windows. The picture on the TV turns to static, and then comes back, as debris falls to the ground around the news crew. Some people in the crowd cheer loudly, happy about whatever they blew up. The newswoman, still bent over for cover, takes back the microphone.

"I'm Linda Shrivers reporting live; please stay tuned."

The television switches to the newsroom, and the regular anchorman takes over. Ron seems more worried than he was just a minute ago. He reaches over and turns down the volume.

Trapped inside the house, they all stay idle for hours. As darkness sets in, the sky becomes filled with an orange glow. It is not from the sun but from the hundreds of fires that are burning out of control. A thick cloud of black and gray smoke slowly drifts over Doc's old house. As it passes by, bits of burning debris fall from it. Looters begin to run though Doc's yard, carrying everything from booze to furniture. Someone attempts to take a refrigerator, but leaves it in his yard; it is too heavy. Al stares out the front window, watching the hot embers drop from the sky. It is obvious that the fires are getting closer.

Al looks at Natalie. "I'm going out front; I need to use the garden hose and soak down the roof before it catches on fire."

Natalie opens her mouth; she wants to tell him to stay inside, but knows it won't do any good.

"Be careful," is all she can get out.

Without warning the power goes out. In a flash, the small house becomes pitch black. For a brief moment, panic strikes them all. Doc lights a match and turns it to a candle. As he lights other candles, Al walks outside and grabs the hose. He begins to saturate the roof with a steady stream of water. Ron comes out and stands as a lookout from the front porch. With all the stuff on the ground, and the sky glowing, it looks as if they are in the middle of a war zone.

A large rock shatters a window just two houses away. Rioters quickly go inside and begin to take whatever they want. Al and Ron can both hear the owners of the house scream in terror. At least twelve people come running out with whatever they can carry. Others arrive shortly after and set the place on fire. They act like they support the cause, Al notes, but they are really nothing more than a roving street gang.

"Ron, go inside and make sure the back door is locked," Al blurts out.

Ron rushes inside, and Doc comes out to see what is going on. With an open mouth, he stares at his neighbor's house. Smoke pours out from the missing window as the flames flicker from inside.

"That's my friend's," he says in a worried voice.

Al frantically sprays the house as he attempts to keep the glowing embers under control. The hairs on the back of his neck stand on end. He turns around and looks at the twenty or so rioters staring back at Doc's house. They are nothing more than street thugs looking for free stuff to call their own. Fear courses through him as he stares at all their angry faces. "Give us what we want and we won't burn your house," one of them shouts.

Doc begins to panic. "What have I ever done to any of you? I'm a black man just like you, trying to make a decent life."

One of them suddenly throws a rock. It whizzes through the air and cracks the old man in the forehead. His limp, semiconscious body falls back onto the porch. Natalie runs outside to help him.

"Now we shall burn you down," the leader yells.

He raises his torch and prepares to throw it through the front window. Al spins around and soaks the torch with water. In a second, the flames turn into a cloud of steam. The leader opens his mouth and prepares to yell something. Mad at this senseless violence, Al squirts the man right in the mouth, stunning him. He quickly moves away as he coughs on the water.

"Do you see what color my skin is?" Al yells, with every ounce of courage he has. They all stop and fall silent. "You want to free yourself from bondage! But we are not the ones who put you there! We are the ones who are there with you! So burning down his house is not going to help you one bit! It only makes matters worse."

Natalie's knees tremble as she watches the group. She feels that they are all going to be killed. Her heart is in her throat; she can't even swallow. She and her friends are outnumbered five to one, and have nowhere to go. Al is afraid, but stands his ground. Ron and Obie stay on the porch and pray that this will be resolved peacefully.

"We are the ones with you," Al repeats in a softer tone. "We're trying to make a living, just as you are."

Strangely, a few of the rioters in the back turn and begin to walk away. Some pick up stolen items off the ground. The leader—a young, tall black man—stands still, with two clenched fists. But then he looks to his side to see that he is standing alone. Al lets out a sigh of relief as the man slowly backs away. Doc slowly comes to his feet, with a large bump on his head.

"My house," he moans.

"It's all right; they're leaving," Natalie explains.

As soon as the coast is clear, Obie runs inside, grabs the fire extinguisher, and heads for the neighbors' house. The owners of the house are already battling the small fire. Al rushes over and uses their garden house to get the blaze under control. With the two of them working on it, the fire is put out, and the damage is limited to the living room.

The night of terror and unlawfulness runs its course. Thousands of people still rule the streets, stealing whatever they can. There are many other street gangs that pass Doc's home. But they see the men standing out front, and leave the house alone. The fires and the mayhem spread out, block after block, as the authorities fight a losing battle. The four performers continue to stand guard over Doc's house as the sun starts to rise over the thick layer of smoke. The power still hasn't come back on, and the street has never looked so dark and eerie. In the distance, the sounds of sirens, fires, and screaming keep them all alert.

As they stay there on the porch in silence, a low, rumbling noise can be heard. They all their heads and look down the street. A row of headlights can be seen coming towards them, and the noise becomes louder. Large green army trucks with white stars painted on the doors pass by. They weave in and out of the debris and burned cars that cover the street. As the canopy-covered trucks cruise past the house, the group at Doc's looks through the open back of one of them, and can see rows of armed soldiers sitting inside them.

"They called in the National Guard," Al says, with a sense of relief.

Natalie watches the long convoy as it continues to go by. "How many did they call in?"

"Looks like all of them," Ron says, without missing a beat. "I never thought I would be so happy to see a bunch of white guys in uniform."

A few hours after the sun rises, the National Guard takes back control of the city, and peace settles down on the streets once again. After making sure that Doc is fine, the gang walks out of the neighborhood, to the nearest place where they can catch a cab. They pass by scores of burned-out buildings and empty shells that people used to call home. With sad faces, they watch the ambulances go by with the injured, and the coroner trucks go by with the dead. It is a disturbing sight for all of them; one that they will never forget.

Natalie's promoters are grateful to see her alive after she was missing all night, and Smokey is happy to see his friends make it out as well. But unfortunately the stress that the riot placed on the city forced the cancellation of both their concerts, and there would be no rescheduling.

"I don't care; I just want to go home," Al says as he hears the news about their concert.

His mind is still focused on the burning houses; he knows not everyone made it out alive. *Burning to death is a horrible way to go.* "The only thing I know for sure is that I don't want to be a fireman," he says softly but with emotion through a tight mouth.

Al and Natalie say their good-byes and part once again. Al's heart feels torn in two. He knows what he did with Natalie was wrong, but there is just something about her that makes him lose control. When he is with her, it feels so good, so right, as if all will be justified later on.

The equipment is loaded up onto the trucks and they head home, anxious to be with their loved ones again. But as they come closer, Al's feeling of guilt slowly push their way to the surface.

* * *

Two hours later the convoy rolls up to Smokey's house. Lorraine and Claudette come rushing out to greet them. Smokey had called home during the night and told his wife that Al and the others were missing, so Lorraine was worried sick.

"Are you OK?" Lorraine asks as she grabs hold of her husband. She holds him and rubs his body, as if there would be missing parts.

As soon as he feels her touch, the guilt from his sin rams its way into his heart. It feels as if someone poured a bucket of paint over him. *Oh man, what did I do? I'm going to ruin a good thing again.*

"Everything is fine," he replies, as he tries not to look her in the eyes. She looks ten times more innocent than she did just a little while ago. "Just had a long night over at Doc Jacobs' house."

He holds her tight and gives her several long kisses, hoping she won't ask too many questions. It would be easy enough to leave Natalie out of the subject, but he hates lying to Lorraine. They all go inside and exchange stories about their trip. Being home reminds Al of the reason he left—Berry and Motown—but now even worse is the thought of what happened last night. Al stands in the back of the living room and stares out a large picture window that faces the backyard. He remains quiet as the others joke around. Lorraine notices him standing there with his hands in his pockets, and comes over to check on him.

"Are you sure that you're all right?" she asks.

Al closes his eyes and nods. "Sorry, I know I'm not much for company right now."

"Is there something you would like to do?"

He turns and looks at all his friends as they play pool and joke around. He loves them all, but right now he just wants to be alone with his wife.

"Yeah. I would like to take you and a picnic lunch and go down to the lake. We could sit and relax, and let the world run itself for a little while."

He puts his arm around her, and they stand there holding each other as they sway back and forth. Hurting inside, he holds her tight, as if it would wash away some of the guilt.

"That's sound nice. I'll explain it to Claudette. I'm sure they won't have a problem with it."

* * *

They leave Smokey's and head home so they can pack a lunch. While Al was gone, Lorraine bought some new furniture. She was hoping it would cheer him up, but it is only another reminder of the IRS raid, and all the money they say he still owes.

On the way back to the car, Al picks up the newspaper from the front sidewalk, and without looking at it, tosses it in the car with the food. In near total silence they drive to the lakeshore and park the car.

It is a beautiful day, with only a few small, white clouds in the sky. A cool breeze runs across the lake and up onto them as they unfold a blanket and lay it on the grass. In the distance is the sound of boat motors; others are enjoying the summer day too.

"Would you like some wine?" Lorraine asks.

"Sure, I'll open it for you."

The two sit down on the blanket and watch the boats go by as they sip on some red wine. Al feels a lot of pressure on his heart, and he can't put his finger on what exactly is causing it. Hoping to get his mind off of it, he reaches over and grabs the newspaper. He unfolds it and looks at the front page. There in bold color is an aerial shot of the riot zone. Scores of burned-out buildings seem to go on forever, as smoldering fires try to come back to life. The caption below reads, "Five thousand troops called in to stop violence; more than a dozen dead and eleven hundred arrested." Right next to that is a picture of several US troops over in Vietnam. They are loading dead bodies onto a helicopter.

It is just another grim reminder that Frankie Gaye is over still there. He can't even bring himself to read the caption. The anguish and pain in his heart grows. He wants to break down and cry, but he can't, not in front of Lorraine. She reaches out and touches his shoulder, and he almost jumps out of his skin.

"Al," she says softly. "Please tell me what is on your mind."

He stares at the two pictures and shakes his head. He remembers his own personal hell trying to protect Doc's house for one night, and can't imagine how those troops over in Vietnam are doing it day after day. He can't bear to look at the pictures any longer. He quickly folds the paper and places it behind him. He keeps his head down low and his eyes closed as he prepares to talk.

"You know,when I was a kid . . . if I had a question about the world, all I had to do was ask my mother, and she could tell me what was taking place. Now here I am with kids of my own, and if they were to ask me—" He stops, looks up, and holds his emotions at bay. "If my own boys were to ask me 'What's going on?' I couldn't tell them, because I don't understand it myself. Why is God's green earth turning into such a cold and evil place? And why can't I explain it to my boys?"

Lorraine only has to think about it for a moment. "Your mother is a wonderful woman and she has a nice way of explaining things. And when she doesn't understand things, she always asks others."

Al almost smiles. "And I don't?"

"You do, but maybe this time you shouldn't do it with words, but with music."

He sits up as his mind shifts into gear. "I should ask 'What's going on?' in a song." Suddenly he perks up. "Yeah, yeah, I like that."

Al grabs a notepad and a pencil, and begins writing. He pours his heart into the lyrics; they begin to form down the page. He lets his feelings go, and it only takes a few minutes before the song is complete.

"What are you going to call it?" Lorraine asks, as she hands him a sandwich.

He takes one bite from his sandwich, and thinks about it briefly. " 'What's going on?' " He smiles and nods. "I think that sums it up. What do you think?"

"I think it's a wonderful title."

* * *

First thing in the morning, Al goes downstairs to Obie's place to show him the lyrics. In silence, his friend reads them over as he walks back into his apartment. Al follows him in and closes the door behind them.

Obie stands about five foot ten, and always has a gleam in his eye when it comes to music. He loves to smile and have a good time, and best of all, he loves to play his guitar.

"I like it, man," Obie says with a large smile. "It a serious song for a serious time."

"You think you could add some guitar to it?"

"Can Obie add some guitar?" he repeats, as if the question were a ridiculous one.

He lights up a cigarette and walks over to his guitar and amp. With the cigarette hanging out of his mouth, he begins to play as Al sings the lyrics. They run though the song twice, and then stop. It sounds good, real good. They know they have a hit; they can feel it.

Obie looks at him. "You going to ask Smokey to do this?"

Al glances at the lyrics and shakes his head. "Smokey enjoys doing love songs, and this is more of a protest song."

"Well, we got plenty of folks to choose from."

"I was hoping Marvin would do it."

Obie takes a long drag off his cigarette, and then watches the smoke pour out his nose. He squints and points his cigarette at Al. "You got something there, man. Marvin has a nice voice and could do wonders for this song."

That evening Al calls Marvin. He reads the lyrics to his friend, but Marvin seems less than enthused about it. Although Marvin never says anything, Al feels that he is having the same IRS trouble as himself. He tries for two days to convince him to do it, but he won't give in and record at Motown, and that is who he is under contract with. If either one could find someone to take black artists, they would be facing a messy lawsuit. Feeling that he needs a change of pace, Al calls him again on the third night.

"Hey, Marv, it's Al."

Marvin gives him a heavy sigh. "Are you going to ask me to do that song again?"

Al switches the phone to the other ear. "No, relax, man, just relax. Do you remember Ken Holiday?"

"Yeah. That is one mean bass player."

"Sure is. He just called me bragging about some big, white, convertible Cadillac that he bought. He wants to know if the gang would like to take a ride out into the country for a little road party."

Marvin is silent for a moment. "You know, that sounds nice, Al. I could use a little time away. It would be nice to act like one of the guys again."

Al knew exactly what he was talking about. So many out there want the fame and fortune, but once they get there, they wish they could go back and just be an ordinary person that can stroll down the street without being asked for autographs and pictures.

"Well, all right, I'll tell him to pick us up in the morning."

* * *

The next morning Ken Holiday shows up, just as Al said. He is a short, slender black man with a love for adventure, and a bigger love for large cars. The huge, shiny, white Cadillac is gorgeous and brand new. Ken drives up with the top already down. Ron, Al, Marvin, and Obie all stare at it and drool as he stops in front of them. Ron's face lights up as he looks it over.

"A big, white, brand-spanking-new car filled with five black men. You know every cop in the state is going to think we stole this from their grandmother," Ron says with a chuckle.

Ron and Ken sit up front as the others pile into the back of the luxury automobile. The large eight-cylinder roars to life, and they speed away. As they pass the city limits, Ken opens the glove box. There is a large bag of marijuana inside of it.

"Come on, guys, let's light up and party!" Ken says, as he winds down a narrow country road.

They spend the entire day laughing, smoking pot, and having a good time. After several hours pass, Ken decides to turn around and head back home. He speeds down the narrow roads, and barrels into the rural area of Detroit just before dark. Al, who is still sitting in the backseat next to Marvin, looks over Ken's shoulder at the speedometer. He is going almost twice the speed limit.

"Ken, slow down before you get pulled over," Al says.

Being pulled over is the last thing they want. They all know it would mean harassment and a search, and that is bad enough. But this time they have enough pot to warrant felony charges for drug trafficking. That could mean ten years in prison, and nobody in their right mind wants that.

Ken lets off the gas, and the heavy vehicle immediately slows down. Al feels more comfortable as he watches the needle on the speedometer drops down. He puts his arm across the backseat. As he does this, he notices a police car that pulls out from a side street and begins following them.

"Ken, are you speeding?" Al quickly asks.

"No. I'm doing the limit."

"Well, we've got company."

Ron turns around, and instant panic flushes over him. "Oh great, five black men in a stolen car with a bag of weed."

"It's not stolen; I bought it," Ken blurts out in a high-pitched voice.

Ron looks even more nervous as he looks over his shoulder again. "The weed or the car?"

"The car, fool."

"Explain that to him," Ron says, motioning towards the police. "This is great. First Al starts a riot, and now we're drug trafficking."

"Just relax, Ron, act natural," Al says, without looking back. "He may just be going this way."

Ken stops at a red light; they all keep their eyes straight ahead and keep their mouths shut. Ken casually passes the bag of marijuana back to Al. The light turns green, but Ken doesn't notice; he is too busy staring at the cop in the rearview mirror.

"Go," Al whispers.

Ken pushes his foot on the gas pedal, and the car slowly drives off. Suddenly the cop turns on his red circular light. All of their hearts skip a few beats as the siren lets out a loud squeal.

CHAPTER 10

"Damn. We're all going to the big house," Ron whispers.

"Just shut up," Ken quickly says through gritted teeth.

Two white police officers get out of their car and slowly walk up on them. Al closes his eyes and thinks: *Please don't be the blonde-haired one with the blue eyes.* He opens his eyes, and luckily, it's not. One stays near the back of the car as the other walks up next to Ken.

"Driver's license and registration."

Ken hands him the paperwork as everyone else sweats bullets. The officer looks over the registration and compares it to the name on the license. He lowers the stuff, and takes a look at all of them. All their eyes follow his hand as he reaches down and opens Ken's door.

"I need all of you to step out of the car."

It was the words they didn't want to hear. That meant they were going to be searched.

"Is there something wrong, officer?" Ken asks as he slowly gets out.

"We got a report of a white car speeding down the road, and you guys look mighty nervous now that I have pulled you over. Why? Do you have something to hide?"

"No," Ken answered, but his voice was weak; he was obviously lying.

"Why don't the rest of you boys come on out of there too?" the other officer says.

The men line up along the police car. One officer searches them while the other searches the car. All eyes are on the one in the car. He looks under the seats, in the glove box. He even takes the keys and searches the trunk.It is summertime and the men have thin clothes on, so the search is over quickly.

"They're clear," says the officer who did the search.

The other tosses Ken's driver's license and registration on the front seat. His gut is telling him that there is something to be found, but he can't find it. He places his hands on his hips and glances at the car one more time. It is only for a second, but it feels like an eternity to the men.

"Just make sure you're doing the speed limit," the officer says as he walks back to his car.

At first they just stand there, not knowing what to do. Then they do their best to walk back to their car without running. Acting as casual as possible, they all get back in. Ken starts the car and they drive away, leaving the police car behind. The red circling light slowly vanishes from sight.

"Whoo!" Ken shouts. "That was a close one."

Ron turns around and wipes the sweat off from his forehead. His eyes dart all around the back. What did you do with it, Al?"

Al has a devilish grin on his face. Everyone is dying to know where he put the bag of marijuana. He reaches into the folded flap of the convertible top and pulls it out, then holds it up like a trophy.

"Ta-da. I hid it just behind me. Sometimes the best place to hide stuff is out in the open."

"Man, you saved us," Marvin says.

Al reaches over and squeezes his shoulder. "You're my friend. I'll always take care of you, and I hope you'll do the same for me."

Marvin knows exactly what he is talking about. He stares at the floor and is silent for a moment. Neither one of them like Motown, but their love of music keep them coming back for more.

"All right, Al, you got it."

"Got what?" Al asks, pretending he doesn't know what Marvin is talking about.

"I'll sing your song. We can do 'What's Going On.' "

Al puts his arm around him and shakes him a little. "Thanks, man. You're not going to be disappointed. I promise you. It's a blockbuster, baby, a number-one hit. I can just feel it."

* * *

Late the next evening, Al, Obie, and Marvin sneak into Motown Records and record the song "What's Going On." They work through the night, and leave before Berry comes in.

Although they all still work for Motown, they don't want to tell Berry about the project. Not yet, at least; they want to make sure it is complete and ready. Afterwards they all feel great about it; they know the song will do well.

At five thirty in the morning, Al walks into his apartment. He is tired from being up all night, but happy about how his song came out. Lorraine is sitting at the table, drinking coffee and reading the newspaper. She stands up and greets him with a warm kiss.

"I sure did miss you last night," she says while holding him. "So how did it go?"

"Great," he replies, full of enthusiasm. "I really like that one. It's going to be a hit, I can just feel it."

"I'm so happy for you, sweetie," she says as they hug one another again. But then she turns to a more serious note. "I received something in the mail yesterday, and we need to talk about it."

"Uh-oh, this don't sound good."

She walks over to the table and sits down. He follows her. With a small smile that shows her pride, she slides a large, yellow envelope to him. On the front of it he sees the letters UCLA. *I know she has been working hard for this, but did she actually get it?*

"What's this?" he asks.

"I got the job!" she replies with a huge smile. "UCLA wants me to come work for them. It's the job I've been trying to get for years."

"That's great," he says, with all the excitement he can muster. *What about my music career? What am I going to do? Things here are starting to pick up again.*

"It's a lot more than I make now," she explains.

Yeah, but what about my music?

"No more cold winters for us."

But Motown is here.

"Maybe with the extra money we can get square with the IRS."

His eyebrows rise. "That's a good point. When does this all happen?"

"If I accept the job, my first day is a month from now."

Al almost falls over. He was hoping she would say in six months—or even better, next year. "Wow, that's fast. I guess they want a response pretty quick too, huh?"

She's still exulting about the job offer; he can see it in her face. "Yeah. I am supposed to call them tomorrow night . . . if not sooner," she adds, hoping he'll tell her to *call now and take the job*. Lorraine is tired of watching her husband work so hard for the peanuts he's been receiving at Motown Records. She knows that they can do better in California.

"Well, I'm happy for you, honey." He kisses her on the forehead and walks away. "I am exhausted, so I'm going to bed for a while."

"So do you want me to call them?" she asks softly, feeling slightly let down. She was hoping that he would jump on the opportunity to get out of Detroit.

Al walks back to his bedroom, gets undressed, and climbs into bed. The pillow never felt so soft as he curls up. But instead of sleep, he lays there with his eyes wide open. *Man, what am I going to do? I don't want to lose her. She has been the breadwinner all along, and I really love her. Maybe I can talk to Berry about writing and producing from California. Yeah, that could work. She could have her job, and I could still have my music.*

* * *

Al rolls over and looks at the clock; he didn't realize he had already been laying in bed for several hours. Groggy, he stands and stretches. His eyes are still half shut as he walks out into the living room. Lorraine had gone to work some time ago. He plops down on the couch and stares at the wall, as his mind slowly awakens. He reaches for the phone and calls Marvin.

"Hello?" Marvin says in a half-asleep voice.

"Hey, I just wanted to see if you were awake."

"I'm trying to be."

"Thanks for recording that song last night, I mean that."

Marvin perks up. "No problem, I like it. But we can't keep hiding from Berry; sooner or later we are going to have to tell him, if we want it released."

Al sighs. "I know, that's why I am calling you; let's just do it today and get it over with. How does three o'clock sound?"

"Sounds good. I'll see you then."

They hang up, and Al walks off to the bathroom to take a shower and try to wake up.

At two forty-five that afternoon, Al is standing outside of Motown Records. He feels rather nervous; he hasn't talked to Berry in months. Marvin drives up in an older car and parks across the street. Al walks over to greet him.

"Ready for this?" Al asks.

"Ready as I'm going to get. So let's go show this man that we can make some music."

Together they walk into Berry's office. The boss's whole face changes as soon as he sees Al comes in. The last time he saw Al was during a hostile moment.

"Well, if it ain't Mister Gaye and Mister Cleveland. Isn't this a surprise? What brings you two back into *my* little studio?"

Suddenly Al's mind goes completely blank; his stomach begins to turn as he thinks about the IRS and all the money he owes. It takes him a second to gather his thoughts; he doesn't want to get upset.

"Ah . . . we've got a new song, and we would like to release it. This is one in particular that we think you'll love; it's titled 'What's Going On.' "

Berry sits there in silence as he taps his pencil on his large, dark, wood desk. He knows that he and Al don't see eye to eye. Nonetheless, Al writes number-one hits, and is a gold mine to have work for him.

"All right, let me hear it," he finally says.

Enthused, Al turns around and places the tape on the reel-to-reel player. *He's going to love this; it speaks of the times. It makes a statement.* The song "What's Going On" plays through. Al and Marvin force themselves to stand still and not sway to it. Berry never moves a muscle; he doesn't even nod to the music or tap his fingers, as he usually does. The song ends. Al anticipates that Berry will want to listen to it again, so he immediately begins rewinding it.

"What kind of garbage is that?" Berry asks.

Al and Marvin are both shocked; they thought for sure he would like it.

"That's a protest song," Berry states.

Marvin defends the song. "It's a statement for today. All the things that are going wrong in this world."

"It's crap," Berry interjects quickly. "This company has done extremely well with love songs for a good reason, gentlemen, and that's because love songs are what the people want to listen to. This . . . this protest thing won't make it anywhere. It's a waste of time and money."

"This is a number-one hit," Al says.

Berry shakes his head. "No, it's not, and I'm not going to release it." He pauses and looks at the two of them. "Now, do you have any music worth my time? If not, I have an appointment to go to."

"No, this is it for now," Al replies softly. "But this is a good song; it speaks for our minds and our souls."

The boss glares at them, making it clear that he has heard enough. "Then I guess we are done. Good day," Berry says, not wanting to discuss it anymore.

Marvin turns and walks out. Al stands there for a moment, wanting to say something; he wants to yell 'WAKE UP!" at his boss, but doesn't. He slowly turns and leaves. He follows Marvin out to the street. In total disbelief, they lean on his car and stare at the small building.

"Do you think he is right?" Marvin asks.

"No, not for a minute. I tell you that is a hit. I know a hit when I write one, and this is a hit."

"Well, maybe over time we can get him to release it."

Al pauses as his mind shifts to his wife and her new job. "Time is what I don't have, my brother. Lorraine and I are moving to California."

"What?"

"She got a job at UCLA. I can't possibly expect her to turn it down. And besides, we need the money so we can get the IRS off of our backs."

Marvin's mouth hangs open as he stares at Al. He waits for his friend to tell him that he is joking, but it doesn't happen.

"How long until you go?"

"A month, maybe less." He smiles. "You know, in a way I'm looking forward to it. A change of pace would be nice right about now.

Not to mention that the music industry is beginning to grow out there at a rapid rate."

Marvin agrees with him, and starts to consider the idea of moving himself. Then he thinks about the reel-to-reel tape. "Hey, we left the recording in Berry's office."

"Yeah, I know. I did it on purpose, hoping he would listen to it again and like it the second time around. Don't worry, it's just a copy. We still have a few weeks to get him to release it; hopefully we can do it before Lorraine and I move."

"I'll do my best."

* * *

The next few weeks seem to fly by. Al calls Daryl and Ted to keep them abreast of the move. Marvin and Al have at least five more meetings with Berry, but he will not budge from his position on the song. He feels there is no reason to take a chance on protest music when things are going so well.

"So you're leaving us," Berry says as he hears the news from Al.

There isn't a whole lot of sincerity in his voice. It is more as if he were talking to just any Joe off the street. Of course, that is the way Al feels towards him, and they both know it.

"Yes. My wife has worked hard for this, and I can't stop her now. But I can still write and record over there, and send it to you."

As much as Al hates this, he has to do it; there are not a lot of record labels that promote black artists or black songwriters. It doesn't matter how he feels about Berry; Motown Records has the power to launch his songs the way he feels it should be done.

"All right," Berry says. "That sounds fair enough. Did you know there's a lot of talent out there in California? I was thinking of moving the company over there, so I'll let you know."

This last statement comes as a surprise to Al. Berry had never mentioned that in the past. Al leaves on a high note; he is apparently still in good standing. He hopes that, with this new development, Berry will start sending him some royalty checks. As he walks out to his car, he is finally feeling good about leaving. He returns happily to his wife.

There he finds Lorraine chest deep in belongings that are already packed. The different-sized cardboard boxes are stacked up all over the place, with little walkways between them. She doesn't know that he is there. He stops in the doorway and listens to her hum a song. He smiles. It is one of his.

"You're not excited, are you?" he asks.

She turns and looks at him with an ear-to-ear grin, her face glowing in anticipation of a new job and a new life somewhere far away. Away from Motown Records, and away from the constant reminders of the IRS raid. Even though the government knows they are moving, and will surely still expect payment, it feels to Lorraine like she is leaving it behind. They will not have to worry about it until they are settled in their new home, and right now that seems to be a long time from now. The first year of the new decade is half over, and she is ready for the challenge.

"Nope, not in the slightest."

"Are the movers still coming in the morning?"

"Yes, first thing, according to them. They asked me not to call anymore."

"How many times did you call?" Al asks in a high-pitched voice.

She shrugs her shoulders, and looks like an innocent child. "I don't know, about ten."

Al laughs and walks back outside to check the mail. He still holds on to the dream of receiving another large royalty check. But there is nothing from Motown Records. Even the statements he used to get are no longer coming in. Instead, all he finds are several bills and two notices from the IRS. Al's heart shifts gears and beats oddly as he opens the first envelope. He and Lorraine are making payments, but it doesn't seem to be doing any good. The money they owe is being taxed and penalized at such a high rate that their payments are doing little to bring the total down, and there is nothing they can do to stop it. Without showing them to his wife, he takes the notices and stuffs them into his suitcase; he doesn't want the news to ruin her trip.

Two days later, Al and Lorraine are quiet as they drive across the country. Although Al would never tell his wife, part of him feels lost and confused. Everything that he knows about the music industry is on the East Coast. Now that they are moving, he will have to start all over again—make new contacts, find a decent company and new talent. *I can do it. I know I can. My name is established, and it will be a lot easier than last time*, he tells himself.

"You hungry?" Lorraine asks in a boisterous voice.

"Yeah, sure. Why are you being so loud?"

"I asked you three times. What were you thinking about?"

Al is quiet for a moment as he watches the white lines on the highway pass rapidly. "Aw, nothing much. Just things we need to do to get our new house going."

She reaches over and squeezes his hand. "I know you better than that, Al. Don't worry, I have faith in you, and so does the Lord. You will keep writing songs, and you will still be a success."

He smiles. "Thanks, babe, I needed to hear that."

They take their time and enjoy the trip across the country. The green, tree-filled countryside fades in the distance and is slowly replaced by arid desert. Feeling the need for a little excitement, they stop in Las Vegas. Al likes the town. For some reason he believes this isn't the last time he will see it. *What a great place to start a music business*, he thinks. Anxious to get to California, Lorraine only wants to stay one night so they can get on their way. Al wants to stay longer and research the area a little, but reluctantly goes along to please his wife.

CHAPTER 11

A year passes, and the pair is finally settled in. They found a nice house to rent, and they call it home. Lorraine is doing very well at her job. Unfortunately, Al has not been doing so well. His music career seems dead for the most part; he doesn't know how to pick up the pieces and start again. He struggles to hold onto his dream of making music.

At first he spends many hours listening to the radio, hoping that he will hear his song "What's Going On," but it apparently hasn't been released. It's depressing, so he stops listening to the radio. Both of his sons have been out to visit on a couple of occasions. Daryl has noticed the difference in Al, and tries to encourage his dad to write again, but his effort only lasts while he is visiting in California. As soon as he is gone, Al sinks back into depression. Without Daryl around, the only reminders of his former career are the constant IRS notices and bills.

Man, I have to get some help with my career, he thinks. *I just can't sit here any longer. But who can I go to? The only person I know on this side of the world is Natalie.* Al's pulse rises with the simple thought of her.

All this time he has been doing his best to stay clear of her. Every time her pretty face enters his mind, feelings of guilt rush into his already-stressed heart. He wants to remain faithful to his wife. Finally, out of desperation, he breaks down and decides to call her—just to help him get his career back, he tells himself.

The phone rings three times before he hears her voice, and it sounds so sweet, just like he remembers.

"Hi—" she says.

"Hey, it's me, Al."

"—You have reached the Natalie Rose residence. If you wish to leave a message, please do so after the beep."

Al's shoulders slump once he realizes that it is only a recording. He waits for the message tone.

"Hey, Natalie, it's me, Al Cleveland. I know we haven't talked in quite a while . . ."

Then he hears a click. "Al?"

"Uh, hey, you're there."

"Yeah, I just walked in the front door. You sound close by; are you in town?"

"Sure am; I live here now. I hope you don't mind, but I would like to get together. I need help with my music career. You're the only person I know of who could get me back on track. I seem to be at a dead end."

Natalie seems surprised by his comment. "Well . . . OK. Why don't you come over to my place tomorrow, and we can discuss things?"

Instantly, memories of how her shapely body looked, and how those green eyes seemed to glow, rush into his mind. He does his best to banish those thoughts.

"Sounds great. I'll see you soon," he replies, with an upbeat tone.

"Hey, bring your bathing suit; we'll go to the beach," she adds.

The following day, while Lorraine is at work, Al heads for Natalie's house across town. His pulse is rapid as he pulls up and stops in front of her large home. He sits there for a moment, drying his sweaty palms on his slacks. The last time he saw Natalie was in Detroit. *What a night that was.*

Al looks over the place she calls home. *Damn, look at that house, she's doing well. She must be making some good money.* He stops, gathers his thoughts, and gathers the courage to get out and see her again. *Just friends; no more fooling around, Al.*

He gets out of his car and walks up the long, curved walkway, passing manicured bushes and shrubs. Her house is very large, and is covered in perfectly laid stone. He makes it to her large, wooden, double door, and straightens out his clothes quickly before ringing the doorbell.

Natalie opens the door. Her eyes light up at the sight of her old friend. She is wearing a white bikini, and has a small, black, mesh beach robe around her. As in the past, her beauty takes Al's breath away. She hardly says a word as she jumps into his arms. It feels so good for him to hold her again. His large hands rub her back. Deep inside, he begins to wish he married her when he had the chance. His eyes open wide, and he casually pushes her away.

"You look great. You don't believe in aging?" he asks.

She smiles. "Thank you. You look great too." Natalie looks him up and down. He is wearing slacks and a white, button-up shirt. "Tell me that you brought your bathing suit, because we are going to the beach."

"Yeah, my stuff is in the car. Are you ready to go?"

"In a minute; why don't you bring your things in and change first? Then we can take my car."

Al gets his belongings and changes in her bathroom. He keeps the door closed, feeling funny about it. She doesn't appear to be coming on to him, anyway.

"So you've been in town for a while," Natalie says through the closed door.

He opens the door and looks at her, surprised that she knows. "How did you know that?"

"I have a phone, and I talk to Ron," she giggles.

He comes out of the bathroom wearing a T-shirt and his bathing suit. "Man, I haven't talked to Ron in a while. How is he doing?"

"Great; he's ready to come out here."

"What?"

"Yeah, didn't you hear? Berry is moving Motown Records here, and most of the gang is following him. They should be here today or tomorrow."

Al's knees go a little weak. He never really thought that Berry would come out West. Natalie begins walking towards the garage, and he follows. Al's mind is a million miles away; he's not sure how he feels about Motown moving out to his corner of the world. But whether he likes it or not, they are coming.

"Ron seemed pretty happy about coming out here and teaming up with you again."

"Well, I'm looking forward to it," he replies sincerely.

Al's mind drifts back to his old boss and their last conversation in Detroit. He has not heard a word from him since—not a letter, not a phone call, and especially, not a real royalty check. The only ones he receives now are garnished completely by the IRS. The vast space in between Al and Motown has been nice, though it is costing him his career. But since Berry is going to be in California, Al can probably persuade him to release the "What's Going On" album. He wants that more than anything right now.

Natalie opens the garage door, and then climbs into her small convertible sports car. It's a brand-new 1971 Midget, with all the luxuries. Tall as he is, Al has to squeeze in. Even with the seat all the way back, it doesn't offer him much legroom. Natalie plops down in the driver's seat, and snickers at his cramped condition.

"Sorry. I didn't have you in mind when I bought it," she says with an ear-to-ear grin.

"It's OK, I'll make it," he groans as he adjusts himself.

Then her soft smile fades as she looks at his bare legs. She places her hand on the right one, and slowly rubs it. At first it makes him nervous, but then he realizes she's not really doing it in an affectionate manner.

"Your leg is swollen," she states.

"Yeah," Al replies nonchalantly. "It does that every once in a while; just retaining some fluids, I guess. Probably had too much salt in my food last night."

She looks at the leg again and shrugs. "OK, but you might want to see a doctor. What does Lorraine say about it?"

He shakes his head and mumbles, "Nothing."

Since Al pays it no mind, she doesn't either. He does his best to act like he isn't worried about the swelling in his leg, but the truth of the matter is that he has been concerned for quite some time. He has been wearing long pants on purpose for a while, so his wife hasn't noticed his condition. For some reason he can't pinpoint, he's not sure if he wants her to see it.

Natalie starts the car and backs out of the garage. Soon they are on their way to the beach, with the top down. It is a perfect day, not a cloud in the sky, and the temperature is a nice 80 degrees. They both know that the beach is going to be perfect.

A few minutes later, they stop on the parking lot facing the beach. Natalie pauses to smell the air; she loves the smell of the salty sea. As for Al, he can take it or leave it. Whether in Pittsburgh, Detroit, or Los Angeles, as long as he is making music, he is happy. Natalie sits up on the back of her seat and looks around.

"I love coming down here on weekdays; the beach is so empty," she explains. "Everybody is at work, so I can come down and not be bothered with signing autographs and stuff. And for a few hours, I can just be a regular person."

"I imagine it is a tough price to pay. But it is something you worked so hard for."

Al climbs out of the small red car and squints as he looks around the bare beach. He watches as the large waves come crashing in with a loud rumble. A cool breeze rolls off of the ocean, carrying the sounds of seagulls with it.

"Where do you want to set up?" he asks.

She points over to a rock pier. "I usually go over there. In the past I've seen dolphins swimming around." Her cheery tone captures his heart once again.

He does his best to keep his guard up as he walks over to the trunk of the car. Natalie comes over and unlocks it. Inside the trunk is a blanket, a cooler, and a battery-operated record player.

"What are you going to do with that?" he asks, pointing to the record player.

"Play some of my favorite music, silly," she says, bumping her hip against his.

OK, we are in public and I saw her pack the cooler chest. I don't think there is any booze in it. So if she plays a little romantic music, I can still keep my distance. No mistakes, Al; we're just going to talk business, and then I'm going home to my wife.

Al grabs the portable record player and the cooler as Natalie picks up the blanket. Together they walk over to her favorite spot. Natalie spreads out the blanket and kicks off her shoes. She walks around briefly with her arms open wide, taking deep breaths of the fresh air.

"Don't you just love it out here?" she asks.

"Yes, I do," he replies, taking off his sandals.

He sits down on the blanket and watches her as she walks along the edge of the water. He silently goes over things he wants to say to her, hoping she will help with his stagnant career. She walks up and down twice, and then joins him on the blanket.

"Mind if I play some music?" she asks.

"Of course not," he quickly replies, hoping that they will soon be talking about what projects they can work on together. As she pulls out a 45, he thinks romantic thoughts, and then he hopes it won't come to that.

Natalie opens the record player, puts the record on the turntable, and, without saying a word to him, she turns on the small machine, letting the music start. She has a devilish grin as the first few notes are played. Al suddenly turns and looks at her with wide eyes.

"That's mine!" he cheers. "That's . . . that's 'What's Going On'; I recorded that with Marvin almost two years ago!"

"Sure did," she replies.

In total disbelief, he listens to his friend sing the song that he and Obie put together. "How did you get it?"

Natalie looks at him as if he were from another planet. "I bought it in the store, you goofball. You don't listen to the radio much, do you?"

"No, not anymore; it became too depressing. How's it doing? How long has it been out? Do people like it?"

She laughs at his nervous, restive tone. "Well, Mister Cleveland, your song, "What's Going On," has been out for a few weeks, and it is number five on the charts right now. And it is still climbing and doing very well, so I think it is safe to say that people like it."

His eyebrows cross. *Why hasn't Berry contacted me? No one told me it was being released after he's been holding on to it all this time.* "That explains why you were so surprised when I asked you for help with my career."

She laughs. "You took me by total surprise on that one. I'm thinking to myself, hey, the guy has a song on the charts and I don't, yet he needs my help? I should be asking him to write me a few songs."

He smiles as he listens to the music. "I suppose that did sound pretty silly."

"You need to talk to Berry as soon as you can."

He immediately looks away. "I don't know about that. It seems that he likes to keep me in the dark about what is going on."

"That's not a good reason to avoid him, Al." She reaches out and takes his hand. "You wrote that song; it is yours and Obie's. If you see him and tell him he needs to renegotiate your contract, he will. He'd be crazy not to."

"Think so?"

"Yes. After all, it worked for me."

He squeezes her hand, and they look into each other's eyes. His heart pounds as he feels they are about to kiss again. But oddly, she looks away, and gently withdraws her hand. A soft breeze brushes her hair across her face, blocking her expression.

"What is it?" he asks.

She shakes her hair out of the way, looks at him, smiles, and looks away again. Slowly her eyes drift downward, and she stares at the blanket in silence.

"Oh my, are you serious with someone?" he asks.

She doesn't answer his question, and suddenly he feels lonely. Somehow he had come up with the notion that he would always be her one and only part-time lover, as if he could keep her on the side like a good book, to read whenever he wanted to. The song comes to an end. Natalie lifts the arm of the record player and begins the song over again.

"You don't have to do that," he says.

She smiles, keeping her eyes on the record player. Al is beginning to feel that he is right. There is a man in her life, and her heart belongs to whoever it is. But from the time she first met Al in New York, she wanted him, and wanted to be with him forever, he thinks. She begins to sing the song in perfect tune with Marvin's recording. Al smiles at her playfulness.

"All right, backup singer. I'm beginning to feel self-conscious."

She laughs, breaking her beat with the song, and lightly hits him in the arm. He hits her back, and the two begin to wrestle on the blanket. He grabs hold of her, flips her down to the blanket, and pins her to the ground. She struggles to get out from under him, but he is too strong for her.

"You big tub o' lard," she groans out as she giggles.

Al leans over; he wants to kiss her. Her lips look so full and tender. He wants to taste her again. But he suddenly stops when the sounds of other people talking drift their way, and they both realize that they are in the public eye. He lets her go and they both sit up. *That's all I need is for someone to take a photograph of us, and for it to be posted for Lorraine to see.* Natalie casually looks around and makes sure no one is taking pictures as she straightens out the blanket.

"You know, Al," she says softly, as she recovers her train of thought. "You've been really important to me over the years. You've been my lover, my confidant, and my good friend. We made our choices in life, and spent time together here and there. But now I wish we had spent more time together."

"Me too, baby. But we are together now," he adds, nudging her.

She offers a small smile and shakes her head, keeping her eyes out on the ocean. She draws in a breath and prepares to speak. "I need to tell you something, Al."

A heavy sigh escapes from Al's mouth. "Uh-oh, this sounds serious. Should I be worried? Did you have a kid from me ten years ago that I should know about?"

She hits him again. "No."

"Well, that's good, because that would be a hell of a lot of back child support that I would I owe. You know it's like that one time—"

"I'm engaged."

"Wha—" He chokes on his words as his heart stops; it seems to be resting in his throat. She doesn't need to repeat it—he heard it, but he can't believe it. "Engaged? Who? How?"

She laughs and acts innocent. But her smile quickly vanishes. "Years ago, when we first met, all I wanted was my career, to be on the stage, singing and dancing, with all eyes on me. Traveling from place to place sounded so romantic back then. But now I am growing older, and I am doing it *alone*. I want someone to know the everyday me, not just the entertainer. I want a family—a husband and children."

"Please tell me that you love this man who asked you to marry him."

She gets up on her knees and takes his hand. "I do, Al; he is my business manager, Bobby Harris. We've been seeing each other for some time now. Oh, Al, please be happy for me."

Al is extremely flattered that she is concerned about his feelings in the situation. "I am happy, very happy for you." He reaches over and hugs her, and they slowly rock back and forth for a few brief seconds.

They break apart, and she wipes away a few tears of joy. "You were my first big love, Al Cleveland. I am grateful for all we shared, and I have always wished things went differently between us."

"Me, too," he admits painfully. "There is hardly a day that goes by that I don't think about that." He pauses as he remembers that he is deeply in love with Lorraine as well, and that she is his wife. "I wish you a lifetime of happiness with your new husband."

He leans over and kisses her on the cheek. They spend a little more time on the beach, and Natalie tells Al all about Bobby, and what a wonderful man he is. She is really looking forward to settling down.

Later, they pack up their few belongings and return to her car. Natalie feels so relieved that she has told Al the truth. Al walks to the car with a smile on his face. He spent the day with her, and nothing happened. *This is OK; I can go home with no guilty feelings whatsoever*, he tells himself. He places the cooler chest and record player in the trunk, and climbs back into her small car.

Back at her house, they hug one another, and he kisses her on the cheek again. From this point on, they are no longer lovers, but are still the best of friends, and they are both OK with it.

"I'd like to come to your wedding."

Natalie's eyes light up. "I would love it if you were there. Oh, that makes me so happy. Thank you, Al."

* * *

Al drives back across town to his home. Out in front of his house is a four-door brown car that he doesn't recognize. His garage opens, and his eyes widen as he sees Lorraine's car already parked inside.

"Hey, she's home early," he thinks aloud.

Suspicious thoughts fill his mind. Who is she home with, and what is she doing? He quietly exits his car and heads for the back door of the house. He stops with his hand on the doorknob. From inside he can hear a man's voice. He brings his ear closer to the door, but he is unable to make out the words. *Come on, Al, why would she bring another man home when she knows you could be here at any moment?* He opens the door and enters the kitchen.

Inside, he looks across to the dining room. Lorraine is sitting at the table with her back to him. She's drinking a cup of coffee, and doesn't bother turning around to greet her husband. Sitting across from her is Ron Jolley. Ron has a rather concerned look on his face as he stands up.

"Hey, there's my buddy," he says to Al.

Al is happy to see him, and the two embrace. "Man, when did you roll into town?"

"Just a little while ago. Lorraine had to come out and find me. A guy could get lost forever in this big city."

Al quickly notices that Ron is acting a little different. He's being more serious, more cautious about his words. Walking over to his wife, Al places his hands on her shoulders and leans over to kiss her.

"Don't touch me," she growls angrily.

Al stands up and lets go of her. He doesn't know what is wrong. Ron clears his throat

"Hey, bud, I gotta go," Ron says.

Al's eyebrows cross. "What do you mean? You just got here."

"I know." He hands him a piece of paper. "Here's my number. Call me if you need anything. Good-bye, Lorraine," he adds cautiously.

"Good-bye, Ron, I'll see you later," she says pleasantly.

Oh great, if she's kind to him and mean to me, it means that I am the one in trouble. What did I do now? His shoulders slump. *Man, I just had such a nice day too.* As Ron walks out the front door, Lorraine walks into the kitchen with her empty coffee cup. Al stands there and watches her as she rinses out the cup and places it in the dishwasher.

"Do you think you could tell me what is wrong?" he asks.

With her back still towards him, she reaches out and grabs the counter in a death grip. He can see her knuckles turning white. As she takes a deep breath, Al can feel her anger spreading across the kitchen.

"Where in the *hell* were you today?" she asks in an icy tone.

Al knows that she is really mad; she doesn't cuss. His mouth hangs open as he tries to come up with a lie to cover up his tracks, as he has done so many times in the past. "Out." he replies softly. *Out? That's the best you can come up with?*

Lorraine turns around, her arms tightly folded across her chest. She still won't look at him. Anger and disappointment cover her face.

"Seeing how you weren't home, Ron called me and asked if I could meet him because he was lost." She pauses as her lips tremble with anger. Her voice becomes a little louder and uneven. "I had to drive all the way across town, and I passed right by little Natalie Rose's house! And look out front, there is my husband's car parked right there for everyone to see that he's visiting that home-wrecking slut."

Al's mouth hangs open; his mind goes blank. *Al, just tell her the truth; we didn't do anything.* "Yes, I was with Natalie. But the only reason I went over there was to discuss my fading music career."

Lorraine's eyes are still fixed on the floor; the tears begin to fall. She quickly wipes them away, not wanting to give Al the satisfaction of seeing her cry. Then she shakes her head. Suddenly she looks up and glares at him. Without warning she throws the dish towel at him; it harmlessly hits him in the chest. Luckily she had already put the coffee cup away.

"You fooled around with her on your first wife, Ella! And I strongly believe you slept with her when those riots were happening in Detroit! And now . . . damn you, Al," she yells, teeth gritted.

"No, honey, you have it all wrong."

She clenches her fists and glares at him again. "I don't know why I bother to stay with you."

Al stands there as she storms off. She slams the bedroom door, and he jumps at the loud noise. He waits a few minutes, then walks down the dark hallway and stops in front of the bedroom. Gently he turns the doorknob, only to find out that it is locked.

"Lorraine, please let me in," he says softly through the door.

"Leave me alone!" she barks back.

"The only reason I went to see her was to asks for help with my career. We didn't do anything; she is engaged to her business manager, Bobby . . . Bobby someone."

"She's a home wrecker, so I really don't care if she is engaged or not. She'll sleep with anyone!"

Al places his hand on the door and does his best to control his brewing anger. He begins to contemplate breaking the door down. *Please, Lord, help me deal with this. I know I have done wrong in the past, but this time I was good.*

"Lorraine, all we did was go to the beach. We had a few sandwiches and sodas, no alcohol or anything. She had a record player, and she played mine and Obie's song, 'What's Going On.' I didn't even know it was released."

"I didn't either; Ron told me before you got home," she replies softly, with a sniffle.

"Did he tell you how it's doing?"

"No."

"It's number five on the charts. Isn't that great?"

"Fabulous, Al," she says, with no enthusiasm whatsoever.

His head makes a thump as it hits the door lightly. "I love you." There is no reply. "Berry is moving Motown Records out here."

"There goes the neighborhood," she mumbles.

"I'm going to demand a new contract. One with a bigger cut in it."

The door unlocks, and she opens it. She stands in the way; she still won't let him inside. Still filled with anger, she crosses her arms over her chest. "And what if he says no to a new contract?"

"Then I won't do any work with him. I'll find some other way of promoting my music. It shouldn't be hard with a song on the charts."

He reaches out to touch her, and she moves away. She won't even look him in the eyes.

"Don't touch me, Al," she says as she walks back to the bed and sits down on the edge of it, her back towards him.

He decides it would be best if he stays in the doorway. That way if she throws something, he will have a chance to react before it hits him.

"I love you," he says again.

"I never said you didn't. But the problem is that you love a lot of women. I just happen to be the one you live with too."

"I do more than just live with you. I married you, Lorraine. I swear, I did not fool around on you with Natalie." *Not this time, at least.*

"And most likely the only reason you didn't is because, number one, she's engaged, and number two, you guys were in public."

Damn, she is good. I swear sometimes that woman is the devil in disguise. "So does that mean you forgive me, seeing how I didn't do anything?"

Lorraine isn't sure whether to believe her husband or not. In the past she has caught him telling some pretty shady stories.

"I am still mad at you, Al. I want to be left alone for a while."

Al nods and slowly walks away, hoping that in a short period of time, all this will smooth itself out. Back in the kitchen, he rehearses what he will say to Berry when he sees him. As the hours pass, he can envision himself marching into Berry's new office and demanding a new contract. The thought of victory feels great as he stares at a pile of IRS notices on the kitchen counter. The pressure from the federal government is increasing. The massive debt is being held over their heads like a noose. *God, when will this nightmare ever end?* The American Dream seems so far out of reach for them. Even a savings account is out of the question. Any extra money is given to Lorraine's friends for safekeeping, just in case the IRS decides to pay another surprise visit.

CHAPTER 12

The next morning, Al is sitting at the breakfast table with his eyes firmly fixed on the phone. In front of him is a plate covered with the crumbs of his already-eaten toast, and an empty coffee cup. Scattered over the table is today's newspaper. The entertainment section is the last part he reads. It has a long story about Motown coming to California. On the front page is a picture of the home Berry had already bought; it is a huge mansion, and it turns Al's stomach. His eyes stay on the phone hanging on the far wall. *Come on, ring already. Ron, don't let me down.* He takes a deep breath and tries to be patient as his fingers subconsciously tap a beat on the table. Finally the phone rings, and he jumps out of his chair, sprinting across the kitchen and answering it before it can ring again.

"Hey, it's me."

"Damn, Ron, what took you so long?"

"I have some bad news. Berry said he didn't like it out here, so he already left and went back to Detroit."

"What?"

Ron starts to chuckle. "Just kidding. Hey, is Lorraine still there? Man, she was mad as hell at you for pulling those little panties again."

"Ron, I didn't do anything."

"Yeah, come on—this is your buddy Ronnie, baby, you can tell me all about it. So, how was it?"

"There is nothing to tell, Ron. I didn't do anything."

There is silence on the phone, as if Ron can't believe what he is hearing. "Wow, you're serious. Are you feeling OK? Maybe you should go to a doctor or a shrink. I don't know, you could even try a veterinarian or a voodoo lady . . . something."

Al smiles and laughs lightly, then turns serious. "It ain't nothing like that."

He pauses and sighs. "It just isn't the same between Lorraine and me; we've kind of grown apart since we've been here, and I don't need to make things worse by fooling around."

Al flashes back to old times, when he and his wife seemed closer, a lot closer. The hot flames that fueled their passion for each other are dwindling as time passes. Over the last few months they have been doing their own thing; they have distanced themselves from each another. It's not that they are fighting, because they would have to talk more in order to have an argument. He thinks it's the stress from the IRS that is driving them apart.

"Well, maybe after you meet with Berry things will get back on track, back to the way they were before," Ron says, snapping Al out of his musings.

"I hope so, but I just don't know anymore. So tell me where the new office is so I can pay the little man a visit."

"Are you sure you wouldn't rather open our own recording company?"

Al sighs. "Ron, we've talked about this before. I think it's great, but do you have the money?"

"No," Ron moans.

"Then just give me the address."

"OK, I'll give it to you, but I wish I could be there to see it."

A half hour later, Al drives downtown to see his old boss. Motown has leased the upper half of a fourteen-story building. Construction crews work at a feverish pace to add a few more offices and sound studios. The old, gray, concrete building sits at the very edge of the section of LA with all the skyscrapers. Al's stomach does somersaults and his hands turn cold and clammy at the thought of the meeting. He parks the car and walks toward the building. He knows that this has to be done; he has a right to some of the money that is pouring in from his latest single, "What's Going On."

With a steady step, he enters the lobby. He runs through the well-rehearsed scenario that he wants to have take place in Berry's office once again. Every word and every statement has been carefully thought out and planned. There is going to be no surprises; he is ready for this.

He stops at the building directory and looks to see where his boss's office is. He smiles and feels victorious once he finds it listed on the top floor. *Well, at least I'll have a nice view as I do this.*

He pushes the call button, and keeps his eyes on the digital numbers on top of the elevators as they count up and down. "Ding, ding," the bell of an elevator on the end chimes, calling its waiting passenger. Al walks down to it, stepping to the side as others walk off the elevator. He is the only one going up. He walks in and sees that the walls are covered with mirrors and gold trim. He pushes the fourteenth-floor button and looks at himself in one of the mirrors. *You may not look like a million bucks, but you write songs worth a million bucks.* The sliding doors are almost closed when someone sticks a hand in between them. The doors reopen, and Al turns around. A short black man with a hat and a suit enters. Al looks at the person's reflection; it's Berry. He has a beard now and looks a little bit heavier, but it is definitely Berry. Al's mouth falls open as his mind goes completely blank; it isn't supposed to happen like this. Berry looks up in the mirror; their eyes meet.

"Well, look who it is," Berry says, slowly turning around. The shorter man seems to have all the power, all the confidence, in the world. "Mister Cleveland, are you coming to pay me a visit?"

Al stands there for a moment, speechless, heart pounding and mouth gone dry. "Yes, I am," he finally answers. "I noticed you released the 'What's Going On' song that Obie and I put together."

"Yeah, I did." He pauses, shrugs, and makes a frown, as if it was nothing but a headache. "Don't know why I did, though. It's not going to be a good one."

"I suppose that's why it's number five on the charts and still climbing."

Al's statement stumps his boss. Berry sighs and stares at him in silence. The elevator dings again, and the doors open to the fourteenth floor. Berry leads the way as he walks off. Al follows him down the hall, past the construction crews. Parts of the walls are covered in plastic as the offices are torn down and rebuilt to the specifications of Motown Records. At the end of the long hallway is a set of dark, wooden, double doors. Berry heads straight for them and pushes the heavy doors wide open.

"You have an appointment in ten minutes, Mister Gordy," his secretary says.

"Thank you; this should only take a moment."

He walks into his spacious office, and casually hangs up his jacket and hat in a small closet. The room is decorated with all the appointments of a spoiled life, complemented by its own sound system. The furniture and bookshelves are done in dark oak. It reminds Al of a lawyer's office. Sitting behind a new desk that seems bigger than some small countries, the proud owner folds his hands onto his desk, signaling Al to continue. Then Berry smiles at Al. Nervously, Al rubs his hands together in an effort to warm them up.

"So," he says, making the first move, "if you give me your proper address, I can send your royalty checks. I'm sure you've been waiting for them."

"I've already given you my address, twice. That's not why I am here."

Berry leans back in his large, high-back, leather chair. He knows where this is leading, but he will still play the game. He raises his eyebrows, as if the news will be totally surprising.

"Well then, why don't you tell me what's on you mind?"

"It's my contract; it's time to renegotiate." *There, I said it. It's out in the open, now let's hear what you have to say about it.*

Berry sits up and looks at him as if he is shocked to hear it; as if there was no one else on the entire planet that has ever asked for such a thing. "Renegotiate? All of a sudden, just like that?"

Al stands firm, not budging an inch. "There is no *all of a sudden* about it. I've been working under the same contract for years and years. And all this time I have hardly received a dime. All my money has gone to pay for improvements in the sound room and elsewhere," Al says sternly, as he taps his index finger on the large desk, insinuating that it was his money that paid for all the office furniture.

Berry leans back in his chair and rubs his chin as he gathers his thoughts. For him, this is a massive chess game, and each move has to be made carefully, strategically. His secretary comes in and sets a cup of coffee in front of him.

"All right, I give in, I will redo your contract." He calmly takes a sip of his coffee, hoping that Al will be satisfied with that and leave.

The time to act is now, Al; you have him running, now get him. "I don't want to see anything under 25 percent of the royalties."

Berry practically chokes on his coffee as he sits up. Using a napkin, he wipes away the spilled liquid from his chin. "Twenty-five percent; are you crazy? I was thinking more like 6 percent, and that's being generous."

"You can save the 6 percent for your junior writers. I feel I have proven myself by writing several number-one hits."

Berry remains silent. He stares at the wall with a tight mouth; the meeting is not going as planned. Al has changed over the last year. He is much more independent, stronger.

The secretary comes over the intercom. "Mister Gordy, your next appointment is here."

"Give me just a minute," he says softly.

Shoving Al out the door at a time like this would not be a good idea; it would be foolish and costly. Berry leans back in his chair and stares at Al. The man was asking for a lot, and he isn't sure how to deal with it.

Finally he speaks up. "Well, Mister Cleveland, I'll do my best. Check back in a couple of weeks, and we'll see."

Al knows what he is doing. He is giving him a couple weeks to cool down; right now, with a song on the charts, he is a hot commodity, and he feels it is time to take full advantage of that situation.

"I'll be back tomorrow. If you have a new contract for me, we'll immediately begin working on the 'What's Going On' album. If you don't have a new contract for me, I'll go with one of the other recording studios that have been calling me."

Berry struggles to remain calm. The last thing he wants is to lose Al to someone else. "Who's been calling you?" he asks politely.

There was no one really, but Al wasn't going to say that. He sticks his hands in his pockets and rocks back and forth, from the balls of his feet to his heels. "Just some of your competitors."

Berry looks down and shakes his head. Being brand new in town has its disadvantages; he isn't sure what his competitors are up to. "I'll let you know. Don't call us, we'll call you. Now if you'll excuse me, I have another appointment."

Al walks out, feeling a little unsure of what will come, but overall he knows he did the right thing. With his chest sticking out with pride, he marches back down the hall to the elevators. Standing up to the boss makes his feet feel lighter than air. *He's going to do it, Al, there is no doubt about it.*

* * *

Al drives straight home, and doesn't waste a moment before calling Ron with the full details of what happened. They are both very excited. After the phone call, Al remains at home and waits for Berry to call. Hours pass, and the offices at Motown close for the night. Slightly upset, Al begins to make dinner for Lorraine, who should be home any minute. As he is pulling out pots and pans, he hears her car pulling into the garage. With a smile on his face, he walks out to greet her.

"Hey, baby," he says, giving her a kiss.

The move comes as a surprise to her, it has been a while since he has done that.

"What's the special occasion?" she asks.

"Motown; they're here in the big city with us," he says, as he snaps his fingers and dances.

"Oh," she mumbles, grabbing several books from the backseat of her car.

Lorraine has enjoyed their time away from Motown. The IRS raid is still a vivid memory for her, and their house shows it. It is taking some time to recover from the blow, and they are still paying the government for money that they never saw.

"I told Berry I want 25 percent of the royalties, and if he doesn't give it to me, I'm not working for him anymore."

Lorraine stares at her books as she slowly nods. She has been very busy studying for her doctorate. She thinks about the large amount of royalties; she doesn't believe that Berry would ever part with that kind of money.

"Well, I wish you the best of luck with that one," she says evenly as she walks into the house.

Al wishes they could be close again; he wants her to have more enthusiasm about his career. He follows her quickly. "You don't think it will happen?"

Lorraine stops at the counter and sets her heavy books down. She takes a deep breath. "I just don't want to see you get hurt again, Al. I don't want the IRS coming to our house again and taking everything we own." She pauses as she chokes back her emotions. "We've been through that once, and once was too much."

"Well, unless he gives me what I want, I'm not working for him."

"OK. So, what's for dinner?" she asks, changing the subject.

* * *

The next morning Lorraine leaves for work once again, and Al hangs around the house waiting for Berry to call. Several hours pass, and the phone doesn't ring once. Disgusted, Al decides to take a drive down to the beach. He puts on some shorts and a T-shirt, and grabs a beach towel. Just as he is about to leave, however, the phone rings. Al is certain that it is Ron, calling for a status check. Al answers the phone.

"Hello?"

"Hello, Mister Cleveland?"

It's Berry's secretary; he recognizes the voice in a second. His heart begins to pound and his mind races; the thought of making some money, some real good money is exciting.

Be cool, stay calm. "Yes, it's me."

"Mister Gordy would like you to come down and sign your new contract with Motown Records. He would also like you to come in and do it today, so you can get started on the 'What's Going On' album. Is that possible?"

Al smiles; it's the biggest one he has had in years. He swears his lips are touching his ears. His voice is filled with joy. "All right, I'll be there in just a few minutes." He hangs up the phone and begins to jump around in the kitchen. "Yes! Yes! Who's the man? Who's the man around here?" he asks the empty room.

A half hour later, Al approaches Berry's secretary. He is brimming with excitement, but he does his best to act casual. She announces him to her boss, and then sends him into the spacious office. Berry is on the phone talking to Marvin as Al walks in. Berry motions for Al to take a seat on one of the chairs in front of his desk.

"Yeah, Al's here now," Berry says to Marvin. "Now that all of you have new contracts, I want you guys to get started immediately on the new album . . . all right, sounds great . . . I'll talk to you later. Bye."

He hangs up the phone and folds his hands. With a strange smile he looks at Al. "Well, Mister Cleveland, you drive a very hard bargain. I may live to regret this later, but I am giving you your 25-percent cut." He slides the new contract over to him.

Al smiles as he picks up the thick package of paper and looks it over. His eyes fall right on the royalty distribution section, and it clearly states that 25 percent goes to him. Al feels very confident about it. He has to fight the urge to jump up and down.

"Don't worry about a thing, Berry, you won't regret this one bit," Al says in his cool, calm voice.

Al continues to read it over. He scans for any mistakes that he might have missed the first time. He is leery about signing it, but it is exactly what he asked for.

"I'm glad to hear that, because we have a lot of work to do," Berry replies.

* * *

A week later, Marvin, Obie, Al, and several other songwriters go to Ron's apartment in West Hollywood to put together the "What's Going On" album. All of them work long hours, day after day, for two straight months. As the weeks pass, they record "Wholly Holy," "Save The Children," "God Is Love," "What's Happening Brother," and many more to make up the album.

Marvin puts his heart and soul into each and every lyric as they are recorded. He gives an extraordinary performance. Once all the songs are finished, Al, Marvin, Ron, and Obie all go to Berry's office to let him listen to it. As the last song stops, the four of them stand there in silence, waiting for Berry to speak.

"I'm still not crazy about a protest album," he says, as he slowly rocks back and forth in his large leather chair. "But I feel you should release this as soon as possible."

The men rejoice. Berry will never admit that he likes it to them. After all, he had put down the "What's Going On" title song. However, it's number one on the Billboard charts and holding strong. Admit it or not, Berry knows this will be a good moneymaker for the company.

Two short days later the album is released. It is only in stores for a little while before it zooms up and off the charts, selling over twenty million copies. It establishes itself as Motown Record's benchmark musical accomplishment, and makes the company a ton of money as well.

* * *

"It's here; it's finally here," Al says as he shifts though his mail weeks later.

He has finally received a royalty check, the first under his new contract. With fumbling fingers he tears into the envelope. His eyebrows raise as he looks at the check.

"Lorraine! Lorraine!" he hollers as he runs inside.

He finds his wife sitting at the kitchen table with open books all around her as she studies for a final exam.

"What's all the noise about?" she asks as she continues to read.

"I received a check. Look at this, baby," he says as he shows it to her.

She looks at it and nods. "Good for you, Al. Let's hope he keeps sending them," she replies with a minimal amount of excitement in her voice.

It's not that she isn't happy for him; she's just preparing herself for the letdown that has come so many times before. But this time Al is right; the new contract makes things better. There are still numerous deductions shown, but enough is left over for Al to send large chunks off to the IRS—which, for now, will keep it pacified.

That night, as Lorraine studies, Al goes to a big party, celebrating his new life with booze and marijuana. The drugs are an escape for him; when he is high he doesn't have to deal with life. He doesn't have to think about the IRS or his failing marriage. As the weeks pass and the album sells, the parties become more and more frequent; suddenly they are happening almost every night. With each late night out, Al builds a larger, thicker wall between and his wife and him—one that neither one bothers to tear down. Their marriage turns colder than any iceberg floating in the ocean.

* * *

Late one Thursday night, Lorraine is cleaning up the dishes from her dinner. It's becoming a regular thing for her to eat alone, and she's not sure whether she wants Al around or not. Suddenly the reflection of headlights flash on the wall, and she turns and watches Al park his car halfway on the lawn and halfway on the driveway. She turns her back and cringes at the sight of him stumbling towards the front door. Rage begins to boil in her stomach, preparing to surface.

Al never did come home the night before, so she hasn't seen him for a day and a half. And drunk is no way to come home to an angry wife. He enters the house, not only intoxicated but stoned as well.

"I'm home," he mumbles.

He manages to make it part way across the living room before collapsing on a recliner. Lorraine somehow manages to maintain her composure as she walks over and looks at him. His clothes are wrinkled and somewhat dirty, indicating that he had slept in them. The pungent odor of alcohol drifts off his body and his breath. Given another day outside, he could have been any wino off the street.

"Look what the cat dragged in," she says angrily. "My husband, straight from the gutters of Los Angeles. You look and smell disgusting."

"Leave me alone, woman," he mumbles.

"I am going to leave you alone, Mister Missing Husband! First thing in the morning I am going to New York for the weekend. It's my mother's birthday, and I want to be there, *alone*. Without you," she reiterates, just in case there was any confusion.

She pauses for a moment. Al continues to stare out the front window. His head sways back and forth; he can't keep it still. He belches, then waves his hand at her as if it really didn't matter. His *don't care* attitude causes her blood to boil. Suddenly her anger erupts.

"You know, both my sisters have been married almost as long as us, and they have nice homes, kids, new cars, things to show for their years together! They have all the things that we are missing from our marriage."

He doesn't respond like she wants him to. He continues to sit there, seemingly oblivious to his surroundings.

"What do I have?" she asks loudly, with her fists clenched. "All I have is a drunk!"

Al sits up and begins to straighten some of his wrinkled clothes. Some of her words actually make it into his head. "Maybe you should have married one of your sisters then," he slurs.

Lorraine clenches her jaw. "I don't want you to be here when I get back."

Al smiles oddly. "Of course I won't be here; you get back on the fifth, and I have rehearsals all that week."

Lorraine picks up Al's small brown suitcase and places it next to him; it is already packed with his clothes. "You don't understand. I don't want you here at all. Ever!"

Al struggles to get up from the chair. He picks up the suitcase and heads for the front door. She watches in disgust as he wobbles back and forth. He stops as his forehead lightly touches the wooden door, and he fumbles with the doorknob, as if it were a complicated lock.

"Thanks for the ride, babe," he chuckles softly. "Take care of yourself."

It takes a few minutes, but he makes it to his car, starts it up, and drives away. She watches the taillights fade, and hopes he makes it somewhere safe.

Al manages to drive around the corner, then realizes he can't make it any further. He parks the car on the side of the road. There he passes out in his front seat until morning.

* * *

Three days later, Al moves into Ron's large apartment in West Hollywood, just off of Sunset Boulevard. A while back Ron left Motown Records; he now is working with Jose Wilson at 20th Century Records, and doing quite well. Al feels lonely and depressed about his separation from his wife. He knows she is back in town, yet she has not called at all.

The days painfully pass. They both have aching hearts over the breakup, but the couple hardly talks to one another, except for the occasional short phone call. Lorraine doesn't want him back until he changes. At this point he shows no signs of giving up his wild life. He feels it is high time for him to enjoy life and have a great time.

Although the apartment is Ron's, every night after work Al continues to hold loud parties. It begins to strain their friendship. Early one morning, Ron comes out of his bedroom and finds Al sitting at the breakfast table. He had been at a party somewhere across town, and is still in his clothes from the night before.

"Dude, what's up with you?" Ron asks.

Al has a massive hangover, and slowly rubs his temples. "I'm finally getting to enjoy life," he whispers.

"Doesn't look like you're enjoying it right now."

Ron pours two cups of fresh coffee, and slides one to Al. Then he walks over to the cabinet and takes out some aspirin for his friend. Al takes a sip of the hot coffee as he gulps down the pills. His head is pounding, and the room still seems to be spinning.

"You don't understand. All my life I wanted to make a living off making music, and I am finally doing it."

"Oh, I do understand," Ron replies in a compassionate voice. "I'm making a living off of my own talents like I have always wanted to. But just because I'm doing it doesn't mean I have to destroy my body along the way."

"I don't want to hear any more," Al mumbles as he waves his hand at him. "If I wanted a lecture, I could call Lorraine."

Slowly, Al stands and staggers down the hallway towards his room. He holds on to his pounding head, hoping he can find a dark, silent spot where he can die quietly. Ron's shoulders slump as he watches him go; he hates seeing his friend like that. He knows that Al is living from one royalty check to the next, and things are only going to get worse.

A while back Ron found one of Al's royalty checks. He noticed that his friend was no longer making the extra payments to the IRS, so his checks were being heavily garnished. On top of that, Motown was taking back its usual hefty cut. Ron wants to talk more to his friend, but then glances at his watch.

"Damn, I'm late."

Ron rushes out the door and heads off to work. Al sleeps half the day away, then makes a brief appearance at Motown Records later in the afternoon. As he meanders around the studio, he notices that he feels sluggish and rather tired, even more so than usual. It feels as if his heart can't keep up with his movements. But he quickly reminds himself about the good time he had had the night before, and thinks about doing it again. Ron has to stay late at his job, so Al holds another big party at the apartment in the evening.

Later that night, the large apartment seems small, because it is jam-packed with dozens of partygoers. The people are loud, and the music is even louder. Drugs, booze, and women are everywhere. The entire apartment is filled with a cloud of smoke.

Al stumbles out of his bedroom with his arm over a young woman that he had just met. His glassy eyes stare straight ahead as she giggles and guides him out. Once they are out in the living room, she heads off to see someone else, and Al walks into the crowd, not feeling a thing. *I think I am flying. I can't feel the ground anymore, I feel so light and free*, he thinks to himself as the music plays.

He slowly turns and heads for the open sliding-glass door. The drapes move with the cool breeze coming over the balcony. It carries in the smell of the ocean, but Al doesn't even notice it. There is a couch that sits a few feet in front of the door. He makes it around to the back of the couch, and turns to look at everyone else. The room spins as he is stricken with tunnel vision.

"Am I asleep?" he whispers.

The place is filled with people, yet no one seems to notice him. Suddenly he feels very alone and disconnected. Things begin to slow down. The beating music sounds distorted. He feels a bump; it's his knee hitting the ground, but as far as he is concerned, he is still standing. The music fades, as does all the sounds in the room. All he can hear is his own heartbeat. It sounds slow and without rhythm as his heart struggles to beat. The room grows darker.

A few minutes later, Ron drives up in his car. Before he even shuts off the engine, he can hear the loud music bellowing out from his apartment. He gets out and slams his car door shut. With angry eyes, he glares up at the open doorway, which is filled with people he doesn't even know.

"Ah, Mister Jolley." The landlord comes racing over to him. He is a small white man in a blue bathrobe. His wife stands in the background, with her arms folded across her chest. Most likely she put him up to this. "This has got to stop," he says, pointing to the party. "There are other people that live here, and they have rights too."

"Yes, sir. I'm going to put an end to it right now."

He looks up at his apartment again. Hostility towards all the people there fills his gut quickly. He has to put an end to this or both of them will be looking for another place to live very soon. And Ron isn't about to move.

"Party's over with, Al," he says as he marches up the stairs.

He forces his way through the smoky room and into the crowd of dancing, drunken people, in search of Al. No one pays any attention to Ron; as far as they are concerned, he is just another person joining the party. Ron's plan is to get Al to tell everyone to leave, but he can't find his friend anywhere. Finally he walks over to his stereo and shuts off the music. Dead silence sweeps across the apartment. Instantly, all eyes turn to him.

"Time to go home; everyone out," he says in a voice that is almost a yell. "This is my place," he says, once he realizes that he is receiving some bad looks. "So move it on out of here."

There is some moaning and groaning, but the people begin to file out of his apartment. The last few stragglers come trotting out of the bedrooms and follow everyone else out. Ron doesn't even want to think about what they were doing in his room.

He places his hands on his hips and looks around at the mess. The floor is littered with beer bottles, empty cans, and napkins. Cigarette butts seem to be everywhere; some have even bee put out on his furniture.

"Man, is he in trouble when I find him," Ron groans.

Then his eyes fall upon his friend's legs, which are sticking out from behind the couch. There is no movement in them whatsoever, and he knows that Al can handle his liquor. Quickly he rushes over to him.

Al is lying on his stomach, in between the couch and the sliding-glass door. His arms are underneath him, indicating that, when he fell, he did nothing to brace himself. Ron's mouth falls open as he stares at his dear friend's body. Everything that Al might have done wrong in the past is instantly washed away. Quickly Ron rolls him over. Al's face is lifeless and pale, and there is strange foam coming out of his mouth.

"Oh God, no. Oh please, God, don't do this."

He checks Al's neck for a pulse. There is one, but it is very faint. He rushes over to the phone and frantically dials 911.

"Hello, yes, I need an ambulance right away . . ."

CHAPTER 13

Hours later, Ron leans on a pay phone and begins dialing. It's a phone call he doesn't want to make, but knows he has to. He mashes the receiver into his ear so he can drown out the loud noises in the emergency room. The hospital is unusually busy, full of sick people and crying children. Doctors and aides rush by with people on gurneys, as operators make announcements over the PA system. Ron plugs his other ear with his finger and listens as the phone rings several times.

"Come on, pick up the phone," he whispers.

"Hello?" a groggy voice asks.

Ron hadn't even thought about the three-hour time difference. "Daryl?"

"Yeah."

"It's me . . . Ron Jolley."

Daryl is now a grown man, living on his own. His eyes widen as his heart beats faster; this is not good and he knows it. He and Ron always palled around, but the connection was always Daryl's father. If Ron is calling at this late hour, it is something serious, something to be afraid of.

"What happened to my dad?" he suddenly blurts out, as if he could read minds.

"He's all right . . . well, he's alive. We just got here to the hospital; he was having a party, and I think he got carried away. He's in the ER right now; the doctors are doing some tests on him." It isn't the whole truth; Al is in critical condition and barely holding on to life. And Ron is worried that his son will never get to see his father alive again. "I think it would be best if you came out to see him as soon as possible."

Daryl takes a deep, shaky breath. "I'll take the next plane out there."

* * *

Ten hours later, Ron is sitting in the waiting room on the fourth floor. Al has been moved up to ICU as the doctors continue to watch him. Luckily, they were able to stabilize his heart. The elevators open, and Daryl walks out quickly. He has the height and build of his father. With a tight grip, he holds onto his suitcase. His new tennis shoes squeak on the highly waxed floor.

Ron notices him coming and stands. The two embrace as Daryl's nervous eyes look down the empty hall.

"How's my dad?"

"They're not telling me a whole lot right now. But they have him in a room right over there, where they can monitor him closely. They did tell me that he is stable, though."

Daryl doesn't like that one bit. He bites his lower lip and stares down the hall. No news is usually good news, but he knows it doesn't always work that way in the hospital.

"That's all they told you?"

"They might tell you more; I'm not a family member."

"Yeah, you're right. let me go talk to them."

Daryl is an emotional wreck as he walks up to the nurse's station. He checks in by signing a logbook and showing the nurse his ID. Pleading his case with the three nurses on duty, he tries to get any news, but they won't release any information about his father until he talks to the doctor who is taking care of him.

"Can I see him, at least?" he asks in a high-pitched voice.

"You have fifteen minutes, that's all," one of the nurses says. "He needs to rest."

The nurse motions across the hall. Daryl didn't realize he was that close. Turning around seems harder than ever. It's the fear of facing the unknown, not knowing whether or not he will ever talk to his dad again.

But Daryl turns anyway, taking slow, cautious steps towards the large room. He knows this is going to be hard to face. A wall of windows faces the nurse's station, so they can see everything that is happening. He can hardly bear to look through the glass at his unconscious father, lying in the bed with wires and tubes coming out of him. With wide, worried-filled eyes, he gazes at Al. Some of his dad's color has come back, but he still looks different; his face looks swollen, more rounded.

The room is completely silent except for the beeping of the heart monitor and one machine that is helping Al breath. Daryl's ears begin to ring in the eerie silence. His eyes follow the IV and the tubes entering Al's mouth that are keeping him alive.

A lump forms in Daryl's throat as his eyes well up with tears. He does nothing to stop his crying; it's killing him to see his dad like this. He had held his composure all the way across the country, but he can't hold it any longer. Fearful feelings flood his heart as he thinks about touching Al. He is afraid that his dad's hand will be ice cold. But he builds up the courage, and touches him anyway; he reaches out and takes his hand. He allows himself a small smile as he feels the warmth off his dad's hand. Tears roll down his cheeks as he remembers all the time they spent together over the years. He closes his eyes and takes a deep breath as he listens to the steady rhythm of the life-support equipment.

"Lord," he says with a shaky voice. "I know my father wasn't walking on the right path. but he is a good man, a caring man. Please don't take him home yet; please let him stay with us for a while longer."

He opens his eyes and looks at his dad once more. Somewhere deep in his heart he is expecting a miracle, a miracle that will bring his dad back just the way he remembers him, but it doesn't happen. Al doesn't move a muscle. Daryl squeezes his hand, and notices one of the nurses watching him. He knows his time is already up. He doesn't want to go, to leave him like this. But staying there would most likely do more harm than good.

"I have to go, Dad," he whispers. "But I won't be far."

He lets go of his father's hand and slowly walks out of the room, keeping his eyes on him. In his heart he is saying good-bye, just in case things don't go right. Daryl nods to the nurses and walks down to the waiting room with his hands in his pockets. Daryl pictures a funeral where he is crying over the casket.

"Well?" Ron asks as he sees him enter the waiting room, which is cluttered with old magazines.

"No news. They said I have to wait for the doctor to talk to me."

Daryl sits down, buries his face in his hands, and prays silently again. A TV is on in the corner, but neither of them bother watching it. They both sit there for another hour and a half before the doctor comes in.

"Hello, Mister Cleveland. I'm Doctor Rayson."

Daryl looks up. The doctor is a short, thin, white man with black glasses and brown, curly hair. He doesn't seem to be a real social type, which oddly makes Daryl feel more comfortable, because that most likely means the doctor is very smart, he tells himself.

Daryl stands and shakes the doctor's hand. He gets the impression that the doctor is nice, and quite caring.

"What's the deal with my dad?" His voice is still shaky and filled with emotion.

"Well, it's hard to tell right now; we're still waiting on the test results. Your friend Mister Jolley here told me that he was smoking—" He pauses as he flips through his chart to make sure he said the right substance. "—marijuana, and it seems to have been laced with something else that his body could not handle."

"What do you mean, 'handle'?"

"It appears that your father has some type of heart disease; the chemical reaction of the drug basically shut him down." The expression on Daryl's face says it all. "I'm getting the impression that you didn't know he has a problem at all."

Daryl's mouth gapes open as he envisions his father living the rest of his short life in a hospital bed, tied down with dozens of wires and tubes.

"What kind of heart problem does he have?"

"Hopefully the test results will tell us that. But for now, we just need him to become conscious again. As for you two, you should really go home, get something to eat, and get some sleep. Just give the nurses your phone number, and they can call you if anything happens."

"Thank you," Daryl says as the doctor walks out of the waiting room.

Daryl stands there for a moment and gathers his thoughts. He searches his memory, trying to think of the last time he saw his dad, and if there was any sign of a heart problem. Nothing come to mind. Then he thinks about his father lying alone in that room. He feels wrong about leaving his dad at the hospital alone while he goes to sleep, but he knows that he is exhausted; he has barely slept in the last twenty-four hours.

"We can stay here if you want to," Ron says.

Daryl can see the compassion in Ron's eyes, but he can also tell that he is in desperate need of sleep. "No. The doctor's right; we should go get some rest, and besides, I am starving."

The two go back to Ron's apartment. Daryl is shocked to see the mess left by the large party. Even though they are both extremely tired, they begin to clean things up. The first thing they do is open all the doors and windows to help get the stench of booze and smoke out. Then they start in the living room and kitchen, and make their way back to the bedrooms.

As Daryl cleans up his father's room, he discovers some men's clothing that does not belong to him or his father. He carefully picks them up with his thumb and index finger, as if they were covered in germs, and tosses them into the garbage bag. Underneath the clothes, he finds a large bag of cocaine. He pick it up and stares at the five-pound, clear, cellophane bag.

"I hope this isn't your stuff, Dad," he whispers.

He thinks about throwing it away, then decides to hide it under the bed for now. He tries to come up with a good reason for keeping it, but he can't. He keeps it anyway. As he picks up empty beer cans from Al's dresser, he smiles as he sees pictures of himself and Ted that had been taken over the years. Sitting in the center of the dresser is a notebook filled with songs that he and his dad wrote together. Daryl sighs and thinks about his father as he picks it up and thumbs through it.

"You OK?" Ron asks from the doorway.

"Yeah, just old memories, that's all."

"The place is reasonably straight. I'm going to hit the sack for a while."

"Thanks for everything, Ron."

"Don't mention it. Your dad is going to be fine, you'll see."

Daryl is already bracing himself for the worst. "I hope so."

The two go to separate rooms, and fall asleep for several hours. Later, stomachs growling, they both get up and stumble out to the kitchen. Ron makes some sandwiches as Daryl looks around the apartment.

"Does Lorraine know?" Daryl asks.

Ron slides two plates on the table. "I've called several times, but haven't been able to get hold of her."

His eyes shift to several trash bags piled up in the corner. All of them are filled from the party. "My dad was out of control, wasn't he?"

Ron sits down and takes a healthy bite out of his sandwich. "I guess so. I didn't realize how bad until last night. I hope he can pull through this."

They both eat their dinner, then head back to the hospital, hoping the test results are in. Once again Daryl signs in at the ICU, then walks in for a short visit with his father. He feels better when he notices some of the life-support equipment has been taken out of the room. That has to be good, right? If there is less equipment, his dad must be holding his own.

"We took the breathing tube out," Doctor Rayson says as he enters the room.

Daryl turns and looks at him, and immediately wonders if the doctor has been working all night, or if he had started a new shift.

Daryl's eyebrows raise. "So things are looking better?"

"Oh yes, much," the doctor replies as he walks over and checks on his patient. Out of habit, he looks at his watch as he checks Al's pulse. "We did a CAT scan, and his brain is functioning perfectly normal. So there is no brain damage, which is very good. Now if we could just get him to wake up from his coma, then we would be doing great."

"What about his heart?"

Doctor Rayson picks up a large yellow envelope and pulls out several full-sized chest X-rays. He places them on an X-ray viewing wall and turns on the light. The fluorescent lights flicker to life, showing the black-and-white photos. Daryl walks over and stares at them with an open mouth.

The doctor continues. "We had a cardiac specialist come up and take a look at these. He could probably do a much better job at describing what's happening to your father, but . . ." He pauses as he points to the X-ray just to the left of the heart. "Look here, see this gray area on the left side of his heart?"

Daryl squints; he can just make out a slightly fuzzy, gray-shaded area. To him it really doesn't amount to anything. But it provides all the clues the right doctor needs to see. Al's heart has suffered, and it is now damaged.

"Yeah, I can see it."

"That's the problem. It's caused largely by stress. Of course, your dad's wild life wasn't helping it at all. Was he under a lot of stress in the past?"

"Yeah, he has huge IRS problems and everything. So, what does this mean? Is he going to die?"

"Well, not real soon," the doctor says with confidence. "With the right medication, we can prolong his life for at least another ten years. You see, his heart is like a battery that is slowly winding down; there is no pain, but he will feel sluggish from time to time, and there will be localized swelling."

Al moans, and they both turn to look at him. Daryl's eyebrows rise as he hopes his dad will wake up, but he doesn't. The doctor turns back and begins to pull down the X-rays. Daryl slowly walks over, praying he will see more signs of life, but his dad remains still.

"Can he hear us?" Daryl asks.

"Yes, he can. I've heard of coma patients waking up and telling about whole conversations that took place while they were asleep. So watch what you say to him," he says with a smile.

* * *

A day later Daryl comes back again to find his father in the same position. Ron has returned to work, so Daryl spends the day talking to his dad. Then, with nothing left to say, he starts reading out loud; he reads the newspaper, magazines, and anything else he can get his hands on.

The sun travels across the sky, and Al is checked many times, but he shows no signs of waking up. His son begins to fear the worse, and that he will have to make the call to stop feeding his father intravenously. It has been on his mind since he first saw him lying there, but with each passing moment, it seems more like reality.

Al's soft groggy voice snaps him out of his daydream.

"Dad? You're awake!" He quickly reaches over and clicks the call button for the nurse. "You're back," he says happily.

"What are you doing here?" Al pauses and looks around the room. Confusion fills his sleepy head. He tries to remember what happened, but his mind is filled with large blank spots. Short glimpses of the party flash in front of his eyes. "Where am I?"

"You're in the hospital. You were smoking pot that was laced with something, and you OD'd. Ron found you and called an ambulance. He notified me and I came out here to see you. Oh, Dad," he says, squeezing Al's hand. "I am so glad that you are back."

"Well, look who's awake," the nurse says happily. "I'll go page the doctor."

Al's brow scrunches down; he can hardly remember a thing. "How long have I been asleep?"

"Three days. Three very long days, Dad; you scared me half to death."

Al tries to sit up. The simple movement causes his heart to race and his muscles to go numb. He wisely decides not to move anymore.

Another doctor walks in quickly. He smiles when he sees that Al is awake and fully alert. "Welcome back," the doctor says as he checks Al's pulse. The room falls silent as he stares at his watch. "Well, your pulse is fine." He holds out his hand. "Squeeze my hand as hard as you can." Al does it. "Good, now the other one."

Al squeezes the other hand; he is already feeling tired again. "How bad off am I?"

The doctor pulls a lighted scope from the wall and looks into Al's eyes. "Not bad at all, Mister Cleveland. You should feel a little groggy and confused right now; that is perfectly normal. For the time being, don't do anything strenuous, and in the morning we'll get you started on rehabilitation, so we can get your muscles going again."

"Rehabilitation? How long is that going to take?"

"That depends on you. But after what you put your body through, I would plan on a good month."

"A month? But . . . but I have work to do."

"Strain yourself and the only thing you'll be working for is a grave," the physician states, with no sympathy in his voice.

Al tries desperately to remember the party, but only bits and pieces come to him. It's like his life is a thousand-piece puzzle that has been dumped on the carpet, and a person with no hands is trying to put it together.

The doctor writes something down on Al's chart and leaves the room. Al watches him leave, then stares out the row of windows and watches the nurses work behind the front desk. Suddenly his eyes shift and he glances at all the life-support equipment around him. The noises and beeps they make seem so much louder than they did just moments ago. His eyes follow the tubes that lead from clear bags straight into his arm. He knows they were feeding him and giving him medicine to keep him alive.

The reality of what he had done rams into his heart like a freight train. He stares at the wall and tries to remember something, anything, about the party. Who he was with, what songs were played, what they ate . . . but nothing comes to mind. He glances at his son, and the expression on Daryl's face tells him that death was close, very close.

"I must have been nearly—" he stops himself, as he almost can't say the word. If he did say it, he would be admitting that what he did was wrong, and totally foolish. Then he says it anyway. "I must have been nearly dead when Ron found me."

Daryl sits on the edge of the bed, very relieved to see his father awake. "Yeah, you were. He told me that you had foam coming out of your mouth and everything."

Al's voice becomes small. "Are you disappointed in me?"

His son doesn't hesitate for a moment. "Hell, no, Dad. You know that you and I have smoked pot together." Al nods, remembering that they had done it many times. "You just have to slow down. Well, way down. The doc said you have a heart condition."

Al looks away; deep down he has known he has some type of heart problem for quite some time. "How bad is it?"

"I guess it's not too bad." He pauses and watches his father's eyes as they become heavy. "You're real tired, aren't you?"

"Yeah, son. But I'm afraid to fall asleep again. I just want to make sure that I can wake up."

"I'm sure you will, plus I'll be right here with you."

Al falls asleep once again, and begins to snore loudly. Daryl calls Ron and Lorraine to explain what happened. He stays by his father's side throughout the night, and is there in the morning when his father wakes up again.

Early in the day, they begin working on getting Al's body back into shape. In just the few days he has been there, his strength has been greatly diminished. Two weeks pass; Al has been moved off of the ICU ward and given his own room. Daryl flies back to Pittsburgh, packs his stuff, and moves out to California to help his father. He makes it there two weeks later. By that time, Al is being released from the hospital.

"You know, son, you didn't have to move all the way over here."

"I know that," Daryl replies, as he carries his father's suitcase out of the hospital. "I want to help you, and besides, California's winters are a lot nicer than the ones in PA."

"That's for damn sure."

They head back to Ron's apartment. Al feels much better, and knows he must watch his diet and exercise now that he has a heart condition. His spirit soars once he realizes that their newest album is still number one in the nation. He decides he wants an even bigger cut of the royalties that are pouring into Motown Records, so the very next day he heads into Berry's office.

"Fifty percent?" Berry yells. "You have got to be kidding! You are already the highest-paid producer I have!"

"I am also the best one," Al says calmly. "Fifty percent is what I am worth. If you can't do that, then maybe I should go elsewhere."

Berry's eyebrows cross with anger as he folds his hands on top of his desk. His body stiffens as he prepares to take a stance. "Your contract stands at 25 percent; there will be no changes."

"Then I guess we are done," Al replies as he stands up.

Berry does nothing to stop him as he walks out the door. Even before Al is out of the building, he is feeling good about his decision. He is tired of working for someone else, and he is feeling held down by

Motown Records. Now he will be able to freely express himself through his music.

* * *

"Wow, you walked out just like that?" Ron says as Al tells him the news. His round face is bursting with a large smile. "I wish I was there to see it. Does that mean you want to get started on our project?"

"I think it's time that we showed the world our talents."

"What project is that?" Daryl asks.

"Doorway Enterprises," Ron replies, his head held up high. "Our own music company. We will no longer be held down by the *man*."

"Ron and I have been talking about it for some time," Al adds. "We think this town needs a good, honest music company, one that won't rip off its own employees."

"I like it," Daryl says. He thinks of how nice it will be to work with his father, writing music. "When do we get started?"

The two older men look at each other, and suddenly smile. "Now," they both say.

* * *

Two weeks later, Daryl drives up with his father to their new offices on Sunset Boulevard. They both sit in the car and watch as the small, lighted sign, which reads, "Doorway Enterprises," is put into place a few feet above the entrance. Ron and Al have borrowed enough money from the bank and devout friends to give the company a good kick-start. Ron decides to keep his job at 20th Century Records; it's a conflict of interest, but it is great for roping in raw talent.

The building they have leased is small but efficient. It has a small front lobby, one recording studio, and two back offices. Dark, low-pile carpeting covers the floor, while the walls are simply painted white. It's nothing very pretty to look at, but it will get the job done.

"I can't believe this is finally happening," Daryl says. "I've wanted to do this for so many years."

"You're not the only one, son." Al turns and watches as cars pass by the small sign on the busy street. He knows that it will only be a matter of time before their first superstar steps through the door. "What do you say we go inside and get started?"

Daryl's enthusiasm brings new life and energy to Al. Daryl has his father's gift for music, and demonstrates it every time he writes a song. Soon Doorway Enterprises seems to be a force to be reckoned with. They select local talent like the California Girls, and hook up with Charles LaMarr, manager of the Chambers Brothers as well as Three Dog Night. LaMarr urges Clive Davis, president of Columbia Records, owned by CBS, to help Doorway by putting some of their talent on network television. The potential deals are numerous and wonderful, but always seem to be just out of their reach.

Even with the high-powered help, something is still missing. Al does not possess Berry's managerial skills, nor is he creative enough to force something out of nothing when it comes to business. Over the next few months, things slowly wind down. Money becomes tighter and tighter. Ron stands in the back office, rubbing his head as he stares at a stack of unpaid bills. He walks down the hall to Al's office, and listens to Al as he struggles on the phone to make a deal.

"All right, well, please give us a call if you change your mind," Al says, and hangs up the phone.

Ron plops down in a chair and stares at the floor. He hates what is going on, and the money matters are causing him to lose sleep at night. "You couldn't get the deal?"

Al shakes his head. Ron already knew the answer to his question, but thought he'd ask it anyway. Daryl comes over and stands in the doorway; his tall build seems to make the door look smaller.

"Come on, guys, let's get to work," he says.

Neither one moves. They both stare at each other with blank looks; there is something going on that they haven't told Daryl about yet. Revealing the secret they've been keeping seems inevitable now.

"I think we are done," Al says softly, staring at the desk.

Daryl can't believe what he is hearing. "What? I know things are slow, but come on. We can still last for a while."

Al glances at Ron. He knows that his friend put up a small fortune to get this thing going. If they don't act soon, all that money will be gone for good, and that is something Al doesn't want on his conscience.

"We have received an offer from another company to buy out the contracts we have," Ron says quietly.

Daryl's mouth falls open, and he wants to protest, but his dad speaks up first. "If we sell out now, we can pay off all our debts, and still have enough left over so we all get a little piece of the pie." Daryl opens his mouth to talk again, but his dad continues. "If we wait another week, we take the chance of losing everything, and Ron has the most to lose in this deal, son."

Daryl is quiet as his father's words sink in. He hates quitting, but he can also see the concern his dad has for his lifelong friend. It only takes a few seconds to realize that his dad is right; it's only fair. Ron stands, and is silent for a moment as he straightens out his clothes.

"Why don't you call the buyer and tell him he has a deal?" Ron says softly, not wanting to admit defeat out loud.

As Ron leaves the room, Daryl comes in and plops down in the chair. He understands the reasoning behind selling the contracts, but he hates it anyway. He kicks his foot lightly against the desk. Al picks up part of a newspaper and hands it to his son. Then Al grabs the phone and starts dialing.

"Hey, Steve, it's me, Al. I just wanted to let you know you have yourself a deal. Well talk to you tonight."

Daryl can hear the man's voice come though the phone. "That's great, Al; I'll talk to you later," the man says.

Al hangs up the phone and watches his son read the paper. "Well?"

Daryl is a little confused about his dad's motives. "This lists an AM radio station for sale in Pittsburgh."

"Yes, it does; some doctor owns it, and I was thinking about picking it up. I can put the down payment on the lease with my piece of the pie."

"Do you want me to go along too?

"The more the merrier. There is only one other black radio station in town, so competition can't be that bad."

"But it's AM."

"If we play good music, people won't care."

Daryl looks at the clip from the paper again. He realizes that it is from the Pittsburgh Press.

"Hey, how did you get this?"

"Your mom sent it to me."

"Mom?"

Al laughs. Warm memories of Ella resurface as his heart flutters. "Yeah, son, your mom and I still talk once in a while."

*   *   *

Doorway Enterprises was launched quickly, and it goes out that same way. A few days later, Al and Daryl are packing their belongings and getting ready for the long drive back East. As he empties his father's room, Daryl stumbles across the large bag of cocaine that he had hidden when Al was in the hospital. His father never did ask about it, so Daryl figures it isn't his. He pulls the bag back out and stares at it.

"You ready to go, son?" Al asks as he walks down the hallway.

Not wanting his father to see the bag, Daryl quickly throws it in the suitcase, and closes it.

"Yeah, all set in here."

"Good, then let's go get us a radio station," he says, grabbing the suitcase. "I called the doc; he knows we're coming."

Daryl watches his dad with the suitcase, and wonders if he did the right thing. He follows his father out to their large, green, four-door sedan, which is hooked up to a U-Haul trailer. There they find Ron waiting. After saying their good-byes and promising to keep in touch, they head off on their journey.

CHAPTER 14

They drive straight across the country, rarely stopping. As always, they are on a tight budget, and they don't have the time nor the money to stop and smell the roses. As the miles pass underneath the car, signs for Pittsburgh eventually begin to pop up. *This is it, Al, the place where it all started. We can start over here again, and make things happen. Soon the airwaves will be filled with your music.*

As they press on, large, heavy raindrops begin to fall. They ping off of the roof and slap against the windshield. The whole street is saturated within seconds. Their minds drift back to the sunny days in California as Al reaches over and turns on the windshield wipers.

The rain continues to come down, and the windows fog up. They can feel the humidity in the air, something they've grown accustomed to feeling less of. Daryl stares out the window as they enter the city. Watching the familiar buildings go by, he wonders how it will be to see his mom again. It has been quite some time since he's been home. Once they are settled in their new home, they will only be a four-hour drive apart, which is a lot closer than before.

He holds up the paper with the address to the radio station and reads it to himself. He knows that part of town. It is an older section, but still not too rough. Somehow crime has stayed away from this tiny section of brick buildings that were built at the beginning of the twentieth century. He turns and looks at his dad. Once again, his face and neck seem swollen. That's one of the side effects of his heart condition. He has been driving a lot, and looks very tired.

"Did you take your medication?" Daryl asks."

"Yes, Mother," Al replies with sarcasm. This daily question never goes without being asked.

"It's just that I'm worried about you."

"I know, son, I know. I'm starving. What do you say we stop and get something to eat?" Al usually changes the subject when it comes time to talk about his health. To him, talking about it is almost like admitting that life is going to come to an end before he reaches the level of success that he so desires. That is something he is definitely not going to do. And he doesn't want his son worrying about it any more than he already is. But there is another thought that surfaces from time to time when Al lets his guard down . . . death. Such a lonely word; it scares him more than anything else. He doesn't want to die, not yet, not for a long time."

"There she blows," Al says, as he stops in front of the radio station.

They both look out the rain-covered windows at the small, brick, four-story building. The bottom floor is the radio station, and it has a large picture window. The top floors are leased apartments. One small sign hangs outside with the radio's call letters on it. The hand-painted sign sways back and forth in the gentle wind."

"Too bad we couldn't get one of the apartments right upstairs; that would be great," Daryl says."

"Yeah, I already asked the doc about them, and he said they were all under leases, and will be for some time. Let's go get a bite to eat. We can grab the paper and start looking for a place close by."

They stop at a fast-food joint and tear through the want ads like two hungry wolves. This time they are in luck. There is a two-bedroom apartment for rent, and it is very close to the station; in fact, it's only half a block away. The rent is very reasonable compared to others that are listed. Daryl stands and digs through his pockets for spare change.

"I'm going to call this person before it's too late," he says, as he trots off to the pay phone. Within the hour, they are in the apartment, looking around. It is a small, quaint one, with hardwood floors and whitewashed walls. Over by the old windows, they can see the layers of paint that have been put on over the years.

The place is old, but nice and clean. It is also partially furnished, making it that much more inviting. Daryl looks out the window at the quiet street three stories below. He and Al both know that this is the best place within five miles, and since they only have one car, it is perfect, because they can walk to work.

"Will you be able to handle the stairs, Dad?" Daryl asks, a note of concern in his voice.

Al nods. "The doc says I need some exercise, and going up those stairs is just that." He turns and looks at the landlord. "I really like this place," Al says to the five-foot-tall landlady who is standing in the front doorway.

She's a tiny woman with a slender build, but there is a certain toughness in her eyes that says *don't mess with me*. She appears to be older than Moses. She probably even helped the Hebrews leave Egypt. Her accent is strong, thick, but neither one of them can put a finger on its origin. It must be from somewhere in Europe—Poland, maybe.

"Thank you," she says with a smile. "The people before you said the same thing. They said they would call me back at three o'clock to give me an answer."

Daryl looks at his watch; it's five until three. "We'll give you an answer now; we'll take it," he says.

The lady smiles. "That's very nice of you, son, but to be fair, I should wait until the others call me first." Al's shoulders slump as the little lady turns around.

"Wait!" Daryl says. He pulls out a chunk of cash, most of his portion from selling the contracts at Doorway. "I'll pay you the deposit plus the first three months rent, all in cash."

The lady spins around so fast it is like she is a teenager. Her eyes are as big as silver dollars as she stares at the wad of money. The only noise comes from Daryl, as he counts the money out on the counter.

"Well," she says with a huge smile. "I guess I can just tell the others that the place is already rented out. After all, they didn't put down a deposit."

"Then we have a deal," Al says.

"Yes, we have a deal."

* * *

The next morning the clouds part, leaving behind a hot, humid summer day. The two wake up in their new apartment. The rooms are still bare, as they have very few belongings. It will take a lot to get them going. Shortly after, they are ready to meet the doctor at the radio station.

"What happened to the people that had the station before?" Daryl asks his father, as they walk past their car.

"As far as I know, it was a news station that was run by the doctor himself, but I guess he wants out, and figures it will be a lot easier just to lease it with the option to buy it."

They head towards the station, walking on an old sidewalk laced with cracks and bits of green grass. As they approach the building, they can see some lights on inside. Al watches through the front window as an older black man inside moves things around. They walk up and open the front door. A bell on top of the door rings as they enter.

"Are you the Clevelands?" the older man asks.

"Yes, we are," Al replies, extending his right hand. "This is my son Daryl, and I am Al Cleveland."

The man, wearing gray slacks and a plaid shirt, shakes Al's hand, and then Daryl's. He is of medium height, with a slender build, and seems very pleasant and intelligent. Al looks at the top of the man's balding head, which is surrounded by half a white Afro that is cut short. Daryl figures he is in his late sixties.

"Well, it's nice to meet the both of you. I am Doctor Freedman; most everyone around here calls me Freddie. I trust you both had a safe trip."

"Everything went fine. I hope you weren't waiting long for us," Al says, wanting to get down to business.

"No, not at all. I'm sure you two didn't come all the way down here to chitchat, so let me show you around the place."

If they take their time, the tour will last about three minutes. Two of those minutes are spent with the doctor telling about the new bathroom he just finished. Indeed, he is a talented man, and does fantastic handiwork.

The small front room is the office, lobby, and boardroom. The back room is the sound room, and the spot for broadcasting and recording, if they should decide to do that. It is very small, but clean and tidy. As Al talks with Freddie, Daryl checks over the equipment. He envisions himself as the DJ, playing music while countless people are listening. He sits in the stool and spins around once before running his fingers over the controls.

"How does everything look, son?" Al asks, as Daryl walks out of the sound room.

"Looks good to me."

Al smiles, feeling good about the deal. "Well then, Freddie, you have yourself a deal. We would love to lease this place from you."

Freddie's smile fades slightly. "You told me on the phone that you were going to buy it."

Al didn't receive the lump sum from Doorway that he expected, and as usual, all his royalty checks had dozens of deductions and IRS garnishments on them. He has to be smooth in order to pull off this deal, so the seller will also be happy.

"I do want to buy it . . . right after a one-year lease, and then we'll give you a balloon payment." Freddie is silent for a moment as he thinks about it. At his age, he doesn't feel like waiting for the money, but being paid on the lease for a year straight sounds nice. Then he smiles, and slowly nods his head. "All right, sounds like a good deal. I'll have my lawyer draw up the papers, and I'll get back with you later today." The two men shake on it. Later that same day, all the papers are signed. Al and Daryl are filled with excitement as they load up the station with their albums in preparation for their broadcasting debut the next day.

* * *

"Good morning, Pittsburgh, this is your new radio station, Hittsburgh, WXVX 1510 on your dial," Daryl says with a lot of enthusiasm. 'We're going to start off our day with one of my favorites, 'I Second That Emotion.'" He begins the song and glances at his watch; it's 6:01 in the morning. Daryl will work until about twelve, and his dad, who is still sleeping, will work from noon until six at night. They figure that twelve hours a day should be enough to get the radio station going at minimal cost. Once his dad takes over, Daryl will try to find some advertisers, the same thing Al will be doing shortly.

The weeks pass, and the two have very little luck lining up any takers to advertise on their station. It is something they really didn't expect. And this single obstacle might as well be a hundred-foot wall that they are trying to climb.

Wanting a little help, Daryl contacts the papers; one of them, the *Pittsburgh Press*, is interested and does a story on them, titling the article "Motown Finally Comes Home." After the story is out, they gain a strong audience, and receive a ton of phone calls and requests, but still the advertisers won't sign on. For some reason, they feel that they are being blackballed, but they don't know why.

"I think the hardware store down the street might buy a spot," Al says as he walks in to take Daryl's place.

"Might?" he replies as he sets down the headphones. His voice instantly changes tone.

"They might take a spot? We're outdoing the stations on the FM side of things, and they *might* take a spot?"

Al knows his son is getting frustrated, so he tries his best to remain calm. "It's not my fault, so watch your tone."

Daryl looks down and nods. "Sorry. I just can't believe that we don't have any advertisers yet." He leans back, lets his head hang over the edge of his chair, and stares at the ceiling. "What are we doing wrong?" Al flops down in the chair, already looking exhausted. He has been up for several hours, trying to get takers, but his fatigued appearance is largely due to his heart condition. The two haven't had much sleep, and due to the crunch on money matters, not much food either. Daryl looks at his dad sympathetically.

"I'm sorry, I didn't mean to snap at you, Dad. You OK?"

"Yeah, I'll make it."

"Did you eat today?

Al gives a half smile. "A little. There isn't a lot to eat up at the apartment, and I knew you would be hungry."

Daryl leaves, feeling a little disgusted about the whole situation, and quite worried about his father's health. He makes it back to the apartment and opens the bare refrigerator to see if there really is anything at all to eat. They have three slices of bread and some butter; that is it.

He stares at the old, empty steel racks that seem to be laughing at him; he slams the old refrigerator shut.

"Man, prisoners eat better than this," he mumbles.

Daryl's mind flashes back to the bag of cocaine, which is the only thing still in his suitcase.

He stops and shakes his head. "Ain't going to do that. Can't." Then his stomach growls loudly and fiercely. He knows that if he doesn't do something, he will have nothing to eat today or tomorrow.

Reluctantly, he walks back to his room and pulls his suitcase out from under the bed.

Daryl stares at the clear bag of coke. His heart races and his palms become sweaty as he thinks about the money he could make with it. The risk and excitement of breaking the law causes a tingling sensation to run up his back. He takes the bag out to the kitchen and begins to divide a small portion of it into small bags; the rest he puts back in the suitcase, way under his bed.

He comes back to the kitchen and quickly shoves the small bags in his front pocket. His breaths become more rapid as his thinks about the illegal act that he is about to commit. He stops at the front door, and places his head on the cool wood frame.

"Be cool, stay low and out of sight," he whispers to himself. "I've seen many drug dealers do it, and I know I can get away with it."

He opens the door, then rushes through the hall and down the stairs. He almost runs out onto the street. He scans the street for police cars, as if they already know what he is doing.

* * *

Hours later his dad comes home, tired from a long day's work. His stomach has been growling for hours. The only thing he's eaten today was an apple that someone gave him. Daryl hears him, and walks out of his room to greet him.

"How did it go today?"

"Not bad; had a lot of calls for requests," Al says. "I think there are some girls that are really beginning to like you."

Daryl chuckles. "That's funny, Dad; with my luck, they're probably in junior high. I bought some groceries. Would you like me to fix you something to eat?" Al sits on a barstool that is in front of the breakfast bar. He knows that neither of them has much money, so the grocery list must have been real short. He begins to wish that he didn't drag his son into this.

"So what's for dinner?" Al says, preparing himself for another peanut butter and jelly sandwich.

"Whatever you want, Dad," Daryl says as he opens the old refrigerator.

Al looks over as the door swings wide open. He gazes upon an icebox filled with fruits, vegetables, and meat. Daryl reaches in, pulls out a gallon of milk, and sets it down in front of his father.

"There you go; I know you love a cold glass of milk with supper."

Al looks at the milk, and then back at the full refrigerator. "That's like fifty, sixty bucks worth of groceries; where did you get that kind of money?"

Daryl pulls out a few fresh steaks, and flops them on the counter. "I sold a few things," he says casually, as he gets a frying pan out from the cabinet.

"Sold a few things?" Al quickly looks around the apartment. What little they have is still right where they left it. "What things?"

"Stuff," Daryl mumbles as he turns on the stove, hoping that his dad will let it go.

Al stands up; he knows something is not right here. His voice becomes sterner. "What stuff, Daryl?"

Daryl stares at the small, blue flames flickering on the burner. "When you were in the hospital, I cleaned up your room. I found a large bag of coke."

"Cocaine?" he asks loudly.

Daryl motions his hand for his dad to lower his voice. "Yes, cocaine. I went out today and sold some of it. We need the money, Dad."

"What?" he yells. "Daryl, I didn't raise you to be a drug dealer."

"I know dad, but—"

"Don't *but* me, son!" Al grabs the milk jug and rips the top off. Without warning he starts pouring it down the drain in the sink. Daryl sees him do this, and grabs his arm, stopping him.

"What are you doing, Dad?"

"This is blood money you bought this with, and I don't want any part of it!"

Daryl stands eye to eye with his father, and is much stronger. They struggle for a few seconds, and then Daryl pulls the milk jug away.

Al backs up. He wants to yell some more, but he can't catch his breath. His face turns pale, and his knees become weak.

"Dad, just relax!" Daryl pleads. "Here, sit on the couch."

Al clutches his chest as Daryl walks him over and sits him down. His breaths are short and choppy, as his muscles become weaker. He struggles to talk, and can barely get the words out.

"My . . . my pills."

Daryl's eyes dart towards the kitchen, and then to his dad's bedroom. "Where are they?"

"On . . . my . . . dresser," he groans in between breaths. He feels his heart is about to explode.

Daryl runs off to the bedroom, and comes back a second later. His nervous fingers tear open the bottle and spill several pills into his hand. Al reaches up, takes one, and places it under his tongue. It only takes seconds for the pill to start working. His son stays close as he calms back down. Al relaxes for a moment as he waits for his head to stop spinning. Daryl keeps an eye on him as he returns to the kitchen and begins to cook dinner.

Al remains on the couch. He doesn't say a word, and is still upset about how his son got the groceries. A few minutes later, Daryl returns to his dad with some cooked steak and vegetables. He hands him the plate. Al stares at the food and shakes his head.

"I didn't raise a drug dealer."

"No you didn't, Dad. You raised someone who will do what it takes to survive. Come on now, it's right there in front of you, just take a bite."

Al doesn't want to eat it, but he knows they are both starving. He sighs and reluctantly cuts off a piece. He slowly brings the hot chunk of meat up to his mouth and begins to chew on it.

He closes his eyes; the savory flavor makes him moan. It feels like it has been a hundred years since he's eaten anything good.

"Good stuff, huh?"

Al's stomach growls for more, so he immediately begins cutting off another piece. "Yes, son, it is," he replies with as little excitement as possible. "This doesn't mean I want you out there selling that crap all the time."

"Of course not, just until we find some advertisers. Now, I am very tired, so I'm going to bed. Don't worry about the mess; I'll clean it up in the morning."

"Thanks for dinner," Al says, with a mouthful of food.

* * *

The next morning Al is sound asleep when Daryl gets up and goes to work. A few hours after that, Al stumbles out of bed and gets ready for the day. He spends hours trying to promote their radio station and get someone to advertise, but as the day passes, he realizes that it won't happen yet again. He walks through the rain and returns to the small station. The front door is locked, so he uses his key and enters. With a smile on his face and his chest sticking out with pride, he sits down in the small front office and listens to Daryl singing as he plays "What's Going On." Al picks up the phone and buzzes the sound room.

"WXVX, Hittsburgh radio, how can I help you?" Daryl asks.

Al disguises his voice. "Yes, I would like to speak to the greatest son in the world."

Daryl laughs. "Dad, come on, I'm busy."

"Well, it's about time for you to go home, so get."

Al hangs up the phone and walks to the back room. He looks around; it is obvious that Daryl has cleaned up the place. He takes off his wet windbreaker and hangs it up on a hook on the door.

"How are things going in here?"

His son seems as if he is on cloud nine. "Just fine, still loving it. In fact, one of our avid listeners is coming over here to meet me any minute now."

Al looks at the top of the cabinet. Daryl has dusted it. "This place sure is clean. I take it that this avid listener is of the female persuasion."

An ear-to-ear grin forms on Daryl's face. "Why, yes, it is." There is a knock on the front door. "And that would be her now." He stands and sets the headphones down. He stops and points to them. "Oh, you've got it, right?"

Al chuckles. "Yes, son, I do. Have fun; I'll see you tonight."

Daryl struts towards the door. "If I have a lot of fun, you won't see me until morning."

Al plops down in the chair and cues the next song to begin playing. He doesn't want to say anything to his son, but he's noticed that his energy level is way down, and his leg is swollen quite badly. *Maybe it's just the poor diet I've been on*, he tells himself. He knows all the time he has spent on his feet isn't helping the problem either. So he decides to slow down a bit, and rest for a few days.

* * *

As the months go by, what was once considered wrong has become tolerated, and then accepted. Daryl continues to sell the cocaine and other drugs, on a low-key basis. He keeps the operation small, just enough to make ends meet. Al's small royalty checks are coming in, but the IRS is still garnishing for back taxes, so it does very little to help. As the days fly by, they both not only stop looking for advertisers, they begin to turn them down as an act of defiance. But Al feels very guilty for having his son do all the dirty work of drug dealing, and he begins to carry around a small portion of it, just in case he can make a sale. After he closes the radio station, he bundles up in his winter jacket, and heads out to meet Daryl at a bar a few blocks away.

He hops in his old sedan and drives down the street. The sides of the road have large chunks of half-melted snow left over from the last two snowstorms, which caught the city off guard. It is early in the season, but Christmas decorations are already beginning to pop up in the windows of apartments, reminding everyone that the holiday is fast approaching.

The bar is named "Lucky's." It's a well-liked locals' spot, and like most others in the vicinity, it is small, and filled with noise and smoke. Its several tables and chairs are always full, and the small pool table sports heated games. Almost everyone is very friendly, so Al and Daryl enjoy going there.

Al walks in; the place is crowded as always. His eyes search the drifting layer of smoke, and then he spots his son's head, sticking above the rest. They both have been there many times in the past, and they know most of the clientele. Al makes his way over to the bar and joins his dad, as the bartender gives him a beer."

"Thanks, Steve," Al says to the bartender.

They both lean on the old bar and silently stare at the TV sitting behind the bar. They are watching news clips of a Monday Night Football game that just ended. Daryl sips his beer and shakes his head.

"Do you think Pittsburgh will make it this year?" Daryl asks.

"Of course." Al pauses and smiles. "Then again, I think they'll make it every year."

A young, five-foot-tall lady with long, black, braided hair walks up to them and stands next to Daryl. Al looks over at her. She is wearing white slacks and a matching blouse. Her bright green eyes remind him of Natalie, which means he likes her even without knowing her name. At first Daryl doesn't see her, so she gently bumps into him.

"Oh, you're back. Hey Dad, I want you to meet Linda, one of our avid fans."

Al looks over and shakes her hand, pretending that he didn't notice her before. "It's nice to meet you, Linda. How are you today?"

She smiles; she can't believe she is meeting the person who wrote the songs that she loves. "I'm fine, and it's nice to meet you too. I love your music, Mister Cleveland."

"Thank you, it's nice of you to say that, and please, call me Al."

They engage in small talk for a while, but before they know it, it is time for Daryl to take Linda home. He doesn't want too stay out too late, as he has to be at the station to open it in the morning.

"Do you want one last beer for the road?" Steve asks Al.

"Why not? It will only help me sleep tonight." Al stays at the bar and enjoys his last beer before they close for the night. He looks around; the place is slowly beginning to empty out. Behind the bar is a large mirror. Staring at his own reflection, he thinks about his life, and wonders where it is leading. Guilty feelings overcome him, as he knows that Daryl is still doing all the dirty work, selling drugs. He tries to think of a way to help. In the reflection, he notices a woman who comes over and stands next to him.

"Can I just have a glass of water?" she asks Steve.

"Sure you can," he replies, as he quickly fills a glass with ice and water, and slides it to her.

Al looks over at the lady. She is a black woman, close to his age. She stands about five foot eight. Judging by the way she carries herself, she appears to be rather intelligent. He looks her up and down, and notices that she is dressed casually, but with a touch of class, something that catches his eye."

"How are you doing?" Al asks.

"I'm all right," she states. "Just trying to sober up a little bit before I go home."

"Yeah, unfortunately the party is coming to an end."

She laughs. "That's my problem; I don't want it to come to an end. I'm always looking for that extra kick in life."

Al is silent as he thinks about what she just said. *She seems like the type of girl that would want what I can give her.* He touches the single bag in his pocket. *I can make some of the money, and take the burden off of Daryl.* He holds tightly onto his cold beer; adrenaline kicks in, causing his palms to become sweaty. *Just relax and make some quick cash.*

"Do you mean something besides booze?" he barely gets out.

She shrugs. "Yeah, sure. Why, do you have something?"Al quickly looks around to make sure no one is watching. "I have some cocaine," he says softly. His heart is racing as he thinks about getting it.

She gives him a devilish grin. Her eyes seem to twinkle with the thought of getting high. "Let me see it," she whispers.

He reaches into his pocket and pulls out one small, clear bag.

"How much?" she asks."

"For you, twenty bucks."

She calmly reaches over to her purse, and pulls out her wallet. Al's heart begins to pick up its pace as he thinks about the excitement of doing this. His eyes are glued to her wallet. She looks past him and tilts her head up. Suddenly the woman turns and shows him a police badge.

"You're under arrest for distribution of a controlled substance," she says.

Another man grabs Al's arm from behind.

"Just relax and come with me, sir," the man says.

Steve looks at Al sadly as they walk him out.

CHAPTER 15

The city is covered in a blanket of cold ice. The sun has yet to come up to melt it.

The phone rings in Al's apartment. Daryl is sound asleep in his bed. The phone rings again and again as he slowly stirs to life. With his eyes still shut, he reaches over and picks it up."

"Hello?" he moans with a blank mind.

"Daryl, it's your dad, wake up."

He struggles to gain consciousness. "Am I late for work?" he mumbles.

"No, you're not, son; I've been arrested." The words send electricity racing through Daryl's sleepy mind. Suddenly his eyes open wide.

"You've been what?"

"Arrested. I need you to get the bail money for me."

"Well . . . what were you arrested for?"

"Selling drugs," he says in a soft tone, as an embarrassed feeling sweeps through him.

"Dad," Daryl says loudly, as if he were the only one who should be doing that.

"Don't *dad* me, son, just be at the courthouse at eight in the morning so you can post bail for me."

"How much is bail going to be?"

"The cop told me it's going to be about eleven hundred," he says, knowing that they don't have that kind of money.

"All right, all right, I'll be there at eight." Daryl attempts to sleep for a few more hours, but he can't rest, knowing his dad is in jail. He gets up shortly after sunrise and begins counting the cash that they have. His stomach turns as he counts the last few bills; he comes up three hundred short. Daryl knows that there is only one way to raise that kind of money in the time that is needed. In his room, he pulls out the familiar suitcase. As much as he hates it, he makes up several small bags to take to the street once again.

A while later, he is bundled up in his winter clothes and walking around the streets, looking for potential buyers. It is not his usual time to be out, so he isn't able to sell to many of his regulars. After a couple of quick, small sales and one large one, he has enough money to post bail. As he turns around, he notices someone watching him. It is another black man close to Daryl's age, but as big as a mountain. The young man looks mean as hell, and is staring Daryl up and down. Daryl isn't sure what to do, but he doesn't want a confrontation; after all, that could lead to the police, and right now he has enough drugs and cash on him to put him away for quite some time.

Daryl looks the other way, and begins walking across the street. The man throws his arms out, and continues to stare at Daryl."

"I think you are in the wrong neighborhood!" the man yells in a deep voice.

Daryl ignores him."

"I'm talkin' to you!" the man says loudly.

The man inside Daryl wants to stay and fight; common sense tells him to keep walking, or he'll never get his father out. He continues to walk away at a steady pace, heading towards his apartment. He takes several risks, cutting through alleyways that are lined with garbage and graffiti. His stomach turns; the stench of urine and other bodily wastes is overpowering. It becomes stronger as he passes groups of vagrants that are huddled in the ice-cold back doorways, trying to feel the heat from the other side.

He leaves that scene of desperation, and travels for a couple more blocks. A strange sense of relief comes to him when he sees his apartment building. It's as if crime could never touch it; an invisible wall seems to protect the old, brick building, and he feels he will always be safe there.

Once inside, he empties his pockets of the drugs. He arranges the money in the proper order, so it looks more like he just got it from a bank rather than from a bunch of different people. His fingers are still numb with the frozen bite of winter. He opens his mouth and lets his hot breath escape over his hands. It feels as if thousands of needles are stabbing into them as they slowly thaw. "Man, I miss the warm weather," he whispers to himself as he bundles up again. His mind travels back to California and its hot beaches.

He hits the cold, partially snow-covered streets again, and walks to the bar to retrieve their car. Glad to be out of the cold, he drives to the center of town, to the old courthouse. He stares at the large building with its Roman-style columns out front. They seem to cast light on the city.

The architecture has remained unchanged over the years; it is a fortress of justice, he decides at second glance.

As always, the marble floors in the old building are spotless and highly polished, as if that is the way life should be, clean and free of scum. He makes it through the large lobby and walks into the courtroom. He stops near the ten-foot-tall double doors and looks around. It is empty except for a few other waiting family members. A small grin forms on his face. It is the picture-perfect courtroom; the one he has always seen on TV.

He sits on a hardwood bench in the back and watches as four detention guards lead several prisoners in, including his dad, who appears rather ashamed about the whole thing, and can barely make eye contact with his son. Al sits down with the row of inmates, and waits for his case to be called.

Daryl looks at the wrinkled clothes that his dad slept in, and the tired gaze in his eyes. Obviously, he didn't sleep much the night before. Then Daryl looks at the others with him; they all look like piles of trash compared to his father. Al was the only one who seemed to care about his appearance and character.

"All rise, the Honorable Judge Stemmings presiding," the bailiff says aloud.

They all stand and wait for the judge to come in and sit down. The judge, wearing the black robe that gives him power over people's lives, climbs the few steps to his high bench, and sits down on his large chair.

"Be seated," he says unenthusiastically, and without looking up.

He looks over the files; he seems somewhat upset about the line of people who were arrested the night before. A five-year veteran of the this courtroom, he had been brought up in the ghettos, and being black himself, he doesn't like to hear any sob stories about living a hard life. He figures that if he conquered that lifestyle and became a judge—one of the few black ones at the time—so can everyone else out there.

One by one, he goes through their files and calls them to the front. He gives them a chance to plead their cases before issuing a sentence, a later court date, or a fine. The last case is called; it's Al's.

"Alfred Cleveland," he calls out in a loud, booming voice.

Al stands, walks out past other prisoners, and stops in front of the judge. He keeps his head low. "Here, your honor," he says in a voice that is barely audible.

The judge stares at Al, and then back at the file. There was one thing he really didn't like, and that was repeat offenders. "I don't recognize your face, but tell me, why do I know your name?"

"I'm a songwriter, sir. I had my hand in the 'What's Going On' album, and songs like 'I Second That Emotion.' "

Al didn't feel like giving a long speech about his achievements, so he leaves it at that.

"And now you sell drugs for a living," the judge quickly adds, with no mercy in his voice whatsoever.

"I made a mistake, sir," Al humbly replies. "But I wasn't trying to sell them; I was just going to share them with the lady." He purposely adds the last part, knowing full well that it changes everything; he is no longer dealing, he just has possession, which means he can't be sentenced today.

Judge Stemmings has heard it all before, and figures Al would enter a "not guilty" plea, so he doesn't even bat an eye. "Well, that mistake gives you a court date in one month, and bail is set at one thousand dollars. You are dismissed," he says as he bangs his gavel against his desk.

Everyone is told to stand again as the judge leaves the courtroom. Then Daryl watches his dad being escorted out by the guards. He goes across the street to the detention center and pays the bail in cash. It takes another hour for his dad to be released.

"Hey, jailbird," Daryl says to his father as he comes out.

Al is very tired and doesn't like the situation one bit. "Let's go home, son, I want to go to bed."

"You didn't get to be anyone's boyfriend in there, did you?" Daryl asks, jabbing him in the side as they walk out.

"No, I didn't. I'm glad you can find humor in all this. Do you know that I am facing twenty-five years for trafficking?"

His son stops in his tracks. Steam flows out his nose as the hot air from his lungs is pushed out. "No, I didn't, Dad; I had no idea it was that serious."

"There is nothing they would like more than to send a *brother* up the river. You never know; I might be the one they make the example of."

They walk out of the detention building and down the street to where their car is parked.

It is a good thing that Al was selling the drugs in the bar rather than in his car, or the police would have impounded it as well. Daryl opens the door for his father, and then hops in the driver's seat.

"You know you could leave the selling up to me. After all, I have been dealing all this time without any hassle," Daryl says, before starting the engine.

Al chuckles. He shifts his shoulders to look at his son. "Don't go thinking you're bulletproof or something. If the police know to watch me, how long do you think it will take them to figure out to watch you too?"

Al's statement makes his son feel like he is sinking in quicksand, and it's only a matter of time before he is caught. In silence, he starts the car and drives away. His father's words run through his head repeatedly. He realizes that he is getting comfortable with the drug dealing.

"Maybe I should lay low for a while," Daryl says, as he remembers the other large man staring him down.

"That's a good idea, son."

* * *

Daryl leaves his dad at the apartment and walks to the radio station. Even though he is tired, he looks forward to being back in the studio, playing music. Back at the apartment, Al calls Ron; they have talked from time to time since they left. Ron still keeps the dream of running his own music company alive. So strong is his dream that he going to move to Las Vegas to try again. Al wants to help him, but he feels that he can get the radio station up and running, and that would be great for promoting his own music. With an understanding for each other's dreams, they wish each other good luck, and hang up.

After getting some much-needed rest, Al goes down to the radio station to relieve his son. The streets and sidewalks are already covered with a layer of ice and frost, as the temperature on the cloudless night drops down into the low single digits. Wanting to get back into the warmth, Al hurries to let himself into the small station.

The bells above the door ring as he opens it. The warmth of the building brushes against his face. Once inside, his eyebrows raise as he sees Linda sitting in the front office, answering the phone lines.

"Oh, hey, Mister Cleveland," she says with a warm smile, batting her green eyes.

Al takes off his jacket and rubs his cold hands together. "Hi, hon, are you helping out here?"

"Yup, Daryl can't handle all the phone calls."

Al glances through the window and watches his son as he plays an imaginary set of drums. "Yes, I can see how busy he is. I am sure he must be exhausted from all the work."

He walks over to the other room. Daryl continues to play the invisible drum set to the beat of the song, as his dad stands and watches with a smile on his face.

"You taking this young lady home or what?" Al asks.

Daryl sits up and looks at Linda through the window; she is still talking on the phone. He really wanted to stay and goof off with his dad. "Yeah, I suppose I should take her home. She's looking for a boyfriend."

"I thought she found one," Al says quickly, surprised that they aren't already together.

Daryl frowns, and shakes his head. "Nope, the girl isn't for me; we're just friends."

Can't he see those green eyes? It's all in the eyes, son. "Different strokes for different folks," he mumbles, plopping down in the chair and starting the next song. "I talked to Ron today, and he's starting up Doorway Enterprises again. This time he's doing it in Las Vegas."

Daryl pauses to think about how much loved being part of that, but for right now he knows he has to stay and help his dad. "Good for him. I hope it works out."

You should go there, son; there is a better life than selling drugs. Al could think it, but he couldn't bring the words to his mouth. "Why don't you go home and get some sleep? You look tired."

"Yeah, you're right. I'll see you later."

Daryl takes Linda home, and then hits the streets again. He knows he told his dad that he is going to lay low for a while, but he is worried about losing his steady customers. After all, if they don't buy from him, they will buy from someone else. There is always someone else. He does his best to keep the operation really small, just what they need to get by, plus a little extra.

As Al's court date draws closer, he receives a royalty check, and the IRS lets him have a small portion this time. It is nothing to scream about, but enough money to hire a lawyer.

The fact that he is facing such a long sentence causes him to lose sleep at night. His appetite fades as well. Over the next three weeks, he loses twenty pounds, and his heart condition really begins to show; his energy is way down.

* * *

Tom, a short white man who seems rather strange and never combs his hair, mumbles something. Daryl didn't understand it, and really doesn't care. He takes ten bucks, and hands him the bag. Tom's a factory worker, probably a laborer, Daryl decides. He quickly hops back into his old, beat-up, four-door car, which has more rust spots than paint spots, and heads home.

Daryl walks down the street as large, puffy snowflakes begin to fall. A thick layer of clouds hangs low over the city, holding in some of the warmth, making his nightly patrol more bearable.

From the other direction, headlights shine on him. He turns and sees three cars, none of which he recognizes. They are driving close to one another, and slowly pass by. All the windows have a dark tint, so he can't see inside. Something is making his skin crawl. A strange feeling brews inside of him; one that makes him feel very uncomfortable.

"I don't like this," he whispers, as a huge plume of steam exits his mouth.

He keeps a close eye on the cars as they drive around the corner and vanish from sight.

He stops as he realizes that he is heading in their direction, something he doesn't want to do.

The strange feeling turns into fear; it starts in the pit of his stomach and works its way into his heart and head. His sixth sense tells him to run like a madman; his pride tells him to stay put.

Everything quiets down as Daryl listens closely for any movement; the falling snowflakes seem loud as they land on the wet ground.

A loud, screeching sound comes from around the corner. Daryl jumps and then listens; he knows the sound; he has heard it a thousands times before. It is a power-steering pump squeaking after being turned too far; the cars are turning around. His heart leaps into his throat as his mind screams, "Run!" But his legs fill with panic and freeze. Three sets of headlights shine on the buildings as the cars quickly round the corner once again.

Daryl takes off running as he notices several people hanging out of the windows. Bang! The noise of the first gunshot streaks along the brick buildings like thunder. Daryl runs as fast as he can. The cars speed up as other shooters open fire at him. He can hear them laughing as the popping and loud bangs from the bigger guns fill the quiet street. The bullets ricochet off the walls and sidewalk.

Running as fast as his legs will carry him, he darts down an alleyway that is too narrow for the cars to fit. One of the cars stops right in front of it, and more rounds are fired, right in a row. The flashes from the muzzle light up the narrow passage. Scared for his life, Daryl leaps headfirst behind some garbage cans and into a pile of garbage. He lands with a loud crash as the metal cans are tossed around. Then, after a few minutes, things appear to quiet down again.

Carefully, he looks out; no one is following him. But he can still hear the car engines running; they are close, and the occupants are still watching him.

"And stay out of our neighborhood," someone yells to Daryl. He recognizes the voice. It's the same man that was staring him down earlier. The sound of distant sirens is music to his ears as the gang peels out and takes off for a quick getaway.

Slowly he stands and walks out in another direction. His body is still filled with adrenaline as he jogs down the snow-covered path, his feet crunching the fresh snow. Without warning, a crashing noise comes from behind. It startles him. He spins around and watches a cat run off.

Relieved at his narrow escape, he is able to smile. "Stupid cat." Then he looks down at the ground, following the trail in the fresh, white snow. There, in between his footsteps, are dots of red blood. The blood is fresh and melting the snow. Then he notices he can feel something warm running down his side. Immediately he places his hand under his jacket and against his ribs. It feels totally wet. He pulls his hand out to see that it is covered in his own blood.

"Oh God . . . I've been shot."

CHAPTER 16

The will to survive stays strong as he holds onto his side, which is sending pain through his body. Several police cars are slowly driving around, combing the street for the shooters.

Once again he has to lay low, like a wild animal. He still has cash and drugs on him. Oddly, he would rather hold onto them than seek help.

Daryl hides behind a garbage can in an alley as a cop car slowly drives by. He ducks lower as the policeman's spotlight shines down the alley. His blood begins to pool on the ground as he sits there.

The snow begins to come down harder. The policeman doesn't appear to see anything; the car slowly passes by.

Daryl groans in pain as he stands and runs across the street, hunched over, towards his apartment. He begins to feel dizzy as his vision becomes distorted. "Come on, Daryl. You're too young to die out here in the cold. Get a grip and get home," he whispers, as he feels death's cold hand reaching for him.

Finally he makes it to the front door of the complex.

He closes the thick front door behind him. He knows he has to climb the three flights of stairs. He looks up the stairwell, and his head spins. He looks back down and begins up the steps. With his hand pressed firmly under his jacket, he makes it. His coat is in shreds. Through the hole in his jacket, he can see his hand, but he doesn't remove it; fearful thoughts keep him from looking at the bloody wound. For a brief second, all he can hear is his breathing, and his blood dripping onto the tiled floor.

Lightheaded and dizzy, he climbs the stairs. His breaths become shorter with each passing step. All he wants to do is get home. He'll be safe there, he tells himself. He makes it to the door of his apartment.

Putting his hand on the wall for support, he attempts to fish out his keys from his pocket. Thud. He falls against the door. His hand slides off the wall, leaving behind a long streak of blood. Suddenly the door opens, and he falls into his father's arms."

"Daryl? Daryl!" Al yells."

"Help me, Dad," he moans softly.

Panic engulfs Al. He feels helpless as he sets his son down in the doorway. His wide eyes gawk at Daryl's torn jacket, and all the blood. "What happened to you?"

"I . . . was . . . shot," he whispers, in between breaths.

Al rushes to the phone and calls for an ambulance. Daryl stays on the floor and keeps moving his legs in anguish; his entire side throbs with tormenting throbs of pain. Deep red blood slowly trickles out and spills across the hardwood floor. Al comes rushing back over to him. He kneels down next to him, and takes his son's cold, clammy hand.

"Just hang in there, son, the ambulance is on its way."

Daryl manages to reach into his pockets; he pulls out the drugs and cash. "Hide this," he whispers.

Anger overtakes Al; he grabs the money and drugs, and flings them across the room. The dollar bills scatter everywhere. Daryl tilts his head and watches the money spread out on the floor. He actually contemplates going to get it.

"That damn crap doesn't matter, son!" Al's eyes well up with tears. "Please, hang in there; don't die on me, Daryl. I won't be able to live, knowing that I allowed you do that for a living."

"We did it to survive," Daryl whispers, in a voice that is growing weaker by the minute.

His father shakes his head. "We took the easy way out, and now it is costing us."

Daryl opens his mouth to speak again. Then his mouth freezes; the words never come out. Slowly his eyes roll back, and he blacks out. Suddenly his entire body goes limp. Al begins to cry out loud, as the sounds of charging paramedics echo up the stairwell.

"Noooo! Oh God, no! Help my son, please," Al begs, crying.

Without a word, two men and one woman come in, and quickly check his vital signs. Not knowing what to do, Al backs away and watches from a distance. He is only a few feet away, but it feels so far, and he feels so alone. He prays that Daryl will move, show some sign of life.

"We still have a pulse; it's steady," the man by his head says.

"Can you hear me?" the woman asks loudly. "Squeeze my hand if you can hear me."

She waits for just a second, but it feels like an eternity to Al.

"That's good; stay with us," she says.

Daryl moans as they pick him up and put him on a stretcher. Going as fast as they can, they carry him downstairs to the waiting ambulance. Al runs out behind them and heads for the back of the emergency vehicle. He wants to be right by his son's side.

"Please ride up front, sir," one of the paramedics says as they close the back doors.

Al runs around front and jumps in the passenger's seat. The ambulance races off with its sirens blaring and its flashing lights lighting the way through the falling snow. Al begins to tremble as thoughts of his son's funeral surface in his mind. With wide, frightened eyes, he turns and watches the paramedics cut away his thick, blood-soaked winter clothes.

"He's lost a lot of blood," the woman says. She looks at Al. "Do you know what blood type he is?"

Al's mind suddenly goes completely blank; his mind is racing with emotions, not thoughts. Images from Daryl's entire life flash in front of him.

"Sir, think, do you know what blood type your son is?"

"A positive," he whispers in a small voice.

One of the other paramedics nudges the woman for her to look at the wound that they are exposing. Al leans over and tries to see it, but seeing all his own son's blood makes his head spin. The woman's eyebrows lower with confusion.

"What hit him?" she asks the others quietly.

They shrug their shoulders.

"What's wrong?" Al asks, not being able to look at the wound.

"Nothing," one of the men says, as they try to stop the massive amount of blood that continues to pour out.

Minutes later, the ambulance pulls into the hospital emergency room. Several more hospital workers are standing outside; they help bring Daryl out of the vehicle. The entire crew comes rushing in through the automatic sliding doors. They all pass the crowded waiting room and immediately head to the back, where doctors and nurses are already prepping for him. They run past another set of double doors. Al attempts to follow, but one of the workers stops him.

"Sir, you need to wait out here."

"My son," is all he can manage to get out, as he watches them wheel him away.

The man doesn't say any more; he closes the two heavy wooden doors, blocking any further view. Al's heart begins to thump and he feels lonely, imagining he will never see Daryl again. One of the nurses comes over with a clipboard in her hands.

"Sir, I know this is hard, but we need you to fill this out. His medical history is real important right now."

All Al wants to do is sit down and cry out loud, but he fights the tears and takes the clipboard. With his mind a whirlwind of emotions, he heads back to the waiting room. He glances at the pay phones lined up against the wall. His head hangs lower. He knows that he has to call Ella and let her know. He digs out some change as he tries to think of the gentlest way to tell her that her son was shot; of course, nothing comes to mind. He drops his coins in the slot and dials.

"Hello?" Ella asks in a groggy voice, which reminds Al that it is the middle of the night.

Al tries to maintain his composure. "Ella, it's me, Al," he says in a worried tone, as his voice cracks.

From deep inside her heart, Ella's motherly instinct kicks in. "Oh no, what happened to Daryl?"

"He's OK. You'd better come down to the hospital as soon as you can. We're here at St. Vincent's."

"Oh Lord, what happened to my baby?" she asks frantically.

A single tear escapes Al's eye. He doesn't want to sound overly concerned, but it is growing increasingly harder not to. "He's been shot," he says softly.

For a brief moment there is nothing but static on the line. "Shot?" she asks loudly.

"I don't know who, but he said it was some gangsters down on D street."

"D street. That's a horrible part of town. Oh Jesus, help me." She pauses to gather her thoughts. "What was he doing down there in the middle of the night?"

Silence fills the line again. Al was not prepared to answer that question; his mind races with ideas. Before he can come up with one, Ella comes back.

"Al, you and him have always been close, so I know you know what he was doing; now tell me, what was he doing down there in the middle of the night?"

"Selling cocaine," he replies softly, as disappointment in himself flushes over him.

Al can almost feel the anger coming through the thin telephone line as his ex-wife grits her teeth. "Why is my son selling drugs? Is that what he is doing to support you?"

"Baby—"

"Don't *baby* me, damn it! If my son dies, it's on your shoulders, Al Cleveland. I'll be down there in a few hours!"

"He's my son too," he says softly. Feelings of guilt keep his voice from getting any louder.

Ella slams the phone down, hanging up on him. Al wipes some of the tears off his face and calmly hangs up the phone. *Well, that went well. If she has a gun I'll be laying there next to Daryl as soon as she gets here.*

With wobbly legs, he walks over to the waiting room, which is cluttered with old magazines, and sits down on one of the few empty chairs. He looks at all the other people in the waiting room, and wonders if he has the worst case. They all look so distraught and worried. Some are in their nightclothes; they have obviously been awakened by their personal emergency. He does his best to put his mind at ease as he fills out the numerous forms on the clipboard.

An hour passes, and he finally finishes the last form. The sound of people talking on a two-way radio catches his attention. He looks up and sees two uniformed police officers standing at the nurse's station. One of the nurses points to Al. The policemen turn around and start walking towards him. *Oh great, what do they want, I didn't do anything.*

"Mister Cleveland?" the taller one asks.

"Yes?"

"We'd like to ask you a few questions about the shooting."

My son was selling coke so we can make ends meet, is that all right? "Sure, I wasn't there, but I'll tell you what I know."

One of the officers gets a notepad out. "Do you know who shot him?"

"All I know is that it was someone in a white car."

"Do you know what your son was doing down there at that time of night?"

He has to lie. There is no way he can tell the truth. "I think he was seeing some girl over there."

The phone at the nurse's station rings, and a brief conversation takes place. The nurse stands up. "Mister Cleveland, the doctor would like to see you." Al looks at her with an open mouth. The nurse had no emotion in her voice; he takes that to mean it isn't good news. His entire body freezes with fear; it can't be good if they need to speak to him in private. *Oh God, my son is dead. How am I going to explain this to Ella and Ted?*

The two officers part as Al stands and slowly makes the lonely, heart-stopping journey to the back of the ER. With each step, his legs feel weaker and weaker; it gets to the point where he wishes that someone was helping to keep him upright.

The same worker that shut the large doors on him before is now holding them open. Al glances at the man's face; it seems so filled with sorrow and pity. Al's stomach begins to turn, and he thinks he is going to throw up. He comes closer to the operating room; other nurses and workers begin rolling equipment out it. The surgeon walks out; he looks very tired.

Al's eyes focus on the droplets of blood that are on his gown—his son's blood. The surgeon seems oblivious to the rest of the world as he strips off his surgical gown and tosses it in the hamper, leaving behind the usual, plain, light-green smock. Then he turns and notices Al standing there.

"Oh, are you the father?" the surgeon asks.

"Yes," he replies. His shaky hand reaches over and takes hold of the railing as he braces himself for the worst.

The surgeon sees the sad look draped over Al's face. His own mouth drops open.

"Has anyone talked to you yet?"

Al shakes his head and wonders if he should be sitting down, maybe laying down. "No one has told me a word about my boy."

"Well, I have good news, then."

Al's eyes light up. Have his prayers been answered? Could his son be all right?

"Come with me; Daryl is over here." The two begin to walk together. "It turns out that your son wasn't shot."

Al's mind quickly flashes back to the wound, all the blood. "He wasn't?"

They walk into the room where the surgery took place. Even though the work is already done, the room still seems spotless, with the smell of disinfectant in the air. All the scalpels and other surgical instruments have already been removed. Daryl has just been moved from the stainless-steel table to a regular hospital bed. He seems to be resting comfortably, still unconscious from the anesthesia.

The surgeon walks over, moves the sheets to the side, and lifts Daryl's gown to expose where the wound is. There is nothing to see but a large, chest-sized piece of gauze covering the spot where he was hit.

"According to the chart, he dove into a pile of garbage to escape someone shooting him."

"Yes, that's what he told me," Al says, remembering that is also what he told the 911 operator.

"Well, something in that pile gave him a foot-long, jagged cut all along here." The surgeon slides his index finger from Daryl's back downward and to his front. "And then we found these embedded inside of him." He holds up a clear bag with three pieces of old metal in it; one is as big as a quarter. "When he dove into the pile, he must have impaled himself on these, and then they broke off inside of him. With all the excitement and the adrenaline pumping through his veins, he didn't even notice it. In fact, after we took the X-rays, we weren't sure what he had in him."

Al glances at the X-rays still hanging on the light board. Three dark blotches mark where the metal pieces came to rest.

As the surgeon moves out of the way, Al goes over and covers his son back up. He takes his hand and rubs it against Daryl's. Two tears escape his eyes. He blinks several times, keeping the rest at bay. Al gives a small smile as he feels that his son's hand is warm again.

"So he's going to be OK?" he asks, praying for more good news.

"He's going to need to rest; after all, I just gave him forty-two stitches, and he lost a lot of blood. But there is no internal damage other than a fractured rib. Much better than being shot."

"I'll say," Al mumbles, keeping his eyes on his son.

"So what do you say we bring him upstairs where he can rest and heal up?"

"Sounds good."

As two older volunteers roll him out, Al feels an overwhelming sense of relief wash over him. He builds up the courage to smile, and helps the two older men push the bed onto the elevator. Several more tears of joy escape his eyes as he holds his unconscious son's hand.

"He's going to be fine," one of the volunteers says. "That is a good surgeon he had. One of the best in the hospital."

Al nods, and doesn't bother explaining. The tears are for the guilt that is spreading through his body—guilt for letting his son make a living the way he has been.

They roll Daryl upstairs to his private room and make sure he is comfortable. Al scoots an old yellow chair up next to him and sits down. He places his head on his hands, which are resting on the bed's guardrail. He closes his eyes, praying for healing and forgiveness.

His exhausted body begins to relax as he listens to Daryl's steady, deep breaths.

* * *

"Wow, this is so cool, Dad," a ten-year-old Daryl squeaks out upon receiving a new orange bike with a green-and-white, striped banana seat.

"I'm glad you like it, son," Al says, his voice full of pride.

Al looks over to see Ted already riding his new bike out in the street. It was sixteen years ago, back when he and Lorraine lived in the good part of Detroit; for that brief moment in their lives, the world seemed so carefree and without worry. He had recently received his first, and only, real royalty check. The one without deductions and without the IRS garnishing it. Life was wonderful, and he thought he was sitting on top of the world.

"How did you buy this, and all the new furniture?" Daryl asks, glancing back at the upstairs apartment.

Al looks back; the front door is wide open, and he can see the new couch and lamp standing by the door. He squats down to look his son in the eyes. Young Daryl was so innocent; he didn't know about the evils of the world. His mind was so eager to learn.

"I worked for it, son. You work hard, live a good, honest life, and love the Lord, and He will bless you for it. People who lay around in bed all day and dream . . . that's all they get is dreams. You remember that— you have to work for things, OK?"

"OK," Daryl says as he hops on his new bike. "I love you, Dad," he blurts out, and takes off.

* * *

Al's weak and shaky voice comes out. "I love you too, son."

He can feel tears rolling down his cheeks as his blurry eyes open. Even though the doctors told him that his son would be out of it all night, he desperately wishes Daryl would wake up now. He just wants to hear his voice again, to see him smile once more.

"Please, Lord, it was me who made the mistakes, not him," he whispers in a choked-up voice.

"Prayer, the last refuge of a scoundrel," Ella says with a tongue as sharp as a knife. Part of her anger is due to the drug-dealing that Al allowed to take place, and the rest is old resentment for Al leaving her two decades ago—although she would never admit that.

Al turns around and looks at her. She has hardly aged a bit over the years; she appears to be doing well. Amazingly, in her rush, she found clothes that match her jacket. Her hair must have been in curlers for the night, but she took a few moments to remove them before the long drive over to the hospital.

Al glances at his wristwatch. "You must have broken every speed limit in the city," he says.

Ella is in no mood to play, and quickly changes the subject. "The doctor told me that things went well, and that he's going to be all right."

Al looks back and squeezes Daryl's motionless hand. "Yeah, that's what they told me too."

Ella walks closer; the tension in the room builds. She wants to run up and hug Daryl, but at the same time, she doesn't want to get too close to Al, for fear that she will slug him. The hairs on the back of Al's neck stand on end as Ella looks over her son. Al begins to feel uncomfortable.

Clearing his throat, he says, "Why don't I go get some coffee; would you like anything?"

Ella shakes her head and takes off her coat. Al leaves the room. She stands there for just a moment. Her lower lip starts to tremble; she breaks down and cries. It took everything she had to make it this far, and now that she's here, there is no stopping her tears.

"Oh, Daryl, what happened to my baby?" she whispers, with a trembling chin.

She can feel her body starting to go limp. She knows that if she stands much longer she will pass out, so she sits down and takes several deep, shaky breaths. She looks up at the ceiling and tries to regain her self-control.

Al takes his time getting the coffee, allowing her time to be alone with her son. Ella hardly moves a muscle and barely blinks as she stares at his chest, which is slowly rising up and down in steady breaths. Silently she prays for a pathway from the life that her son is leading straight to a better one, one where the Lord is at the center of it.

* * *

Two days later, Daryl leaves the hospital. His steps are slow but consistent.

Eventually the stitches will come out and the wound will heal, but the emotional scar will last a lifetime for Daryl and his parents. Ella had left the day before, only after it was clear that her son was going to be all right.

As they walk outside, Daryl squints at the bright sun reflecting off the fresh snow that fell the night before. The air is cold, but it feels fresh and free of disinfectants. Al holds onto his arm to help support him. Although Daryl feels he should be the one helping him, and not the other way around, he says nothing.

"I talked to Ron," Al says, breaking the silence. Daryl's eyes search the parking lot, as if the gang would be there to hunt him down.

Paranoia is something new that he will have to deal with. He takes a few more steps, listening to his feet crunch the fresh snow.

"So how's he doing?"

"Great. Things in Las Vegas are perking up; he said he can use some help." They reach their car, and Al unlocks the door for his son. Daryl waits for more of what Ron said, but Al stops there."

"So, what else did Ron say?"

"Nothing, just that he could use some help."

They get in the car and start driving away. Al is beating around the bush about wanting his son to go to Las Vegas. Daryl's mind is a million miles away as the dull pain from his stitches begins; the medication is wearing off.

Al thinks about what he just said, and realizes that being direct is the best—and only—way.

"Son, I think it would be best if you moved to Las Vegas to help Ron with Doorway Enterprises."

Daryl lets out a long sigh that he cuts short as his wound suddenly feels very tight. "You know you can't run the station by yourself."

"And you can't run it by yourself either," Al quickly puts in. "Son, I might be going to jail real soon; my court date is in four days, or have you forgotten?"

Daryl looks out the window at some children playing basketball in a small park. He can still remember doing that himself, back when things were so much simpler.

"No, I haven't forgotten," he moans, not wanting to face the thought of his dad behind bars. He groans as he moves, sending sharp jolts of pain racing though him.

Al loves his son dearly, and all he wants is what he feels is best for him. "Daryl, if I get locked up, and it looks like I will be, there will be nothing here for you."

He pauses as he turns the corner to their apartment. "You can't run the station by yourself, and I don't want you selling drugs anymore. So get while the getting is good. Opportunities like this don't come all the time."

Daryl looks at the floor and nods. "If it will make you happy, then I'll go right after your court date." Al stops in front of their apartment and shuts off the engine. Daryl quickly surveys the surroundings, making sure that no one is watching them. Al notices his son's new paranoia, and feels sympathy for him.

"Dad, if you go to jail, who is going to visit you?"

Al grabs his arm, forcing his son to look at him. "The good Lord will be there for me. I'll be all right, knowing that you're all right; far away from those two-bit punks and their guns."

This is killing Al, but he won't let it show one bit. It hurts more than losing Ella, Lorraine, and Natalie, combined with the IRS raid. He wants to cry, to tell his son that he is scared to death about facing twenty years. He wants to beg him to stay and keep him company while he is serving his time behind the cold, thick walls at the prison. He has come to realize that twenty years would be a life sentence for him, because his heart will not hold out that long.

But he also realizes that the best thing, not to mention the most important thing to him, is for Daryl to get out of Pittsburgh as soon as possible.

Al continues talking as he climbs out of the car. "I've already bought your plane tickets; you leave in two days."

"Two days?" Daryl asks loudly, as he flings open the heavy car door.

That little movement takes his breath away. He pauses as he places his hand over his wound. Al walks around to help him out.

"Two days? Why so soon?" he asks with a slighted tone.

"Because you'll be safer there," he replies calmly, helping Daryl out.

It is half of the truth; he would be safer living outside of their neighborhood. But Al also doesn't want his son around while he is being sentenced, just in case he breaks down. He refuses to do it in front of his son. As far as he knows, Daryl has never seen him cry, and he wants to keep it that way.

The next day Daryl gives in to his father's pleas and packs his bags. All leftover cocaine is flushed down the toilet, giving them both a sense of relief. The last few hours together seem to fly by. Before they know it, it is time for Daryl to get on a plane and head south. He calls his mom to say good-bye, and hugs his dad at the gate before getting on the plane. As Al walks away, his knees shake. Now that his son is gone, the only thing he needs to focus all his energy on is his court date—the thing that is scaring him half to death

CHAPTER 17

The next day, Al sports one of his best suits as he sits in the waiting room of his lawyer's office. He nervously taps his fingers on the nearly empty briefcase sitting on his lap. He isn't sure if he needs it or not, but just in case the lawyer gives him anything, anything at all that would help with the case, he would be able to protect it from the sleet falling outside.

His stomach does flip-flops; thousands of butterflies launch an assault on his midsection. He hasn't had much sleep in days; he stares at the empty, reddish-brown leather chairs in the waiting room. It is early in the morning, and he is the first appointment, just the way he likes it.

The longer he waits, the more his mind wanders. *If I just walk out that door, I could vanish off the face of the Earth. Then I wouldn't have to face life behind bars.* He plots going underground, avoiding the police.

"Mister Cleveland," the young, shapely secretary says with a warm smile. Her voice, unexpected, almost causes him to have a heart attack. "Mister Matten will see you now."

Al hesitates for a second; the thoughts of life on the run are still fresh on his mind. His hands run across the cool briefcase. *Come on, Al, it's just the lawyer, not the judge. What harm can it do to talk to him again? You've already been in there once, and he didn't bite you.* He slowly stands, holding his briefcase in a death grip as he walks into the office. The secretary closes the door behind him.

One look inside, and anyone can tell that this lawyer has money . . . lots of money. He has handled some of the biggest cases in Pittsburgh. George Matten is a very expensive lawyer, but he also has a reputation for getting the job done. In order to get him, Al has resorted to cashing in the balloon payment that would have sealed the deal for the radio station. A lot of money, but a small price to pay for freedom.

The office is done in expensive taste. Dark wood paneling and bookcases filled with law books line the walls. The lawyer sits behind a behemoth of a wood desk that is lined with gold trim. Behind him hang countless degrees and certificates of achievement. He stands, and extends his hand towards his client.

"Good morning, Al. How are you doing today?" Al shakes his hand, his eyes filled with worry.

"Scared to death, George. I think I'm going to die of a heart attack before I have a chance to plead my case in court."

George chuckles. "Sit down, relax, take a load off your feet. You look great. I see you got your hair cut, and that suit looks fabulous. Have you lost weight?"

"George, I appreciate the flattery, but can we cut the BS and get down to business?" he asks in short, choppy breaths.

George's face turns serious. Going over business is something the five-foot-eight man loves to do. He enjoys the challenge of proving someone innocent. Al studies the lawyer's attributes. His dark, freshly cut, brown hair is combed back. His eyes are a darker brown, while his complexion is rather pale. Al figures it must be from the countless hours he spends working indoors. And his clothes are always impeccable. In the past, he has boasted about wearing suits that would cost someone else a month's salary.

"I went over your case. To be quite frank, they have you caught between a rock and a hard place. Selling dope to an undercover cop makes the evidence rock solid."

Al places his hand over his heart. It is aching with a constant dull pain. The thought of a twenty-year prison sentence flashes through his mind; he doesn't think he can make it past ten years.

"So . . . there is no hope for me?"

George picks up Al's file and thumbs though it. "Your past record is almost as clean as Mother Teresa's. I am sure that if we plea-bargain, we can get a reduced sentence."

"You mean, admit I'm guilty?"

"Yes, Al, that is exactly what I mean. I hate doing it that way, but they caught you red-handed."

He stops. Something in the file catches his eye; his eyebrows raise. "But I am working on something—" George suddenly stops, realizing he is about to say something he shouldn't. "We'll just offer a guilty plea, and kind of throw ourselves on the mercy of the court."

"What are you working on?"

"Nothing. Just show up early tomorrow, and be ready to tell Judge Stemmings that you did it; show him that you are remorseful, and tell him that it will never happen again."

"Do you think that will help?"

"It can't hurt."

* * *

The following morning, Al is standing on the steps of the courthouse. Even though it is cold out, he is sweating. He has chosen to wear one of his light-gray suits; he thinks the lighter color would make him look more innocent, though he doesn't know why. He grasps his briefcase firmly in front of him. He knows he doesn't need it, but holding onto it provides some security. His nerves are shot; it is hard for him to sit down. His legs and hands tremble, and his stomach does somersaults. He watches the cars pass by, apprehensively waiting for George to show up. "Come on George, get here already," he mutters to himself.

Al has never felt so alone. Now that Daryl is gone, his life seems so secluded and empty. It is something that he is not used to. In the past he has always had a wife, a girlfriend, or at least a real good buddy to lean on. Now, he has nobody.

Moments later, George appears in his large, black, four-door Mercedes. Somehow he manages to keep it spotless, even in the winter. He drives just past the courthouse, and parks on the side. Al walks over to greet him.

"Morning, George."

"Good morning, Al," he replies as he gets out of his car and pulls out his gold-colored briefcase.

Al notices that he is wearing another two-thousand-dollar suit. It's navy blue. It shines in the sunlight. Al wonders if his own turn will ever come. Will he ever have the chance to enjoy the riches of life?

George takes a moment to look his client up and down. Al's face appears swollen and pasty. His eyes are bloodshot; he looks extremely worried. The attorney reaches out and dusts off Al's shoulders.

"Your clothes are nice, but you look like crap. Are you feeling all right?"

"Of course I'm not feeling *all right*. I told you I was going to die of a heart attack right here."

"Do you want me to call an ambulance?" George is serious. Al looks that bad.

"No, I'll make it." *Maybe I'll drop dead right in front of Judge Stemmings; man, wouldn't that be funny.*

George looks down the street, and then over to the side of the courthouse, as if he is looking for someone. Al can tell that something is disturbing him.

"What's wrong?"

"Nothing, nothing at all," he replies, looking around again. "Let's go inside and review what you will need to say."

They walk across the spotless marble floor in the lobby. The heels of their dress shoes click on the hard surface as they enter the courtroom. George opens the large, paneled, wooden doors, and leads him up to the front. They come to the railing; George swings open the gate and extends his hand, showing Al where they will be sitting.

It is the same courtroom that Al was in before. George has been there more times than he can count, and actually feels rather comfortable there. For him, it is almost like a second home.

More accurately, he decides, it is like an arena, a site for challenges and fights. It is a place where George doesn't like to lose—and there can only be one winner.

The only other person in the room is a janitor mopping the floors. It's still over an hour until the trial begins, plenty of time to go over things. It is common practice for George; it helps his clients feel more at ease when things get under way.

"OK, the judge is going to ask, 'How do you plead?' And then I will stand up and say, 'Guilty,' " George explains.

The word "guilty" causes Al's stomach to tie into tighter and tighter knots, but he understands why he must do it. George instructs Al to give the speech that he plans to give Judge Stemmings as he throws himself on the mercy of the court. Al goes through it and almost breaks down; it is sincere and from the heart. The seasoned lawyer feels that it will work well for Al. All through the speech, George keeps looking at his watch and glancing at the door. He's fidgety and restless about something.

The hour—what Al perceives to be his last hour of freedom—goes by very quickly.

The courtroom fills with onlookers wanting to see the trial of the man who wrote the music that they love. With each passing moment, Al becomes increasingly concerned. His fantasy of being on the run seems more and more appealing. With a sweaty brow, he glances at George. Something is not right; for once the man is not his cool, calm self. His lawyer's actions only make him more nervous.

"Hello, Mister Cleveland and Mister Matten," the district attorney says in a deep voice while taking his seat at the table opposite them.

There is a confidence in his voice that eats at George's ego. The two have battled in court many times before, and though neither one would admit it, they have both been keeping score of wins and losses.

Bam! The DA drops his briefcase on the table. The unexpected noise almost causes Al to jump out of his skin. He gawks at the man.

"Morning," George replies, with an "I can't stand you; I'm just being civil" tone.

The DA, Daniel Rosworth, is a heavyset black man wearing a dark-green suit that looks like it was purchased at a discount store. He stands about five foot ten, and his waist is almost as big as he is tall. He's the type that seems to hate his own race with a passion; he apparently loves to prosecute them.

Al remains silent as he thinks about ways to tell the man where to go and how to get there. Another man pushes open the small gate. He is a large, burly-looking white man. He looks out of place in his suit; he would probably look better in professional wrestling tights or a football uniform. Al looks at the man's short, curly, brown hair, large, bent nose, and beady eyes; the face is familiar.

"That's the other one who arrested me," he mumbles.

George looks over at the large man, and then flips though his files. "Sure is; that's Tom Blackheart. Huh—I guess he is part Indian."

Al looks around at all the others in the courtroom, looking for someone he doesn't see. "I don't see the woman who arrested me. Shouldn't she be here too?"

George smiles; he seems to like the news. "Oh yes, Vicki Washington. She only has five more minutes to get here; it's not polite to show up after the show starts."

Al's stomach turns again. *Five minutes, that's it; five minutes of freedom left in my life.*

He watches as the bailiff enters the courtroom from a side entrance. His weary heart begins to pound; he knows his time is coming. But then he notices that George seems rather at ease that Vicki hasn't shown up yet.

Suddenly George nudges him to pay attention; the bailiff is about to speak.

"All rise, the Honorable Judge Stemmings presiding."

The judge walks in, and everyone stands silently on their feet. Al watches as the man walks over to his bench and scans the courtroom. Although his nerves are jumping, he does his best to remain calm and appear somber. He tries to keep his mind on Daryl and Ted, wishing they were here too, but at the same time, he's glad they're not.

"Please be seated," the judge says as he flips his long black robe under his legs and takes his seat. "Gentlemen, we are a little short of time today, so let's get right down to business." He opens up the file and reads it aloud. "The state of Pennsylvania charges the defendant Al Cleveland with possession and distribution of an illegal substance. How do you plead?"

Just as they rehearsed, Al and George rise from their hard wooden chairs. The lawyer takes a deep breath and prepares to speak. Suddenly the back double doors fly open with a loud crash. A Hispanic man in a dark-blue suit sprints down the center aisle. He is out of breath and sweaty. Al figures he must have run a long distance.

George's eyes light up; he turns his whole body around. The man rushes over to him, hands him several pieces of paper, and whispers something in George's ear.

"Are you sure?" George asks.

The man nods frantically.

Bang! Bang! The judge slams his gavel against the small stand twice. He shows his anger. "Mister Matten, I will not tolerate these interruptions in my courtroom! Does your client have a plea?"

George spins around, a spark in his eyes again. "I am terribly sorry about that, your honor. My client's plea is *not* guilty."

There is a murmur in the courtroom. No one—particularly not Al—was expecting that. The judge bangs the wooden hammer two more times to restore order. Al sits down again, more because he has to than because he wants to. George does the same, tilting back in his chair like he doesn't have a care in the world. He taps his fingers on the table, as if it were the desk in his office.

"What are you doing?" Al asks."

"Just relax; everything just changed. Remember, this is what you pay me for."

Al is shocked; he hadn't been thinking that he had a chance of winning his case. The DA and the arresting officer begin to whisper to one another. Judge Stemmings is becoming angrier by the second.

He stares at Daniel.

"Mister Rosworth, would you care to get things started today, or should I come back at a better time?" he asks, in a voice dripping with a stern sarcasm.

Daniel instantly stands up. "Right now, your honor. We just weren't prepared for such an unusual plea."

"This is America, Mister Rosworth, and here we are innocent until proven guilty," the judge reminds the DA, as though he might have forgotten.

"Yes, your honor," he replies, forcing a smile onto his cold face. "For my first witness, I would like to call Al Cleveland to the stand." Al scoots his chair out, but George puts his hand on Al's shoulder to keep him in his seat.

"Your honor, my client chooses to take the Fifth." George looks at Daniel. "So you can bring him up there if you want, but he has nothing to say."

Again the court fills with murmur, and the judge bangs his gavel down one more time. Daniel continues to stand, but with his shoulders now slumped; he is confused.

"Your honor, this isn't a murder case; the witness still can—"

"The witness still has his rights," the judge interrupts, not letting him finish. He pauses, then asks. "Counsel, do you have anyone else you would like to call up?"

Daniel abruptly appears not to care what George is up to.

"Yes, your honor, I would like to call up the arresting officer, Tom Blackheart."

When Tom stands, his height causes him to tower over everyone else. He strolls over to the stand with large, heavy steps, and takes his seat. The bailiff walks over with a Bible and swears him in. Daniel glances back at George and smiles, as if this case were already wrapped up. The gesture turns Al's stomach—he realizes that he is just a pawn in this game of chess, and that the two lawyers are competing against one another.

"Officer Blackheart," Daniel begins, "how did you meet Mister Cleveland?"

"He tried to sell us some cocaine."

Daniel crosses his arms over his chest and pauses, indicating the significance of this information. "So you set up a sting operation, and he fell into the trap, is that correct?"

"Yes, it is," he replies in a deep voice, staring at Al with beady eyes.

Daniel smiles, confident; his tone exudes arrogance. "It sounds real simple. No further questions, your honor."

The judge turns and looks at George. He is upset and impatient; he doesn't like the ruthless competition between the two lawyers. With years of experience under his belt, he feels this should be an open-and-shut case, and that the lawyers are just wasting his time.

"Mister Matten, I suppose you have some type of defense to this."

George stands up and shoots a smile at the DA. "Oh yes, your honor, of course."

He strides over to the stand with the same air of confidence that his opponent has just exhibited. He stops and leans on the stand, his back towards the arresting officer. He gazes out at the silent audience with a smug look.

"You stated earlier that my client attempted to 'sell us' drugs, and by 'us,' you mean you and Officer Washington?"

"That's correct," Tom states.

"Hmm, that's interesting. How long have you been on the force, Officer Blackheart?"

The DA shoots up from his chair. "Objection, your honor; my witness's work history is not on trial here."

Stemmings looks at both lawyers. "Overruled. I want to see where he is going with this." He nods at Tom. "Answer the question."

Tom is confused; he doesn't know what George is up to. "Eleven months."

"Wow, eleven months," George responds, eyebrows raised. He already knows the answer to the question, of course; but he has to keep up his act. "In only eleven months you made it to drug enforcement. I thought that took years."

"It . . . umm." Tom stumbles on his words as he falls into George's trap. "It does; I'm still a traffic cop."

George acts shocked. His mouth falls open as his hands fly up from his sides. "A traffic cop?"

Once again the DA stands up. "Your honor, I must object; does this have anything to do with Mister Cleveland distributing drugs?"

"Overruled." The judge looks at George. "Counsel, I suggest you take this someplace, and do so quickly."

"Yes, your honor," he replies with a civil smile. "The reason why this is important—" He pauses as he walks back over to his table and picks up a piece of paper. "—is because Officer Blackheart was not on duty. He had just finished a twelve-hour shift and was on his fourth beer when his partner gave him—" He holds up his fingers to make quotation marks. "—the signal." A low murmur fills the courtroom yet again, and the judge smashes his gavel on its small stand. The DA nervously taps his pencil on the table as he considers objecting again.

George passes a signed statement to Daniel and the judge; it is from the cocktail waitress that served Officer Blackheart the beers. The momentum is on his side.

"Now, certainly there is nothing wrong with you having a beer or two after work, Officer Blackheart," Al's lawyer continues, "because you were there to relax and have a good time, just like everyone else in the bar." He raises his voice slightly to get everyone's attention. "You, however, were not there to make an arrest of any sort. Isn't that correct?"

The officer looks at Daniel for guidance, and finds none. He slowly nods.

"Please state your answer out loud," Judge Stemmings says.

"Yes, that is true," he replies softly, he appears to wish her were somewhere else.

"Yes, that is true," George repeats, so everyone can hear it. "You were there relaxing and enjoying yourself when Officer Washington gave you some type of signal. What signal did she give you?"

Daniel explodes from his chair again. "Objection, your honor. Officer Blackheart's police tactics are not on trial here."

"Overruled," the judge says without a moment's hesitation. "Obviously this was not a sting operation, as you had led the court to believe. Answer the question, Officer Blackheart."

The large man glances at Al, and then his head slowly sinks. "She was digging in her purse, and then lifted her head to me," he states, tilting his thick chin into the air, not looking at anyone.

George remains calm; his nerves are again steady, cool. It's his show, and he knows it. "So, initially you didn't know what was wrong. You just had a gut instinct, grabbed my client from behind, and said . . ."

"You're under arrest," lawyer and witness say in unison.

"Objection, your honor; he's leading the witness," the DA says, his voice wavering with panic.

The judge stops and thinks about it briefly. "Sustained." He looks at George with his heavy brown eyes. "You need to watch your wording."

George nods, smiling again. "Your witness really didn't witness anything," he says, turning to look at Daniel. "He saw one officer digging in her purse, a nod, and then he grabbed my client, that was it. Was there really a crime committed?"

Once again Daniel shoots out of his seat. He holds up a small stack of papers tightly in his hand. "Obviously the defendant has forgotten about the signed affidavit from Officer Washington, stating right here that Mister Cleveland attempted to sell her cocaine. Not to mention they found the cocaine on him."

Daniel hastily hands the papers to George and Judge Stemmings. Even though they both have already seen them, they quickly look them over again. George smiles and strolls back over to the table. He winks at Al, whose heart is pounding like a rolling freight train, and picks up the file that the Hispanic man who had burst into the courtroom at the last second had handed him.

"I'm through with the first witness," George says. He pauses for a moment, as Officer Blackheart goes back to his seat with relief. "Good old Officer Washington, making an arrest on her time off; now that is dedication. That's a loyalty that we don't find often in these dark days—"

"Do you have another witness to call to the stand, or are you through?" Judge Stemmings interjects, a no-nonsense tone in his voice. "If you care to write a book about Officer Washington, I think you should do it on your time."

"Forgive me for rambling, your honor. I would like to call one more witness."

"Then make it quick, Mister Matten."

George knows exactly when to draw a situation out and when not to. "Your honor, for my next witness, I would like to call on Officer Vicki Washington."

George spins around, holds his hand out, and looks in the crowded courtroom for the officer to stand. Heads turn in all directions, looking for her, but no one rises to their feet. Slowly he lowers his hand.

"Officer Vicki Washington, please come on down," George says again, making sure his request is heard and his point understood.

He looks at Daniel and shrugs. Tasting victory, he walks over to his opponent's table and sets Officer Washington's signed affidavit down. He taps it several times, knowing that Daniel is aware it is about to become null and void. George looks at Judge Stemmings, and then glances at his gold watch.

"Where is Vicki Washington? She was subpoenaed like everyone else, yet she did not show up."

Daniel has tried all night to get hold of the officer, but she hasn't returned any of his phone calls. He doesn't sweat it, though; he knows that the signed document is enough to make a conviction . . . or at least he thinks it is.

The judge holds up the affidavit. "Mister Matten, I am sure you realize that this will suffice in my court."

Daniel suddenly relaxes.

George places his hands behind his back, and rocks back and forth on his feet. "Yes your honor, under normal circumstances it would. But one must stop and wonder—what if the person who signed that was dishonest?"

"Objection, your honor," Daniel blurts out, jumping to his feet again. "Now he has resorted to defaming my witness."

"That is because your witness is in jail,"

George states quickly, before the judge can respond. "Right now your witness, Officer Washington, is being held in the detention center for trafficking; that is the same offense my client is being charged with."

The DA's mouth falls open as all the blood drains from his face. His heavy eyes shoot to the floor, then back up at George. "She could be proven innocent," Daniel replies angrily.

"And so might Mister Cleveland," George says, walking briskly back to his table and snatching the file off the dark wooden slab. "I am not trying to put down Officer Washington, or destroy her character. She has been on the force for twelve years, and has received many awards. But she has also been in rehab three times for drug abuse." He turns to address the audience. "So my question to you is, without a true witness, was my client buying drugs, selling drugs, or just sitting there having a beer when Officer Washington happened to look at Officer Blackheart in a strange way?"

Daniel jumps to his feet and points at George. "He still had the drugs on him."

It is checkmate time for George. "Were those drugs his or hers? I think they were planted on my client."

Instantly the room gets loud again, and Judge Stemmings bangs his wooden hammer several more times.

"That is enough!" the old judge shouts. "That is the last outburst I will tolerate. This court is adjourned; I am moving this into my chambers." His eyebrows angle downward as he glares at the two lawyers. "And I expect to see you two in there with me!"

"All rise," the bailiff quickly says, as the judge stands. The moment Judge Stemmings leaves the room, George rushes over to Al.

"Are you hanging in there?" he asks, filled with excitement.

Al's mouth is slightly open, and there is a thin layer of sweat across his forehead. "I'm making it, but I don't know what to do."

"Just be quiet," George states, his index finger over his lips. "If old Stemmings asks you a question, you just look at me, and I will answer it for you. That's my job, understood?"

"Yeah," Al whispers, as he watches the large police officer walk past him towards the back.

The judge sits down behind his desk and slams the files down. Just like the courtroom, the office is done in rich, dark woods. Both lawyers try to appear calm and not let their emotions show. Behind them are Officer Blackheart and Al, who have also been ordered into the judge's chambers. The two of them are not used to this; both watch wide-eyed as events unfold.

"What in the name of—" the judge cuts himself off before cussing. "Gentlemen, there is one thing I can't stand, and that is a circus in my courtroom. Is that clear?"

"Yes, your honor," George and Daniel both say at the same time.

"I refuse to sit there and have you two clowns make a mockery of the United States judicial system!" Then, as the judge is about to speak again, there is a knock on the door."

"Enter," he growls.

The bailiff sticks his head inside the door and nods once. The judge's face suddenly shows disapproval. He slowly shakes his head. The message that was just given to him was not the one he wanted to hear.

"Thank you," is his curt reply, and the bailiff leaves.

The tension in the room is thick. Judge Stemmings adjusts himself in his chair and looks at the signed affidavit. He reads over part of it, then tosses the document towards Daniel.

"It appears that your star witness has been arrested, as Mister Matten stated earlier. Do you have another witness?"

Daniel's shoulders drop half an inch. "Only Officer Blackheart. But sir, we have the signed affidavit."

"I think that Mister Matten has proven that Officer Blackheart really didn't see anything. And I think you and I both know that Officer Washington's statement is not very credible right now."

"But your honor . . ."

"Do you have another witness? Yes or no," he quickly asks, cutting the DA off.

Daniel's voice becomes meeker. "No sir."

The judge lets out a heavy sigh as he slowly shakes his head. Deep down, he feels that Al is guilty as charged, but there is nothing he can do about it. "Mister Cleveland, step forward, please."

The two steps that Al takes to the front seem long, and they are and hard to take as well. The sense of security he had when his lawyer was speaking for him, no matter how small, is gone. Judge Stemmings appears very mad as he looks Al up and down.

"I think you were selling drugs, Mister Cleveland, I really do. I don't know how much you are paying Mister Matten, and I don't need to know, but it has been very worthwhile for you. Now I have no choice but to set you free." Al's eyes widen; he can't believe what he has just heard. It feels like a ton of bricks has been lifted off of his shoulders.

"But hear my words, Mister Cleveland. I don't ever, and I mean *ever*, want to see you in my courtroom again. And I don't care if it's for a parking ticket. Is that perfectly clear?"

"Crystal" is the only word Al can manage to get out.

"Good. This court session is over with, and Mister Cleveland, you are a free man."

He bangs another wooden gavel on his desk, and everyone turns around, then files out the door. Daniel and George immediately go their separate ways. George strolls down the hall, his chest sticking out with pride. He places his arm around Al, and walks out.

"Are you feeling OK?" the lawyer asks excitedly. The thrill of victory tastes so sweet—he loves to win, and he has just won big.

Al looks at him, his knees still trembling, and his heart beating with an unsteady rhythm. George squeezes his client, reassuring him that everything is all right.

"See, that wasn't so bad," he says.

Al keeps his eyes on the end of the hallway. He can see daylight shooting in through the glass on the door, and it has never meant so much to him as it does right now. It already seems like he's been in prison for years.

"I'm never going to break the law again," he whispers.

George laughs. "Careful, you'll put me out of work."

Al makes it out to his car with rather slow and sluggish steps. He sits down in the driver's seat and takes hold of the wheel, but he can't yet find the energy to drive home. He has to rest in the cold car for nearly an hour before he gains enough strength.

*   *   *

Al walks into his apartment building. Right next to the front door is a row of small brass mailboxes built into the wall. He stops and peeks into the little window; it is packed with envelopes and junk mail.

His fingers tremble from the stress of the day as he fumbles with the combination. He opens the tiny door and grabs the stack of mail. Suddenly the pile slips from his hand and tumbles to the ground.

"Bills, bills, and more bills," he mumbles, picking the mail up off the floor.

His eyes open wide as he spots an envelope from Motown Records. As if it could bite, he hesitates before touching it. *Oh, please let this be a nice one so I can save the radio station.* He closes his eyes and whispers a quick prayer. With one fluid motion, he plucks it from the floor, and tears into it.

He pulls out the paper and looks at the statement. His eyes go straight to the bottom, the total, the grand amount that he will be receiving. His whole body practically goes limp as his heart strains to keep pumping blood. The IRS garnished his royalty check, leaving him thirty-six cents. He wants to cry, but he keeps his composure as he slowly climbs the stairs. His whole chest hurts.

"Thirty-six cents. I write a best-selling album, and all I receive is thirty-six cents. How am I supposed to live off of that?"

CHAPTER 18

Daryl leans back in his recliner, watching TV. He has been feeling better as his wound slowly heals. Ron is in the chair next to him, reading the entertainment section of the newspaper, looking for new talent. The fact that this is Al's court date has caused Daryl to worry all day long. He is very restless; he keeps moving around and tapping his fingers on the armrest.

"Would you relax?" Ron says.

"I'm worried, all right. Why hasn't he returned my call?"

"Have you tried the prison?" As much as Ron hates to say it, he does.

Daryl shakes his head. He won't admit it, he is afraid to call there, afraid to find out that his father is to be locked up and will never see the light of day again. Suddenly the phone rings.

Both men sit up, and Daryl jumps to his feet. He takes two steps before grabbing his side. The wound is still fresh and the stitches tight. The phone rings again as he picks it up.

"Hello?"

"Daryl."

It's Al; his voice is soft and weak, as if it hurts to talk. Immediately Daryl fears the worse. His body stiffens with fear.

"Dad, are you OK?"

Al is still on the verge of crying; his voice wavers as he talks.

"I'm just to tired of it all, son. I'm so sick and tired of it all. I did what I set out to do and became a music man, and what do I get for it? A kick in the crotch, that's what I get. When you work hard and pay your dues, you're supposed to get your rewards, right?"

Daryl is silent for a moment. He wants to speak, but for the time being, the words won't come. He thinks his dad has been sentenced already. Nerves begin to tie his stomach into knots. He ponders his dad spending the rest of his days in some cold, dreary cell.

"Thirty-six cents," Al mumbles as he stares across his dark room. He slowly sits up from bed; his chest has been hurting for hours, and a part of him wishes he would just die. "After court I received a royalty check; it's for a lousy thirty-six cents."

"After court?" Daryl's eyes search the room for a clock. He spots one; it is late back there. "After?" he asks, with a high-pitched voice. "What happened in court?"

Al's mind is overwhelmed by the day's events. "Remember that lawyer I went to talk to?"

"Yeah, Matten, that real expensive one."

"Well, he got me off the hook. To tell you the truth, son, I still don't know how he did it, but he got me off scot-free."

Daryl perks right up. "Well, that's great, Dad! You're a free man."

Ron gets up and walks over, his eyebrows high. "He's free?" Daryl nods. Al laughs lightly, but it is a pain-filled laugh that is laced with sorrow. He shifts the phone to the other ear and picks up his royalty check for another depressing look. He speaks with sadness.

"I am really sorry I failed you, son."

"What? You . . . you didn't fail me, Dad. I am so proud of you. You have done fantastic work."

Al emits a shaky sigh and sniffles. His eyes water; even though he is alone, he bats back the tears. "A father shouldn't lean on his children during the hard times; it is supposed to be the other way around."

"Man, you and I have been like the best of friends, much more than father and son, and I love it that way."

Al looks around his dark room for pictures of Daryl, as if he has forgotten what his son looks like. "Maybe I was wrong for letting that happen."

"Dad, you're upset because of Motown, and that wasn't your fault—anyone could have fallen into that same trap. And we both know a lot of people have; just ask anyone who has dealt with Berry."

Al is silent as he ponders his son's words. Meanwhile, Daryl desperately wants to cheer him up, but he is running out of ideas. Ron walks over and motions that he wants to speak with Al.

"Hey Dad, Ron wants to talk to you." He glances down at Ron's rounded belly; he's put on some weight over the years. "You should see him; he looks about six months pregnant." He smiles as he pokes Ron in the stomach.

Ron smacks his hand out of the way. "Get your damn hand off of me, boy, and hand me the phone," he says, with his round face on the verge of laughing. Daryl turns the phone over to him. "Hey, old man, what are you doing?" Al almost smiles; there is just something about Ron's voice that can always cheer him up."

"Nothing, just sitting here, sulking in the dark."

"Depressed because you didn't get to go to jail—I can understand that. If you'd been in there for just a little while, I am sure that someone would have made you their girlfriend. I bet I know what your real problem is."

Al wipes away a tear and shakes his head, but he plays along. "What's my problem, Ron?"

"You haven't pulled any panties in a while. I can tell by your voice; it sounds higher than normal."

Al laughs. "Is that so?"

"Yeah, You see, over there it's too damn cold out, and all the women are bundled up from head to toe, cutting down your panty-pulling chances."

"Are you sure about that?"

"That's the God's-honest truth," Ron says, holding up his right hand. "I'll prove it to you. How cold is it out right now?"

Al looks out his window. Frost and ice have formed around the edges of the glass. He glances down to the dark, empty street. The streetlight rattles back and forth from a strong, below-freezing wind that's ripping by. Just watching it almost gives him goosebumps.

"I don't know—with the wind chill, about fifteen below."

"Oh dear Lord . . ." He pauses and fumbles with the phone, making noise. "Forgive me, Al, but I almost fell down there. I am willing to bet my whole life savings—that's right, the entire fifteen dollars—that there isn't a single woman walking around out there." Ron beams as he listens to his friend laugh. "Do you know how cold it is here right now?"

"No," Al says, with a big smile.

"It's fifty-nine degrees, man, and to these desert rats, that is cold. Daryl is still walking around in shorts and a T-shirt. People are eyeballing him as if he is crazy. Personally I think that the boy does have a screw loose, but I ain't no psychiatrist."

Al laughs again. "So what's your point?"

"My point is that it's not so cold here, and therefore the women are out walking around, and my point is that you need to pack your bags and come down here with us. I need your help. I think I can line some stuff up with Bill Cosby, and you're my inside connection. You've done some minor stuff with him before, right?"

Al considers the idea of getting away. It sounds great. The winters are long and hard where he is, and it bothers him more with each passing, cold day. And it would be fabulous to be with Ron and Daryl again.

"Yeah, I could probably get us in. But . . . what about the radio station?"

"What about it? Daryl told me that you are supposed to make a balloon payment in a couple of months. Do you have that kind of money, or did you spend it on that fancy lawyer?"

Al falls completely silent.

"You're not answering, which tells me that you spent it on the lawyer. Don't get me wrong. It was worth it for him to get you out of the mess, but that also means you are way behind financially. Just let it go, Al, and come down here; it's going to happen sooner or later anyway, so make it sooner."

There is brief static on the phone line as Al thinks about the offer for a moment. "All right, Ron, you have yourself another deal. I'll take my thirty-six-cent check, cash it, and pack my things first thing in the morning."

"Well, I am glad to see you have the cost of gas and lodging all taken care of. Here, I'll let you talk to your son again." Ron gives Daryl a thumbs-up and hands him the phone. Excitement fills Daryl. He and his dad talk for a little while longer, wrapping up Al's moving plans before hanging up.

* * *

Four days later Al drives over the reddish-brown, bare-rock mountains and into the arid land of the Las Vegas valley, which is open and vast, and is surrounded by mountains.

The middle of the valley looks like an oasis with a small forest of trees growing in it. From a distance he can see a light layer of brown smog hovering above the small city, but is nothing compared to LA. Near the center of the large valley are a few twenty- and thirty-story towers. Most of them huddle together, as if for protection. Only a few dared to venture off on their own, so to speak. They are the casinos, new and old, the main revenue for what would otherwise be a lost and forgotten city.

Al is still driving the same large car that he had purchased ten years ago. The old, light-green, four-door Buick rolls down the long hill on Boulder Highway. The city looks as if it has grown since he was here five years ago. The once-tiny gambling town is now a booming metropolis. He wonders if the growth will stop soon, or if it will continue, ultimately giving him more opportunities.

It's noon during a weekday, so traffic is very light. Following a map that Daryl sent him, he makes it to Lamb Boulevard and travels past old mobile-home parks and apartment complexes. It doesn't take long for him to find the complex where Ron and Al's son are staying.

He pulls in and drives over several large, faded-yellow speed bumps. Each white, stucco-covered building has a number mounted on the front. Unfortunately, the numbers are not in order, so he is forced to slow to a near crawl. Loud, happy kids of all ethnic backgrounds are playing tag. They dart in and out of the parked cars, which sit under protective steel carports.

Al parks next to a large garbage can that is filled with the debris of someone's move. Feelings of uncertainty about his trip begin to creep in. *Maybe it wasn't such a good idea to come here. I hope I am doing the right thing.* He wonders if Daryl will accept him, or if he will be disappointed for not getting the radio station up and running. *Will my own son look down on me for not making real money off of the songs I wrote and produced?* "Knock it off Al, you're being stupid," he thinks out loud. *It's your son; he will love you no matter what.* "It has to get better than this," he whispers.

The sunlight hits him as soon as he climbs out of the car. Al smiles as he feels its warmth heating up his face. He has to admit it is better than feeling the cold sting of Jack Frost any day. Even though it is late winter, he feels quite comfortable in just a short sleeve shirt. It is definitely warmer than here than it is in Pittsburgh.

A set of automatic sprinklers turns off and another one turns on as he approaches the wet sidewalk. He glances up at the second-story apartment where they live now and looks up the stairs briefly. The spaced concrete steps seem so long and so far apart.

"Man, I wish just once we could get a place on the first floor," he mumbles, as he takes hold of the smooth, wrought-iron railing.

He walks slowly up the stairs and onto the balcony that leads to their door. His heavy body makes a loud thud with each passing step. Suddenly the door flies open and Daryl burst out.

"Hey, you made it," Daryl says happily. "I thought I heard someone."

He rushes over and hugs his dad. Instantly all the feelings of uncertainty are washed away as he holds his son tightly.

"So, how was the trip?" Daryl asks, with a slight look of pain on his face.

"Oh son, I forgot about your side; are you all right?"

Daryl smiles and gently rubs away the pain. "I'm fine, it's OK."

"I'm sorry about that. I swear my mind is going with age. Anyway, in answer to your question, the trip was nice, as soon as I left the snow behind," he replies, holding up his jacket.

They enter the three-bedroom apartment. It is small, like almost all of them in the complex, with a living room and an adjoining dining room. The kitchen is so small that it would barely hold the three of them at the same time. The light-brown carpet shows the tracks of numerous tenants, but somehow still looks reasonably new. It definitely isn't a luxury apartment, but it is affordable, and very livable.

"Thought I heard some old man," Ron says as he comes out of the back room. "How are you doing?" Ron walks over and hugs his old friend.

"I'm doing great; glad to be here." Al steps back and takes a look at him. "Man, you do look pregnant."

Ron's face turns serious. "I feel pregnant, so tell your son to hurry up and fix me some dinner."

"Man, I'm not fixing you anything," Daryl blurts out.

Ron looks at Al and taps his own chest. "How's the old ticker?"

"Still beating," he replies nonchalantly. Al figures there is nothing anyone can really do about it, so if the good Lord wants him to come home, he's coming home. Due to the lack of money, he hasn't been to a doctor in a long time, except to renew his medications. Desperate to change the subject, he frowns and looks around.

"Not a bad place you have here. Do I get my own room this time?"

"Oh yeah, you get it all; that is, right after Daryl cooks us some dinner."

Daryl laughs. "What makes you think that I'm cooking dinner?"

Ron stands on the tips of his toes to make himself taller. "What makes you think we still have enough room in here for you?" He does his best to keep a straight face, but fails, and breaks up. "Come on and help me bring up your dad's stuff. And when we're done with that, you can cook us our dinner."

Two hours later, the car is completely cleaned out and everything is upstairs. Al really doesn't have much stuff. He sold most of it to pay for the trip. As soon as they are done, Daryl heeds the command to prepare dinner. He doesn't mind; it is his turn. They have been sharing the duties, even though Daryl has a part-time job he works in addition to the countless hours he spends trying to get Doorway Enterprises launched again.

He sits down on the couch with his dad and hands him a plate of steaming spaghetti. The aroma of the fresh meat sauce fills the apartment, causing mouths to water—except Al's.

Instead, he mumbles a few indiscernible words through tight lips, and sets the plate down in front of him. He is busy reading something in *Rolling Stone* magazine. Whatever the article is, it has captured his attention.

"What are you looking at?" Daryl asks.

Al picks up the magazine and shows him a page. Under his thumb it reads, *"The 'What's Going On' album is still on the charts, and has already sold over eight million copies."* He slowly sets the magazine back down, and then reads the same sentence two more times in disbelief. Stress, pure and undiluted, seeps into his bones and chest, causing his heart to ache once again.

"Thirty-six cents," he mumbles. "Do you realize that if I didn't get screwed out of my royalties, I would be a millionaire right now? We'd all be set, with nice cars and homes." He stops and looks around the small apartment, making sure he doesn't make eye contact with Daryl or Ron.

"Instead, I have a ten-year-old car that can barely get down the street, and we live in a cramped apartment." Anger begins to boil in him; he tries to keep it under control as he grits his teeth.

"I've spent my whole life in apartments or rented houses. Once, just once, I would like to own a house and have a normal life, without the IRS and Motown taking everything from me." He glances at his food, and gently pushes the plate away. "Thank you for dinner, son, but I'm not hungry."

Everyone is silent as Al slowly stands and goes to his room. He closes the door; the soft thud of it shutting strikes an unhappy chord in both Daryl and Ron. Sad-faced, they look at each other. They know that the stress he is feeling is like a cancer buried deep inside. There is no way to get it out, and it will just keep growing, until it finally kills him.

Ron and Daryl quietly finish their dinner, then clean up. Daryl wishes there were something, anything, he could do for his dad, but there isn't; the matter is out of his hands. As Daryl dries the last pot, someone knocks on the front door. Ron walks over to answer it.

"Hey, look who's here," he says, back to his usual happy tone.

He steps out of the way, and a man walks in. His name is Gerald Ramio. He is a Sinatra-style singer with a flare for music. Gerald is Latino, and stands at five foot seven—"and a half," as he likes to remind people. His black hair has a lot of body, and is always combed back, without a single strand out of place. His favorite shirts are button-up ones; this allows him to show off the hair on his chest. The guys like having him around because he has such a positive, friendly aura about him. It's the perfect personality for them.

"Hi, Ron. Hey, Daryl," he says as he walks in.

"So, what's new?" Ron asks, closing the door.

Gerald glances around quickly; he is looking for someone. "Oh, I was just wondering if Daryl's dad got here yet."

Daryl darts out of the kitchen. "Yeah, he's here. Sit down and relax, I'll go get him." Daryl hopes that some company will help take his dad's mind off all of his problems for a little while.

Al is standing at his dresser, slowly unpacking his belongings from his old brown suitcase. In his hand he holds an old, black-and-white family photo of him, Ella, and the kids when they were very young and small. It feels like a lifetime ago. Gently he rubs his thumb over Ella's face. He often wonders what his life would have been like if he had just stayed in the steel mill and kept working. Would the mill have done him in, or would he have coped through the years, with a close-knit family by his side? His dream of owning a house of their own might have come true, if they had saved for it.

"I'm sorry I hurt you," he whispers to her.

Deep down he still loves her; he never stopped loving her through all the years they've been apart.

"Dad?" Daryl asks, as he knocks softly on the door.

Al quickly places the picture on the dresser and moves away from it, he thinks it would take some serious explaining if he were caught near the old photograph. And he doesn't want to explain his long-suppressed feelings . . . at least not now.

"Come in," he says, as he picks up some clothes and other innocent items out of his suitcase. He remains with his back towards the door.

Daryl sticks his head inside. "Dad, there is someone out here that would like to meet you. He's a good friend of ours."

Al takes his time folding his clothes. "Ron isn't trying to set me up with some girl, is he?" he asks without turning around.

"No, it's a guy."

Al spins around and crosses his eyebrows. "He's not trying to set me up with some guy?"

Daryl laughs; it's good to see some humor again. "No. If he tries, I'll let you know."

"All right, then, I'll come out."

Al walks out of his room. Gerald shoots up from the couch, and looks at the tall man coming towards him.

"Gerald," Ron says, "this is our new music consultant, Al Cleveland. Al, this is Gerald Ramio, a sample of our new talent that's ready to hit the big time."

The two shake hands. For Gerald, it is like his dreams are already coming true. He knows of Al's work, and he loves all his old albums. For Al, it will be a challenge to again get someone with raw talent to be noticed—a challenge that he will have to put his heart into, or it will never work.

"So I hear you are a good singer," Al says.

Actually he hasn't heard anything about Gerald. But if Ron was taking the time to represent him, then he must have some talent.

"Yeah . . . well, I mean, I think so." Feeling rather nervous, he pauses and holds up a tape. "I recorded some of my work, if you would like to hear it."

"Sure, put it on."

Al sits on the couch as the music begins. It is obvious that Gerald recorded it at his home and not in a recording studio; the sound quality is seriously lacking. Al is quiet as he listens to it. Just as he thought, raw talent that will need some fine-tuning, but it is definitely workable. As the third song plays, he can't help but tap his fingers to the beat. Gerald carries a tune well, and his voice is soft as velvet.

"All right," Al says with a smile. "I'll take you on. I think we can get you somewhere with this.

Gerald is so happy that he can barely stop himself from jumping up and down. The four of them hang out and talk for a while. Al takes a liking to Gerald; he is reminded of himself when he was younger—so ambitious, and so filled with life and dreams. He knows firsthand that it's like a thirst deep inside that no one else can quench; you have to quench it yourself. Al only hopes that he can really do something for Gerald, but he also knows that they don't even have a recording studio yet.

CHAPTER 19

Two days later, Al is driving down Paradise Boulevard towards the Hilton. It is the largest hotel in Las Vegas at that time, with over three thousand rooms. The massive, three-tiered, white building sits by itself, as if it has its own section of the city. Then again, it's as big as a small city.

The boulevard is thick with rush-hour traffic, as everyone tries to get home after a long day's work. Al stares at the massive building from a block away, and smiles at the beautiful landscaping that surrounds it. Majestic palm trees and well-manicured bushes line its edges. All around the hotel the lush green grass is bordered with fresh flowers. It's enough to make anyone forget they live in a desert. It reminds Al of California.

"It's winter, and they still have flowers," he says with a grin, enjoying the fact that he still isn't wearing a jacket.

He keeps his promise to Ron and Daryl, and pursues a meeting with Bill Cosby. It takes him a while, but through perseverance, he prevails. After making many phone calls from the little black book of numbers that he always carries, and cashing in on favors that people owe him, he finagles his way into a talk with Bill's manager, and he is able to set up a meeting with Bill in his dressing room. It will be a short one, but a meeting nonetheless.

Al is embarrassed about his old, beat-up car, so he doesn't use the valet; instead, he drives around to the parking garage and parks. As always, he is neatly dressed, in black slacks and a white, button-up shirt—simple, good-looking, and efficient. He glances at his watch and realizes he is early, but that's the way he likes it, no rush.

He takes his time strolling along the cement structure with his briefcase in his hand. He glances between the parked cars and cement columns, and watches the sun go down behind the mountains. *It's beautiful, Lord,* he thinks to himself. *Thank you for allowing me to witness this.* Since the time that he almost died in California, he has always tried to take time to smell the roses, so to speak, and to give thanks for them.

A few minutes later, he is in the back part of the hotel. He walks down the long, wide corridors that are hidden from the customers' eyes. This part of the hotel is for employees and business issues only. Workers in a long, continuous line pass by, coming and going. Housemen pushing large plastic carts of soiled linen make their way down, as do other room-service attendants, bringing food up to their guests.

As he continues on, the decorations fade to just plain-white, cinder-block walls, and a light-brown, tiled floor. A string of fluorescent lights hangs overhead, lighting the way. He turns a corner into a smaller hallway, and bumps into a security podium.

"Can I help you?" an extremely overweight guard in his mid-sixties asks.

Al looks past the guard. He knows that Bill's dressing room must be down the hall.

"Yes, my name is Al Cleveland, and I have an appointment with Bill Cosby."

The man sighs, as if he is overwhelmed with work. He takes his time flipping through several pages on a legal pad, taking momentary breaks every time someone talks on the two-way radio, as if an important, life-or-death call could be coming in at any moment.

"I don't see your name," he says, authority in his voice.

I bet I could make it to his door before you could get your fat butt out of the chair that you are glued to. "There must be some mistake; I spoke to his manager yesterday."

The guard shrugs to show he doesn't care. "I guess they really didn't want you to come."

Once again Al looks past the guard. Frustration begins to set in. Then his eyes light up suddenly—this is his lucky day, he thinks as he spots Bill Cosby walking in his direction, engrossed in a conversation with three other men.

"Mister Cosby," Al blurts out.

"Yeah, how you doing?" Bill says with a quick glance as he keeps on walking.

"I'm Al Cleveland. I am supposed to meet you in twenty minutes."

Bill stops and gives Al another look. He points at him, and begins to shake his index finger as he thinks. Then he snaps his fingers.

"OK, I remember . . . the songwriter from Motown Records. You had a hand in the 'What's Going On' album."

Al's chest sticks out with pride. "Yes, sir, that's my baby."

Bill motions with his hand back down the hall past the guard. "My dressing room is right down there. If you could, just wait for me; I'll be back in five," he says, holding up five fingers. Then he and the other three men resume their conversation as they walk away. Al turns and looks at the guard, who is obviously upset about this.

"You need to sign in and get a visitor's badge. And I need to see some ID."

Although this would be a prime time to rub things in, Al doesn't; it's not his style. He feels he has enough to worry about right now without picking on someone who is just trying to do his job. So he pulls out his out-of-state driver's license, and places it on the podium.

A few minutes later, Al walks into Bill Cosby's dressing room. Although larger than most, it is still a small room. The decorations are simple, with a few paintings of mountains and other scenery. One of them seems to be of a series of mountains to the west—Red Rock Canyon, Al decides after a closer look. The furniture and the walls are done in safe, neutral colors that would please the majority of people who would come inside.

He feels rather uncomfortable about being there without Bill, so he remains standing, his hands behind his back. He stays close to the open door, still looking at the pictures on the wall. Within minutes, Bill arrives.

"Hey, hey, sorry to keep you waiting," he says.

"No problem, I'm early anyway."

Bill motions with his hand for Al to take a seat on the small, black-leather couch. As he does this, the well-known star pours himself a glass of water.

"Do you want anything to drink?" Bill asks.

"No, thank you, I'm fine," Al replies, sitting down halfway on the cushion. He wants to look comfortable, but he also doesn't want to appear overly eager. He casually looks at the end table; there is a picture of a young black man in football gear. Instantly he notices a resemblance between the young man and Bill.

"Is this your son?"

"Huh?" Bill turns around and looks at the picture; a proud smile comes to his face. "Yeah, that's my boy. I am so proud of him. Your kids are your life," he says, holding his glass up in a half salute. "Do you have any?"

"Yes, I have two boys myself. I'm real proud of both of them."

Bill finishes the first glass of water, and quickly gets another. Al casually glances at his watch; he knows this is going to be a short meeting, and he needs to get the ball rolling.

"I really like your music," Bill states, as he pulls up a wooden chair and sits down in front of Al. A small coffee table is all that separates the two of them. "Man, that 'What's Going On' album packs a punch. So much feeling in those words you put in there."

Al smiles and nods; it's all he can do. The thought of the album and all the work he had put into it causes his stomach to knot up. His palms become sweaty as he once again becomes infuriated at the thought of the IRS taking every dime that is owed to him, all because of a bad contract. *Focus, Al; stay focused.*

"Thank you, I'm flattered to hear that, Mister Cosby."

"Oh please, call me Bill," the comic says quickly.

"All right . . . Bill."

He feels privileged to be calling him by his first name. It makes him feel that a deal is that much more feasible. "It's my music that brought me here. I work for Doorway Enterprises, and we heard that you have a movie that is set for production."

Bill's head nods slightly, and he shoots Al another smile. He likes it when people do their homework, and it is obvious that Al has done his. "Yes, I do. It's based on my stage act about family life values. The producers want to call it *Bill Cosby Himself*; man, I like the sound of that."

Al laughs. "That sounds like a winner. I would like to get in on it, if you don't mind. Doorway could write an excellent title song for you."

Bill takes another drink of his water, and swishes it around in his mouth before swallowing it. "I like it." Al does his best to appear calm. He folds his hands in his lap, refraining from throwing them into the air and yelling, "Yippee!" *You're there, Al. You're on the home stretch; just stay on track.*

"I'm very glad to hear that," Al says, as nonchalantly as he can. He opens his briefcase and pulls out a contract. "I would like to sign you up so we can get started immediately."

Al turns the contract around and hands it to him. Bill is quiet as he reads it; suddenly the mood in the room changes. Al can feel it, and it makes him uncomfortable. Slowly Bill sets the contract down on the coffee table. He frowns and shakes his head.

For a moment Al is speechless; he doesn't know what to do.

Bill clears his throat. "If I sign this, it's under one condition."

"Name it," Al says, hoping to keep the deal alive.

"I am not willing to put up any money of my own. However, you can use my name to search for additional talent."

This is not what Al had in mind, but it will have to do. After all, it's this or nothing. "You got yourself a deal," he replies, forcing a smile.

Bill signs the contract, and the short meeting comes to a close. The two shake hands and Al departs, as Bill has to get ready for his show.

All the way back to his car, Al's mind races. He knows this is going to take money to do, and as always, money is something he and his partners don't have much of. Alone, he sits in his car for another half hour. He stares at the peaceful city lights, brainstorming, until a plan to finance the project comes to mind.

CHAPTER 20

"But that's your retirement money!" Daryl says in shock when his dad tells him how they are going to pay for it. "You've saved at every chance you could, and there weren't many of them."

"And it's not a whole lot of money," Al quickly interjects. He pauses, rubbing his thumb along his cold glass of ice tea. "Do you have another way for us to pay for the project?"

Daryl's eyes shoot to the floor; the answer is obvious. "I just don't want you working until the day you die."

"Help me write this song and I won't have to."

Al pauses again and lets the tension die down a little. "So are you with us or not?"

"Of course I'm with you," Daryl replies without hesitation. "I'm just worried about you."

"Well, don't be. Everything will be fine, you'll see."

* * *

That night, Al, Ron, Daryl, and Gerald get together and begin writing the title song. They decide to make it a humorous song, so they take Bill Withers' song, "Just the Two of Us," and create their very own, "Just the Slew of Us." After the laughter stops, they practice the lyrics until everyone is right on cue. All agree that it will make a very fitting theme song.

"We need a recording studio," Ron says reluctantly, not wanting to dampen the good mood.

The atmosphere in the room changes; the excitement is put on hiatus. They all sit and think about it for a moment. A good recording studio cost hundreds of dollars an hour to rent, or $10,000 to build. Either way seems out of reach for them.

"I know," Gerald suddenly blurts out. "I have a friend who records in his garage."

"Is it Vinnie?" Ron asks. Gerald smiles and nods. "Yeah, his garage is occupied by Metro Police; he was busted in that last drug raid. Where were you?"

"Obviously not with him."

As they laugh and continue to joke around, Al stands and walks into his bedroom. When work is on his mind, he has a hard time goofing off. Going over to his chest of drawers, he opens his little black book and begins thumbing through the pages.

"Hello, old friend," he says with a smile.

Al looks at a familiar name, which causes a flood of memories. He grabs the phone and begins dialing. The phone rings several times. Nervously, he taps his fingers on the top of his dresser. *Two more rings and I hang up,* he decides. One ring passes; he places his finger on the button to hang it up. The second ring starts.

"Hello?" The man who answers sounds like he has had to run a marathon to get to the phone.

"Eugene?"

"Yeah."

Al has a huge smile on his face. He hasn't talked to his friend in years, not since they both worked at Motown Records together. "Eugene Terrance?"

"That's me. Who's this?"

"This is Al Cleveland."

Al pictures Eugene's mouth falling open; he sounds like he can't believe it. "Oh man, big Al, live and in charge. What's up with you?"

Al sits on the bed. "Same old thing. I'm living in Las Vegas now, and I'm still counting all the money that Motown owes me."

"Ain't that the truth. How's the kids and Lorraine?"

A river of memories comes rushing into Al's head. He clearly remembers introducing the two of them at some forgotten party. It was one of the songwriters' birthdays, and everyone was celebrating and having a great time. That one day life felt so good.

"The kids are fine, but Lorraine and I split up a couple of years ago. Things just didn't work out. Somewhere along the line, pressure built up and exploded, and we both just stopped caring."

Al's voice is still rather upbeat. Not wanting to stir up any old emotions, Eugene offers his condolences, and leaves it at that.

"Why do I get the feeling you called for far more than to just chew the fat?" he says to Al.

"Because you know me too well," Al replies with a chuckle. "I need to ask a big favor of you. I have a potential high flyer, and I need a place to record some music. It's only a couple of songs—in and out, that's it."

Eugene's eyebrows cross; he's not quite sure he understands. "So, what did you have in mind?"

"You know what I have in mind, Eugene."

Then it dawns on him. Al wants him to sneak them into Motown's recording studio after hours. Eugene's heartbeat picks up a little. Some of it is fear; the rest is excitement for the thrill of the chase. He considers it in his mind briefly, then he pictures his life without a job.

"Al, listen, I don't know about that. I mean . . . that could be my job."

"You hate your job," Al quickly states. "And it's the same job I got you years ago, and where are you now . . . in the same spot. Has the old man given you a pay raise at all?"

Eugene doesn't answer; he is quiet for a moment.

A bad feeling comes over Al. He closes his eyes and takes a deep breath. He knows he is asking a lot, too much. Al and Eugene used to be the "best of buds" at work, but that was a long time ago.

Al speaks up again, breaking the silence. "You know, you're right. Never mind, buddy; I can't expect you to do all that for me. I'm asking way too much."

"No, no, hang on, let me think."

Al's brow raises in disbelief.

Eugene continues, "The old man usually leaves every day about five in the evening. After all, things have been kind of slow lately. If you come over here, I could get you in the back entrance and up to the studio. It's just for a couple hours, right?"

Al is so happy he stumbles over his words. "Sure, yeah . . . if you want. That's great. I'll call you when I get to Cal."

"Sure, sounds great. I look forward to seeing you again. I'll talk to you later," Eugene says, and hangs up.

Al comes trotting out of the bedroom, his arms held up high in victory. "We have a recording studio!" he says in a booming voice.

The other three men are shocked.

"How did you do that so fast?" Daryl asks.

"Where?" Ron cuts in before Al can answer.

"California," he says with a smile, thinking about the warm beaches. "We can leave tomorrow to go and record our new song."

Daryl and Gerald give each other a high five. Ron, on the other hand, looks at his old friend in a peculiar way. He feels that something isn't quite right about this. Then his eyes open wide.

"What studio?" Ron asks.

Al sticks his hands into his pockets, and rocks back and forth on his feet. He has a devilish grin; he loves the thought of sneaking into Motown and doing secret recordings under Berry's nose. *It will be a small piece of revenge*, he thinks.

"Motown," he says softly.

"What?" Daryl asks loudly. "How can we go back to them? Haven't you learned your lesson yet? They've ripped us off so many times in the past."

"Only one thing ripped us off, son, and that was unfair contracts, and Motown isn't going to know what we are doing. By the time we get there and are let in, the old man will already be home in his large mansion, none the wiser."

Gerald's voice shoots up in pitch. "We're going to break in?"

"No," Al quickly states, as if that would be totally out of the question. He addresses them as if he is selling something. "We're not breaking in. We're going to be let in by a Motown employee. We're not pilfering anything. We're just going to borrow a little studio for a couple of hours, that's all. We're not going to do anything illegal, because the last thing I want to do is stand in front of another judge."

"Then what are we going to do after we record the song?" Gerald asks.

"We shop for another promoter," Ron says with a smile, as the idea begins to grow on him. "This could easily work."

"Sure could," Al says. He turns around and walks back to his bedroom. "I'm going to start packing so we can leave first thing in the morning."

"I'm joining you," Daryl blurts out, as he darts off to his room.

* * *

The next morning the city of Los Angeles is covered in a thick blanket of gray and white smog. Mountains that can be seen on a clear day now stand as hidden giants, blocked from everyone's view. Cars and trucks are bumper to bumper in a seemingly endless line as they crawl along the concrete highway. The sound of car horns and the sight of people waving their fists cause Al and Daryl to face straight ahead.

"Let's hear it for Vegas," Daryl mumbles.

Al chuckles and grips the steering wheel with both hands, wishing they were going faster.

"I guess that desert city does have something to be desired. After all this is over with, we're going to buy a nice house in the middle of nowhere and retire. Sound good?"

"Sounds real good."

They check in at a small, inexpensive motel just one block from the Motown building. It only has one story and twenty-five rooms, which are in a straight line. The old building has yellow and white paint that is chipping off. The half-lit sign next to the street flashes "Vacancy."

The room they get is small, and the decor dates from fifteen years before. Nonetheless, it is clean and it has a kitchenette, so they can save money by cooking some of their own meals. The two stay inside their room with the drapes closed, occasionally peeking outside when they hear another car pull up. It's like they are working undercover or something.

As the hours pass, they both begin to feel uncomfortable about sneaking into Motown. They know that Berry, like any wealthy man in any town, has a lot of power, and can make things happen. Neither says a word, but if one of them suggests not doing it, the other would follow.

As Al watches TV, Daryl peeks out of the heavy, yellow curtain again. He glances at his wristwatch.

"Dad, what time are we supposed to meet Eugene?"

"Six thirty sharp. Hopefully we can wrap it all up in a few hours."

Daryl clenches his fists. He is beginning to hate the thought of going into that building. "Are we going to have enough help?"

"That's what Eugene said, so relax, son. We'll be all right."

* * *

Al tries to relax as well, and to keep his mind free. He knows that he needs to save all his energy for tonight; he doesn't want to waste any of it now. Daryl is more nervous about it. Doing anything with Motown causes his stomach to churn. He prays that for once things will work out for them, for once they can have an easier life.

The phone rings loudly, causing both of them to jump. Al grabs the old, tan, rotary phone.

"Hello?"

"Hey Al, it's me, Eugene," his friend says softly, trying not to draw any attention.

"You still at work?"

"Yeah. Everything is going according to plan. I called all the musicians that you requested, and just like you stated, they are all willing to help. You're a lucky guy to have that many friends."

"Not only lucky, but blessed too. So, everyone is set for six thirty?"

"Yeah," Eugene says, even softer. Al can hear someone else close by. Eugene begin to panic. "I have to go, talk to you later."

Al hangs up the phone and feels his heart beating wildly with excitement, causing his fingers and legs to tingle. His whole mood changes in a split second; now he is anxious to get in there and do the project. Daryl looks at him and smiles.

"I can tell by the expression on your face that everything is going smoothly."

"You know it. What do you say we eat some dinner before we go there? I can concentrate on work better if my stomach isn't growling."

Confident that things will go as planned, they go out to eat at a diner down the street. The place is very old; it was built in the forties. The location is ideal, because it's close to the Motown building, so it will give them plenty of time to eat and relax before meeting Eugene.

The diner is small, with a tempting aroma of fried foods. In the background the humming machines are making the best milkshakes on earth—according to Al, that is. The furniture is simple, but fitting. The booths are dark blue; the tables are white with little gold flecks . There are several matching chairs and tables in the middle of the room. The aged walls are covered with old, black-and-white photos of forgotten movie stars and performers. Each one is framed and autographed. At one time, the tiny restaurant was a hot spot, a place to be seen. Although it has become more of a fast-food place, the cuisine is still very good.

In fact, all the food is delicious, and Al knows that; he has been here countless times in his Motown days. He and his buddies used to frequent the place; they came here almost daily. He remembers having many good times at this place on their lunch breaks. But mostly he remembers eating greasy foods without any worries or concerns.

There are only a couple of other people in the diner, so the two men take a booth near the back. Since his attack, he has had ongoing issues, and he likes to keep an eye on the entrance. A waitress comes bouncing across the off-white tile floor and up to their table. She smiles, greets the men, and hands them two menus. Before they can say a word, she is off again, getting them two glasses of water.

Al almost drools as he looks over the menu. There are a dozen types of pizzas and fifteen kinds of hamburgers, with just as many kinds of french fries. He stares at the pictures of the pound-and-a-half double bacon cheeseburger, and he can almost taste it. The waitress comes bouncing over again.

"Did you two guys decide what you want?" Her voice matches her bounciness perfectly.

Al puts down the menu and closes his eyes; he is about to do something extremely difficult. He has to stop and take a deep breath. "I'll have a glass of water and a dinner salad, please—oh, with oil-and-vinegar dressing," he says, regretting every word of it. That cheeseburger sounded so much better.

Daryl smiles at his dad; he knows he is dying for a burger and fries, but it wouldn't be good for his heart.

"Same thing for me," Daryl explains, making his meal less tempting to his dad.

The waitress jots it down, and is gone in a flash. Al looks at his son and shakes his head.

"You didn't have to do that, you know."

"I wouldn't if I didn't love you, but I do. So let's eat our salads and go kick some butt in the recording studio."

Al's entire body seems to light up as Daryl says that. He loves his son dearly, and he can see himself in Daryl—the energy, the drive to succeed. *Please, God, let this work out for us. I don't want him to struggle like I have for so many years.*

An hour later they are standing outside the Motown building. The sun has just set as they walk out of their hiding places to the back entrance. They both keep a watchful eye over their shoulders as they come closer to the single glass door. As they approach it, the door opens.

"Hey, guys, come on in," Eugene says, with a quick motion of his hand.

Once inside, he embraces Al and Daryl. Eugene is a six-foot-tall, thin black man. He is always polite, and willing to do whatever he can to help someone. He is also the type that feels just as comfortable in a suit as he does in blue jeans and a T-shirt. So no one ever knows what he is going to wear to work. It just so happens that today is a blue-jeans day.

"Man, it's good to see you guys. It's been long, too long."

"Yes it has," Al says.

Although it is great to see his friend again, he wants to get in, get to work, and get out. They are barely two feet into the building, and he already feels uncomfortable, as if Berry's prying eyes can see every move they make. It is like returning to a POW camp, Al thinks. It gives him the creeps to be back inside.

"Did everyone show up?" he asks, trying to stay focused.

Eugene smiles deviously, and nods. "For you? Come on, you know they did. Man, there are so many people upstairs that it's like a party or a funeral or something."

That many people made Al nervous. The more people that knows about it, the greater the chance that Berry will find out. Al rubs the back of his neck as they walk down the long, narrow hallway, in an attempt to release some of the tension.

"How many people did you tell?" Daryl asks.

Eugene, playful as he is, taps Daryl in the stomach. "Enough to get the job done. But don't worry, just the ones we can trust. I guarantee that."

Moments later, the elevator opens and the men come strolling out onto the fourteenth floor. Without saying a word, they continue down to the recording studio, just a few doors down. Eugene opens the double doors. It's just like he stated; it looks like a party or something.

Al and Daryl spend several minutes hugging and greeting everyone. All of them are like a close-knit family that have stuck together though the good times and the bad, and when they were together, there were more good times than anything else.

"I want to thank you all for showing up," Al says to everyone.

"Can't believe you're working for Bill Cosby," someone says from the back.

"If we do this right, he'll be working for me," Al replies with a twinkle in his eye. "Time is short, my friends, so if we can get in our places, we can get this over with, and go home. And believe me, each and every one of you will get credit for helping us."

They are all handed sheets of music, and begin playing the songs. The first five times through it are rehearsals, as instruments are added or taken out. This has to be done, as it is the first time they actually hear the song out loud.

Two hours pass by in the blink of an eye. Eugene walks close to Al, looks at his wristwatch, and then taps it with his index finger. There is a look of concern on his face. Al knows he is running out of time; another group is coming in to record their album, and he must make sure that they are long gone by the time that group shows up.

Everyone is about to start the song again when Al raises his hands and stops them.

"Unfortunately, our time is up." He hates saying that. He desperately wants it done on the first try, because it is too risky to try again. But out of respect for Eugene, he will wave the white flag and give up. "We need to clear this place out before we are discovered."

"Then we'll come back tomorrow," one of the singers says.

"I don't know about that," Al says softly. He looks at Eugene; his friend just shrugs his shoulders.

"Same bat-time, same bat-station," he says.

Everyone agrees, and they all quickly leave, making sure first that it looks like no one has been in the studio for quite a while. Everyone else walks out the front door, pretending that they were just working late. Al and Daryl sneak out the back like a couple of wanted men, and return to their motel room.

There they go over the songs several more times. Hearing them out loud, they are able to determine exactly where the fine-tuning needs to be.

* * *

The next evening they are at it again, playing and singing—the things they like to do best.

Al and Daryl record the first two songs without a glitch, but the song "Just the Slew of Us" is giving them problems. It doesn't matter how many times they go through it, something is missing. Before they can finish, their time runs out again. Al is beginning to feel guilty about this, so he goes to Eugene, who is behind the mixing board.

"I'm really sorry this is taking so long," Al says.

Eugene just nods, and keeps his eyes on the control board. He is becoming worried about losing his job. He feels that he is in too deep. He thought this would be over the first night; here it is the second, and they still are not done. Everyone knows that they can't keep doing this night after night without someone finding out.

"One more night," Al says in a pleading voice. "If it doesn't work out, then we are done, and I will know we did our best."

Eugene forces a smile as he glances at his wedding ring. He begins to think about how he will tell his wife that he was fired. Meanwhile, everyone puts everything back in its place and leaves.

The third day, they all show up and try again. This time everyone's heart is into it; they are ready to give it their all. On the very first take, the title song is recorded perfectly. Everyone breaks out in cheers, and Al feels like a ton of bricks has been lifted off of him.

"And on the third day, He rose again," Al says aloud, with more joy than he has felt in a long time. He can tell that everyone wants to go home, or at least get out of the building. "I want to thank all of you from the bottom of my heart. I'll keep in touch with Eugene to tell him how things are going, and we'll all get together after the movie is released."

It is a tradition to throw a party for the performers. But neither Al nor Daryl has that kind of money. So with the recording in hand and a lot of good-byes, they head back to the motel to begin the next stage—finding a promoter.

CHAPTER 21

After the session father and son can hardly sleep; they keep dreaming about making their songs work, and hitting the big time. Al climbs out of bed first thing in the morning, and gets into the shower. He is excited about the entire project, and is eager to find a promoter. He hopes that record companies will jump through hoops to get a chance at this. After all, it is easy money; the hard work is already done.

As soon as he is out of the shower, Daryl goes in. After eating breakfast, the two-man team is ready for action.

"Where do you want to go first?" Daryl asks, as he washes their two plastic bowls in the old yellow sink.

Al adjusts his tie in the mirror, and makes sure his hair is perfect. "I was thinking we could head over to 20th Century Records and see Jose. That is one of the bigger ones around here."

They both know that Motown is the biggest of them all right now. But they want to keep that one off of their agenda. The very thought of working with that company turns their stomachs. A fresh company to do the work, Al feels.

A short while later, they make the drive across town to 20th Century Records. It's a modest, four-story building, with silver reflecting windows. They park right out front, and discuss what they want to do before going in.

Then they walk into the front lobby. The receptionist is a new employee—some young bubble girl with curly blonde hair. Her parents were probably kids when Al wrote "I Second That Emotion," so she doesn't recognize either of them. They are ignored as they stand at the front desk. Al becomes inpatient, and clears his throat.

"Can I help you?" the receptionist asks, with a phony smile that lasts only two seconds.

"Yes, we would like to see Jose Wilson, please," Al says.

The young woman seems rather surprised. She adopts a snooty attitude. "Do you have an appointment to see Mister Wilson?"

Al smiles, wishing that she knew who he was, but he isn't going to jump up and down and tell her that he is someone who writes blockbuster albums.

"No, we don't. If you could just tell him that Al and Daryl Cleveland are out here, I am sure he'll understand."

Al barely finishes his sentence when she comes back with, "I'm sorry, sir, but he doesn't see anyone without an appointment."

"Could you please just call and tell him that we are here?"

She just gives him a blank look, so Al decides to try another approach.

"Look, why don't you just tell his secretary—" Her name is on the tip of his tongue, but he can't get it out.

"Linda," Daryl adds in."

"Yes, tell *Linda* that we are here, and if she doesn't know us, we'll leave."

Al leans on the counter confidently. While the young receptionist grabs the phone, his nervous eyes look towards Daryl; they both hope that Linda will remember them. The curly-haired blonde pushes a button on the intercom.

"Linda? There are two men out here to see Mister Wilson. They say that you know them; their names are Daryl and Al Cleveland."

There is silence for just a split second, but it feels like an eternity. "Just a minute; I'm on my way out," Linda replies, then shuts off the intercom.

Al turns and looks out the window. He doesn't want to gloat in front of the young girl, but he can't help but have a smile as big as Texas. The dark-paneled, wooden door opens, and Linda comes out.

"Well, look who it is," she says with a smile. "Jose and I were just talking about you two the other day."

Al shakes her hand with a tender touch. Linda is fifteen years his junior, a very pretty brunette with a shapely figure. He looks her over quickly. She is wearing a classy, navy-blue skirt-suit with a white blouse underneath it. Most of her long hair is pulled up, with just enough left down to tease the eyes.

"I hope it wasn't too bad," he replies in a rather flirtatious voice.

"Of course not." She blushes and slowly pulls her hand back.

Linda is the type of woman who blushes easily, and Al always takes advantage of that. She knows his intentions are strictly honorable. Spinning on her heels, she turns and begins to leads them into the offices.

"So what brings you two into town?"

"We have a new project, and we thought Jose should be the first one to hear it," Al explains. "So has he been busy?"

"Booked solid," she says, opening the glass door to their office. "I can't believe how much business he has received in the last few months."

Al doesn't let his shoulders slump, even though what he really wanted to hear was how slow it was, and that Jose was looking for something great to exploit. Nonetheless, he presses forward with their original mission.

"Wait here for just a moment," she says, pointing to two chairs sitting in front of her desk.

While Daryl remains on his feet, Al sits down. He is already very tired, and his legs are swollen again, causing his feet to go numb. He sits on the edge of the chair, in order to stay alert and focused.

Across the front office is another large, dark wood door. On it are golden letters that spell "Jose Wilson." Linda knocks on the door twice and peeks in. Without saying a word, she walks in and closes the door. She is only gone a moment before she returns. Al immediately stands.

"Mister Wilson will see you now," she states.

The two men walk into the spacious office. Jose is sitting behind his desk, talking on the phone. He holds up his index finger and mouths "one minute" to them.

Jose is a kind man who worked with Ron Jolley for years. He was well known in town for fair deals and good treatment of his employees. He is five foot six, but his heart is a lot bigger than most, and he has never had a problem lending a helping hand to those who needed it. That is something that Al has always admired about him.

He hangs up the phone, and rises to his feet. "Well, look who it is," he says, with a big smile. He walks around his desk to shake both their hands. "I haven't seen you since Doorway was launched."

"It's launched again," Al responds.

Jose motions his hands towards two chairs in front of his desk, so Al and Daryl both take a seat. The office is not as extravagant as Berry's, and is done in lighter-colored woods. But inside, it feels more peaceful and homey, Al decides as he glances around.

"We're stationed in Las Vegas," Al continues, "and things seem to be looking mighty good right now."

Jose sits down in his large, high-back chair, and makes sure he is comfortable before speaking.

"Really, how so?"

"Well, we signed up with Bill Cosby to do the title track for his new movie that's due to come out real soon. We recorded the title song and now all we need is a promoter."

Jose's eyebrows cross for a brief second; something isn't quite right. "Well . . . if you signed on with Bill, why isn't he paying to promote it?"

"He wants no out-of-pocket expense."

"Oh man," Jose says, in a higher-pitched voice. He changes his voice to make it sound more like a gangster. "You know the man has all the money; I mean, come on."

"I know. That's why we came to you, hoping that you would listen to the songs and be willing to help."

Jose is silent for a long two seconds before he frowns and nods. "Sure, why not, put it on. The stereo is right on the bookshelf."

Daryl stands, and takes the recording over. Everyone is silent as it begins to play. Jose seems to like the music, and even laughs at the song "Just the Slew of Us." When the songs are finished, he doesn't ask to play them again. Daryl and Al pick up on that immediately, and hope it means Jose only needed to hear it once.

"Well, as always, you two have a work of art here," Jose says.

Al's body is ready to leap into gear. He feels a deal is coming, and he is more than ready to sign with 20th Century Records so they can head back to Las Vegas tonight. But then Jose becomes quiet, and rubs his chin. "I can do it, but I need you to come up with at least three quarters of the money."

This news is devastating. It is lucky that Al is already sitting down, or else he would have fallen down. His jaw drops as he thinks about how much money that would be. He shifts his eyes to the carpet, in an effort to come up with an alternative way to do this.

"We don't have that kind of money," Daryl explains. "If we did, we could basically promote it ourselves."

Jose holds out his empty hands to them. "I wish I could help you. But I already have fifteen projects that came to me without a dime. I am seriously over my budget right now, and if things don't start happening, I'll be in the poorhouse. Have you tried Motown?"

He doesn't like asking that, not one bit. The last thing he wants is to send them to a competitor, especially a major one. Jose is unaware of the past problems Al has had with Motown.

Instantly Daryl becomes upset. "Motown? Are you crazy? They—"

"Daryl," Al says, holding his hand up for his son to quiet down.

Even though Daryl is a grown man, he still has nothing but respect for his father. He wants to say more, a lot more, but instead he turns around, and quietly takes his music out of the stereo system.

"I am disappointed that we can't do business together," Al says in his soft voice.

Jose nods. "Believe me, Al, nothing would make me happier, but right now I can't, not for at least six more months."

"Six months," Daryl says under his breath, and shakes his head. "The movie will be on TV by then."

As Daryl waits by the door, Al and Jose stand again and shake hands. Al hands him the phone number to the motel where they are staying, just in case things change.

"Thanks for letting us in," Al says with a smile, and a glimmer of hope that the deal will still happen. "Let me know how things work out."

"I will, Al, and don't be afraid to call me here."

Outside, Daryl leans on the car, with his arms folded tightly across his chest, and his mouth even tighter. He is so upset that he can't even look at his dad as he comes out. Instead, he keeps his eyes glued to the sidewalk.

"Relax, son," Al says, opening his door. "Sometimes things happen like this. You have to pick up the pieces and start again."

Daryl is quiet as they drive to the next record company. He perks back up, only to be let down again. It is for a different reason this time, but they are still turned down, and it hurts just as much. Then the next person uses basically the same excuse that 20th Century did. They try again and again, only to be let down each and every time. Al passes out their phone number to more people than he can count. And the companies whose services they are soliciting keep getting smaller and smaller, not at all what they want.

Both men struggle to keep their hopes up. But the picture of success that they painted is slowly becoming blurred. After trying all day, they return to their room to eat macaroni and cheese. Daryl has been quiet for hours, and Al leaves him alone to sort out his thoughts. Instead, he decides to call Ron and give him a status report.

"Hey, Ron, it's Al."

"All right, don't hold up, give me the good news," he says with a chuckle. He wants to cut straight to the chase, and hopes for something that will make him smile.

"The good news is we have the song recorded."

"That's fantastic. I need to hear something good. Gerald moved away on us; he got some singing job up in New York. Can't blame him for going; it pays decent. So right now I don't want to hear any bad news."

"Sorry to burst your bubble, Ron, but I have some; we can't find a promoter."

"Don't tell me that Jose turned you guys down?"

"Sure did, along with almost every other record company in town. I don't know what to do."

"Did you try Natalie?"

Al flashes back to the conversation he had with her. It was rather short and cold; he was upset with him for not coming to her wedding, and for not returning her calls. Al wanted to, but he just couldn't stand the thought of the heartache it would cause.

"She's with Motown right now, and didn't offer any other connections."

Ron is silent for a moment as he thinks about what his friend said. "You still staying away from Motown?"

Al closes his eyes and sighs heavily. "Do you want me in an early grave?"

"No," Ron quickly answers. "You ain't leaving me here alone." He switches the phone to the other ear, and looks at the stack of bills on the counter. "If we don't do something fast, Doorway Enterprises will be belly up in a week. Bill Cosby is almost done filming his movie. All they need is the title song, and all we need is a promoter. If we don't act soon, they will go somewhere else. Remember, he didn't put any money into this, so he don't care."

Al nods and mumbles, "Yeah, I know. I have to sleep on this. I'll talk to you later."

He hangs up the phone, with Ron's words running though his head. He knows exactly what his friend is saying. But the thought of having to deal with Motown again is making his stomach upset and his nerves twitch. Daryl doesn't have to ask how the conversation went; it is obvious. His father can barely touch his dinner. He is already concerned about the prospect of dealing with Berry again.

"I can't believe we're going back to them," Daryl mumbles, as he takes a bite of his food.

Raw and undiluted frustration that has been building up for years rushes to the surface. Al grabs his plate of macaroni, and flings it towards the small kitchenette. The glass plate shatters on the wall, and the tiny pieces fall to the floor. Daryl jumps at his totally unexpected and out-of-character move.

"What do you want me to do, son?" Al asks, with gritted teeth and fire in his eyes. "Where in the hell do you think we should go? Do you have a hidden promoter in your hip pocket that I should know about?"

Daryl shakes his head; he has never seen his father like this before. Al's voice becomes louder.

"Do you think I like dealing with that man? Well, I don't, and I certainly don't enjoy watching the IRS take every damn thing that I earned!"

Al stops and leans on the table. He is out of breath, as his chest sends shock waves of pain outward. Daryl cautiously approaches him, and places a hand on his back.

"Just relax, Dad, calm down. I'll get you one of your pills."

Daryl rushes over to the suitcases, and takes out several bottles of medication. He quickly flips through them until he finds the right one. He runs back over to his dad, and gives him a pill. Al places it under his tongue. In a matter of seconds, he calms down, and the pain fades, but the agony lives on.

"I'm sorry, son, I'm really sorry about that," he whispers, in between deep breaths.

Al is almost in tears as he stands up and hugs his son. He is ashamed about his tantrum; the last person he wants to take this out on is Daryl. Deep down, the last thing he wants to do is go back to Motown and face Berry again. But he really doesn't see any other opportunity. Within minutes his anger subsides.

"It's OK, Dad, you didn't mean it. How about tomorrow you take it easy, and I will go to Motown."

"No," Al replies, shaking his head. "I must face my fears and frustrations one on one, or they will always be there."

Al slowly sits down in the chair; that little burst of anger has taken everything out of him. Daryl begins to clean up the mess. His father wants to tell him not to clean it up, that he will get it, but he feels so drained that he can hardly move.

A few minutes later, everything is cleaned up and put away. Daryl walks back over to Al, who is half asleep in his chair; his head is heavy, and it nods back and forth. Daryl helps him stand, and walks him over to his bed. Al's steps are slow, and somewhat uncoordinated.

"I think things are getting worse," he mumbles in a slurred voice.

Daryl is scared to death, and begins to pray that his dad will live through the night. "As soon as we get that song promoted, I'm going to get you the best doctor money can buy."

Daryl pulls back the covers, and lays his dad down. Al is already sound asleep when his son takes off his shoes and places them by the foot of the bed.

"Please let him stay with me a little bit longer, Jesus. Please don't take him home yet," Daryl whispers, pulling the covers over him.

CHAPTER 22

The next morning Al wakes up while Daryl is out getting groceries, so he has the small place to himself. He rises, and opens the drapes to let in the bright sun. But instead, the sky is covered in a thick layer of gray clouds, which reflects his mood. Tiny raindrops begin to freckle the parking lot. His shoulders droop a little. He still feels sluggish, but better than last night. He looks at the digital clock on the nightstand. It is eight thirty in the morning; Berry's secretary should be in the office already.

Al's pulse rate increases quickly at the thought of talking to his old boss again.

Retrieving his black book from his suitcase, he thumbs through it until he finds Motown's number and Berry's extension. He picks up the push-button phone, and puts the receiver to his ear. The dial tone sounds very distant as he thinks about what to say, and how to express it in the quickest fashion. He wants this to be over with as quickly and as painlessly as possible.

Suddenly the dial tone is replaced by a harsh, pulsating noise telling him to dial or hang up. With the receiver still to his ear, he pushes the numbers. The phone suddenly rings loudly. Al practically dies of a heart attack as he jumps into the air. It takes him a second to realize that he has let go of the phone keys and answered the call coming in.

"Um, hello?" he asks.

It's a woman's voice; one he doesn't recognize.

"May I speak to Al Cleveland, please?"

She sounds a little stopped up, but professional. His eyebrows lift and he almost breaks into a smile. It must be one of the record companies; they probably changed their mind, and they want the songs now. *This is going to be great; it's all going to work out,* he thinks to himself. He pulls the phone away from his mouth and clears his throat, to make sure his voice sounds right.

"Yes, this is Al Cleveland."

"Hi, Mister Cleveland. I'm Susan Larouse with Motown Records. Berry Gordy would like to see you today, if that's possible."

He feels a strange fear. Unanswered questions begin to come to mind. *How does Berry already know that I am in town? Since when do big-time record companies call for appointments? Are we being watched? Or did someone just call Berry?* He knows the client makes the first move. There is no way that things could be that slow for Motown Records.

"Sure, I can see him today," he replies, completely unsure what will come of it.

"That's good, Mister Cleveland. He has an opening at nine fifteen this morning. Can you make it that early?"

He glances at the clock again and visualizes himself taking a very fast shower. "Yes, sure. I will be there."

He hangs up the phone. His eyes are as wide as silver dollars as he stares out at nothing. *Why would Berry suddenly be taking an interest in me? Does he have that many connections in this town to track people down? Maybe one of the other studios called him. Yeah, I bet that's it. It was probably Jose, just wanting to help us out. After all, he doesn't know what happened to me at Motown.* He begins to feel a little more relaxed as he reminds himself that he was going over there anyway, so this just made things a little easier.

* * *

Thirty minutes later, Al walks in through the lobby at the Motown building. The rain outside has been no more than a sprinkle, so the walk was rather enjoyable. But his mind is far from the walk; it is on business, and everything he has do to accomplish his goals. He is alone this time; Daryl is still out buying groceries. But he wishes his son were with him, if for nothing else than just to hold him back from beating Berry to a pulp. Just the thought of seeing Berry again upsets him.

The lobby is very familiar to him—large, with polished, black marble walls, and kept extremely clean. Besides the recording studio, this is the only part of the building that Al likes. He figures it is the only section that Berry hasn't changed.

He nervously clutches his briefcase as he pushes the call button for the elevator. The doors chime as they open. He hesitates before stepping in. *You're not a sellout, Al; this is business and nothing but.* As his stomach begins to dance to its own erratic tune, he gets on. He swears that he can feel the greed flowing down from the upper floors of Motown. The elevator takes off towards its destination high above.

Moments later, the bell dings again, and the stainless-steel double doors slide open. He steps off the elevator, and stares all the way down the hall. At the far end is Berry's office, with its doors wide open like a trap or a snare waiting for its next victim. He forces himself to take the next steps. The building seems so cold and void of any emotion. Sweat begins to bead up on his forehead as some of his muscles become rigid.

He walks down the long hallway, passing by people who are surprised to see him there. Most thought they would never see him again. They gawk with their mouths open as he arrives at Berry's office. The first set of doors are open, so he strolls in, trying to act as casual as possible.

"Can I help you?" the secretary asks.

Al doesn't answer at first; his mind is already on what is going to take place inside the office, and his eyes are fixed on Berry's closed door. Then he realizes that someone is speaking to him.

"Oh . . . I'm Al Cleveland," he finally replies after a several seconds. "I have an appointment at nine fifteen. You called me," he adds, recognizing the stopped-up voice.

She glances at her watch, and then at the schedule on her desk. She nods, reassuring herself, and then stands. "Wait here for just a moment. I'll tell Mister Gordy that you are here."

She knocks on Berry's door, and lets herself in. Al stands there and waits for what seems to be an eternity. He turns around; his eyes shoot down the lonely hallway. For a very brief moment he contemplates leaving.

"Mister Gordy will see you now."

Al spins back around. He didn't even hear her come back out. *Time to go face the little giant*, he thinks to himself. His mind is so preoccupied that he is unable to speak; he nods at the secretary, and smiles.

As he walks in, his knees begin to tremble. It's not from fear, but rather from anger at all the vivid memories of the past. But for now, if he wants the deal to go smoothly, he will have to bury those feelings deep down, and not let them out.

The office has changed little since Al was last in it. On the wall are platinum albums honoring Motown's greatest achievement . . . the "What's Going On" album. The sight of it makes Al's stomach turn. He knows the company is making a ton of money on it—money that hasn't come his way, and that he will most likely never see.

Berry sits in his large leather chair, with his back towards Al. He is talking on the phone while staring out the window, not bothering to acknowledge his guest. This doesn't bother Al; he has seen this kind of thing countless times. It is some type of power play, but it also gives him a few seconds to try and get his stomach to settle down, and to bury his anger, at least for the moment.

"OK, babe, *ciao*," Berry says as he spins around and hangs up the phone. "Well, if it ain't Al Cleveland. Sit down; take a load off your feet."

Al sits down in the chair across from Berry's huge desk. He notices that Berry hasn't offered to shake his hand. It is probably better that way, because he's not sure he would want to shake back. After all, this is business and not friendship; he knows the two should never be mixed.

The middle-aged black man sits there with his hands folded on top of his desk. He stares at his former employee for a brief moment. "A little birdie told me that you have some music that you're trying to get promoted. I am offended that you didn't come to me first."

Can you blame me? "There are other record companies in town."

"None like Motown," Berry quickly adds.

The men both become silent as the secretary comes in and hands each of them a cup of steaming coffee. Al's eyebrows raise as the scent of the fresh beverage enters his nose. Coffee sounds real good, and a jolt of caffeine might help his tired body. He thanks the lady, and takes a sip of the hot coffee. It's strong, just the way he likes it.

"So are we going to sit here and drink all morning, or are we going to play some music?" Berry asks, with a let's-get-this-over-with attitude.

Al nods and stands. He walks over to the stereo. Berry's mood is real hard to read. He isn't being overly friendly, or really mean either. But Al doesn't have a lot of options left, so he's just going to let it flow. *Maybe something else is bothering him. Maybe for once the IRS is after him.* Al starts his songs and stands by the stereo as all three of them play. A very unusual smile forms on Berry's face. It's almost a devious one, but once again, he likes the music.

"It's cute," Berry says after the last song plays. "You say this is for the Bill Cosby movie?"

"Yes, it's already in production, and will be released real soon. So we don't have a lot of time."

"And let me guess, he doesn't want to put up any money himself."

At the last statement, Berry's tone changed to a friendlier one. Things seem to be going smoothly, so Al feels a little more relaxed. He takes a few steps closer to the desk.

"You got it. I don't know why, but he said no money of his own."

Berry nods, and slips into deep thought. Al rewinds his tape and casually sticks it back in his pocket, so he won't forget it. Berry suddenly snaps his fingers.

"Tell you what, Al, I'm going to make some phone calls to Bill Cosby, and if what you said is on the money, you have yourself a deal. Just come back this afternoon, and I will give you an answer about the whole project."

Even from Berry that is good news; Al can't take another rejection.

"OK, that sounds great."

Berry picks up a pen and resumes his work as if Al has suddenly vanished into thin air. The tall man stands there for a moment, debating whether to say good-bye or not. It's as if the heat is abruptly turned off, and cold air replaces it. There is no sign of friendship coming from Berry, so Al turns and leaves.

"How did things go in there?" the secretary asks with a kind voice as soon as Al closes Berry's door.

Al hooks his thumbs in his pockets and nods. "They went fine. I need to make an appointment to see him again this afternoon."

"Hmm, let's see what he has going on today," she mumbles, looking over the schedule. "He has a few minutes between three and three fifteen; are you interested?"

"Of course. Put me down and I'll be here at three. *And not a minute earlier either. The last thing I want to do is spend more time here. It's so cold here it feels like I'm at the North Pole,* he thinks. Al thanks her again, and walks out. He doesn't bother to speak to any of his old friends; right now it just doesn't feel right. He feels there will be time for that later, much later, after the deal is signed, sealed, and delivered.

* * *

"So it looks like we got a promoter," Daryl says, taking a bite out of an apple.

Al nods. He still isn't too happy about the way the meeting went. There had been a cold feeling in that office, and it left him feeling uncomfortable, as if he was really alone in there. *The only one with a beating heart,* he thinks. But then again, he has a lot of resentment for Berry from years ago, and he could be misinterpreting the meeting as a result.

"I'll be glad when this thing is over with, and we can get on our feet again," Al says. "I'm going call Ron and let him know what happened."

The news couldn't have come at a better time for Ron. He is so happy to hear that everything is finally coming together. They both know that Berry is just calling Bill Cosby to make sure everything is on schedule, and that Motown will make its money by promoting the songs. Knowing Al told nothing but the truth, he knows that the deal is practically sealed. Now all they have to do is wait.

The next hours that pass are the longest of Al's life. Both of the Clevelands stay in their small room and watch TV. The clock slowly ticks the time away. But it feels like it is taking ten times longer than it's supposed to. At two o'clock, Al stirs himself up from a brief nap, and begins getting ready for the next meeting.

"Do you want me to go with you?" Daryl asks.

Al shrugs. "That's up to you, son. This meeting is only going to last ten or fifteen minutes, so we won't be gone long. If you want to come along, I'd love to have you."

Daryl decides to go, and once again the two of them walk over to the Motown building. Al carries his briefcase, just like he did that morning, with a tight grip. He keeps telling himself that things will be different this time. This time they have an outside influence, and that will keep Berry in line.

A few minutes later, they are walking down the long hallway towards Berry's office. The only noise is the lonely thuds of their dress shoes hitting the low-pile carpeting. As in the days when Al worked there, the rule of thumb was that if you could avoid the boss's floor, you did. Out of sight and out of mind was the motto.

"I'm back," Al says to the secretary upon entering the first office.

"And right on time. I'll go tell him that you are here."

She walks into his office, and is only gone a few seconds before coming back out. She seems rather happy, and Al knows that secretaries usually reflect the mood of their bosses. So if she is happy, Berry is happy, and that is good.

"Go ahead, he's waiting," she says with a smile.

Al walks into the office. Daryl follows, and closes the doors. As before, Berry is on the phone, but this time he is facing them. He smiles and motions with his hand for the two of them to sit down. Al's observation of the secretary was correct; Berry appears to be in a really great mood, as he laughs and smiles over the phone. He hangs up and the smile remains.

"Well, gentlemen, if we are going to do this, we have got to get to work immediately. I spoke with Bill, and he told me that the movie is going to premier in just one week. That's awful fast, but not too fast for Motown."

Al and Daryl's hearts are racing. They did it. They can't believe it; this is actually coming together. Berry opens a desk drawer, and retrieves a contract. He gently places it in front of Al.

"Al, only your name is on the contract. I wasn't aware that Daryl was coming with you," Berry explains in a sincere voice. "If you want, I can have another drawn up, but it won't be ready until midday tomorrow."

Daryl knows that tomorrow could mean a whole new ballgame, so he speaks up. "No, that isn't necessary. It can stand as is."

"Are you sure about that?" Al asks. He really wants his son to be in every bit of the project, just as he is.

"The man said we need to get this thing going, so let's not waste time playing around."

Al agrees with a nod, and with a very close eye, looks over the contract. He has seen enough of them to spot errors that wouldn't be in his favor. But this one is short, sweet, and to the point. It skips the pages of the legal mumbo jumbo that normally accompanies this kind of document. The contract states that Doorway Enterprises will have the first singles and album release on *Bill Cosby Himself*, for a guaranteed $100,000. If for some reason Bill decides not to release the movie, Doorway Enterprises will receive a bonus repayment for its production costs. The last part Al doesn't care for; it states that the record shall carry the Motown Records label. He doesn't bother arguing it; there is no point in it. Motown is going to do most of the work, so of course they want their name plastered all over it.

"Does everything seem in order?" Berry asks.

He never asked that before. In the past, it was always, "Hurry up and sign; we've got work to do." It feels like the fresh start Al is looking for.

"Yeah, everything looks fine, from my point of view."

Al signs the contract, feeling like things are finally going to work out for him and Doorway Enterprises. Berry watches him sign it, and then buzzes for his secretary to come in the room.

"Yes, Mister Gordy?" she asks, as she sticks her head in the door.

He holds up the contract. "Would you be so kind as to bring these down the hall and make some copies for our new clients?" She takes the contract, and quickly walks off with it. *Clients*, Al thinks to himself, *I like that. Not employee, but an independent client, someone to be bargained and reckoned with.*

Berry clears his throat and stands up. He turns and looks out the window at the city far below. In deep thought, he folds his hands behind his back, and becomes motionless.

"Al, you're no longer an employee with us, so legally I can't have you as a production manager. Do you have anyone in mind here that you would like to assign the job?"

Al smiles; he can't believe how Berry is handling this. "Ah, yes . . . I think Eugene Terrance would be great at it."

It would mean a promotion for Eugene, and Al knows that. He thinks it is a great way to repay his friend for helping him record the songs.

Berry turns around, and looks at him with a crossed brow. "He's a good man, but do you think that he can do this in such a short time?"

Al smiles and nods. "I know he can, because Daryl and I will be there to make sure it happens."

There is no way Al is going to let his baby go yet. He wants to be right there to oversee every aspect of the project, right to the very end, when it is time to go to the premier.

Berry gives a slow nod. But a frown crosses his face. "I want to remind you that neither you nor Daryl are employed here, so if you do that, it will be on your own time."

"Completely understood," Al says.

It makes perfect sense. Motown will have to spend a lot of money on the project, so cost-cutting from the very beginning is expected. The secretary comes back with two sets of copies, one for Al, and one for Daryl. Berry keeps the original, and immediately files it in a large, black filing cabinet.

"Did you bring the tape with you?" he asks, as he closes the cabinet.

Al taps his pocket. "Right here."

"Then why don't you head on downstairs and give Eugene the good news about his promotion. We need to get started right away."

Al stands. "It's a good thing that I work well under pressure."

* * *

The Cleveland team journeys down two flights of stairs, and tells Eugene all about it. He is ecstatic about the news. The first thing he does is pick up the phone and call his wife. Right after that, they begin working on the project. Hours go by without a break; the sun sets, and the rush-hour traffic dwindles to nothing. They keep busy until late into the night. They decide to call it a wrap when nobody can concentrate anymore.

Day after day they do this, until the entire album is completed. It is the soundtrack of the movie, and it contains Bill Cosby doing his skit. Doorway Enterprise's song is an integral part of the album, just as it will be for the movie. All of them agree it will do very well once it is released. The only thing that is holding them up is the print shop. They can't decide on the picture for the album cover. Al isn't sure what they exact problem is, but nonetheless, Berry said he will personally handle it, so Al isn't worried. In all, that's a minor thing that can be taken care of quickly, so nobody is overly concerned; the album is still going to come out on time.

"Are you guys going to New York for the premier?" Eugene asks.

"Oh yeah," Daryl says, giving him a high five.

Al is happy about going, but remains quieter about it. He spent the last of his money on the two round-trip plane tickets and tuxedo rentals. Obviously, money is still a big concern with him. They will be arriving in the early morning hours, and leaving the same day, after they go to the premier. Al knows it's important that they are there to see the movie; after all, his name is on it.

CHAPTER 23

"What are we going to do with the car?" Daryl asks, as he picks up their suitcases.

"The airport has long-term parking, so we'll leave it there along with our luggage. It's just for one day, so it won't be too expensive."

"After this, we won't have to worry about money," Daryl says in a playful voice, as he walks out the door.

Al follows, his eyes to the floor as his mind races with concerns. "Let's hope so. Eugene called while you were in the shower. He said all the albums have their covers, and have been shipped overnight. So everything is on schedule." *It's barely there, but there nonetheless.*

"Did you ever get to see the album cover?"

Without much thought, Al shakes his head. "No. We'll see it in New York. Our songs are on the album, and that's all that matters."

They check out of the motel, and head for the airport. Their plane isn't scheduled to leave until well past eleven at night, so they are extremely early. It's either be early or pay for another day at the motel, so they decide on being early.

Flying a "red-eye" saves them a lot of money, thus making the hours of waiting worth it. They sit and watch countless other travelers come and go. There are a lot of joyous family reunions, and just as many sad, tear-filled good-byes.

The two are traveling very light. Together they have one small garment bag. The heaviest things in there are a few apples. They are wearing black dress shoes and slacks, along with white, button-up shirts that they will also use with their tuxedos. The only clothing in the garment bag are the jackets, bow ties, and cummerbunds. Later they will have to buy a few things to freshen up, so they don't look like jet-lagged travelers.

Eventually their plane arrives, and they board it.

Al's pace has really slowed down over the past week. All those long hours of work have done him in, so he falls asleep before the plane even takes off. Daryl reads a magazine for a little while, then joins his dad in slumberland.

A few hours later the plane is rocking slightly due to some turbulence. The lights in the darkened plane flicker to life. The seatbelt sign turns on with the sound of a chime. Both the men, along with most everyone in the plane, are asleep.

"Ladies and gentlemen, this is your captain speaking. We are currently beginning our descent into New York, so would you please put on your seatbelts and place your trays in the upright position."

Daryl stirs himself to consciousness, and then nudges his dad.

"Dad, wake up. We're almost there."

"I'm awake," he moans, and starts putting his seatbelt on with his eyes closed. He misses several times, and gets frustrated. Finally he opens one eye to see, and clicks the two parts together.

Thoughts of seeing their names on the big screen slowly bring them both to life. Al glances at his watch; it reads 4:58 a.m., and that is West Coast time. *It's almost eight in the morning,* Al thinks to himself. *Just eleven more hours until showtime. This time it's going to be real—real money, and real recognition.*

"Man, we have a whole lot of time to burn," Daryl says with a smile, as he notices his dad staring at his watch. "What are we going to do until then?"

"A whole lot of nothing," his dad mumbles, wishing he could go back to sleep.

* * *

The long morning and afternoon pass by, and they do just what Al said, a whole lot of nothing. The first thing they decide to do is take a taxi to the Apollo Theater, where the premier is being held. They want to be close to it at all times, just in case time slips away from them for some reason. With hours still to go, they travel to a discount department store, and buy disposable razors and toothbrushes. The last thing they want to do is be scruffy at the premier.

With just an hour and a half to go, Al begins to feel nervous. They eat a light meal at a restaurant across the street from the theater. They purposely pick a table right next to the window, so they can see it.

Slowly the traffic begins to thicken. A long, black limousine pulls up, and someone gets out, but Al can't see who it is. He stretches his neck as far as it will go, and almost stands up at his table. He can barely see a couple walking into the theater.

"You know, we can go over there and join those folks; we have tickets," Daryl says, with a laugh at his father's odd behavior.

Al's eyes have a look to them that Daryl hasn't seen in a long time—one of excitement and energy. He picks up their only piece of luggage, the garment bag, and darts off for the bathroom. Daryl quickly gets up and follows him.

They laugh and giggle as if they are a couple schoolboys as they quickly put the finishing touches on their tuxedos, Daryl helps his father with his bow tie. It feels so good to see his father filled with life again.

"How do I look?" Al asks.

"Like a million bucks. And me?"

Al returns the favor and helps him with his bow tie. "Like two million. Let's go kick some butt."

They stroll out of the restroom with a mission-impossible feeling, and they both love it. Al has already made arrangements with the waitress to hold their garment bag until after the show.

They walk outside to find they couldn't have asked for a better evening. There is only a trace of humidity in the air, and the temperature is a cool 68 degrees. They stop and look up at the huge theater; the large marquee reads *Bill Cosby Himself* in giant red letters. Both of them can't help but smile, and bask in their own achievements. Their hard work has paid off, and now it is time to reap the reward.

The smell of automobile exhaust drifting out of the numerous tailpipes is strong as they weave in and out of the cars and limousines. The two make it to the other side of the street, and ascend the long concrete stairs in the center. Al holds onto the brass railing for assistance. The steps quickly zap the majority of his energy, but he doesn't let it show.

The air is alive, and filled with electricity. A rather large crowd
has gathered, and is roped off on the sides of the stairs. They cheer and
clap as different stars walk up the stairs.

Halfway up, cameras flash as the Clevelands' pictures are taken
repeatedly. It's hard not to raise their hands and block the bright lights
from hitting them. Al stops along the way to shake hands with a few
people that recognize him.

They make it to the top of the stairs, and a white-gloved
employee opens a ten-foot-tall glass door for them. The lobby, done in
a rich, dark red with gold trim, is filled with celebrities. It is clearly a
black-tie affair, and everyone is dressed exquisitely. With wide eyes,
Daryl looks at all the people, especially the pretty women walking
around in their formal gowns.

"I think I found home," he says with a smile.

"Down, boy, we're not on the prowl out here," Al replies in a
tired voice.

Daryl looks at his father; it's obvious that he is worn out again,
and ready to sit down. He takes hold of his elbow, and casually directs
him towards the back of the lobby. Along the way, they stop to shake
hands and gab lightly with a few other producers. Contacts are always
important, and this is no exception.

At the main part of the theater, another white-gloved employee
opens the door for them, and takes their tickets. He motions to one of
his coworkers, and the Clevelands are guided to their seats—halfway
down, dead center.

It couldn't be better, Al decides—the perfect night, a perfect
flight, and great seats. Not to mention being with the best son in the
world.

Daryl turns around and looks at the other stars that are starting
to filter in. "How did you get such good seats?"

"Just luck shining down on us," he replies with a drained but
happy look.

Even in his present condition, it feels so good for Al to be at the
premier. He feels as if he belongs here, and that this should be a regular
part of his life. He glances at his watch; showtime is just a half hour
away. It gives him just enough time to relax a little before having to
concentrate again.

As the minutes tick by, the two men sit and point out the celebrities to one another. Movement behind the large red curtain catches their attention. They both sit up as a spotlight turns on, and shines its bright beam down to the stage. The house lights begin to dim, and the audience falls silent.

The curtains open, and Bill Cosby steps out onto the stage. He has an ear-to-ear grin on his happy face, and he seems to float on cloud nine. Al can feel it too. He is so excited to be here; to experience this part of the show is something new and wonderful.

"Thank you all for coming here tonight," Bill says, with his arms open wide. "You all braved the harsh weather outside."

The audience chuckles.

"I know some of you are expecting the album to be passed out to you. Well, if you know Berry Gordy at Motown the way I know Berry Gordy, then you know he likes to steal the show. He decided to give me a few more gray hairs, and have the albums arrive at the last minute."

Ushers begin walking down the aisle, passing them out. Al and Daryl both receive one. They look at the cover; it has a full-bodied picture of Bill on a stage, wearing a green sweater. At the same time, they both flip it over to see the back, but it is too dark to read the fine print, so they just hold onto them. Bill continues.

"Now that you all have a picture of your favorite star, I shall let the movie commence."

Again the audience laughs and claps. The curtains part again, and Bill walks out of sight as the spotlight is turned off. Silence sweeps the theater as the large drapes are pulled all the way back, exposing the large, white screen.

Without any hesitation, the movie begins. Just as everyone expected, the laughter starts with the beginning line. Doorway's song, "Just the Slew of Us," opens the act, and Al's chest sticks out with pride. It feels so good for them to be here, listening to their work being sung for all to hear.

The movie goes on, and they can't help but laugh hysterically throughout the entire thing. It is truly a hit, and it is obvious that it will gross a lot of money over the long run. Al's stomach is sore and his mouth hurts from laughing so much. He is still chuckling when the movie comes to an end, and the lights come on.

As the audience begins to rise and walk away, Al and Daryl stay in their seats. Al wants to see his name on the big screen. His eyebrows rise with anticipation; the actors' and crew's names begin to show. He knows his part will be towards the end; song credits always are.

Daryl sits there and looks at the back of the album. Something catches his attention.

"Dad?"

"Not now, son," he says, with his mouth slightly open.

It's almost his turn. The corners of his mouth twitch, as they prepare to smile. Sweat forms in the palms of his large hands.

"But . . ."

"Not now, son," he says a little louder, as the song credits start to appear.

He leans forward; his eyes open a little wider. He wants to make sure he can see and read each and every word as they slowly roll up the screen. Then it shows up—his song, the one they wrote in Ron's living room. The one they recorded at Motown. The song title goes by in large white letters for everyone to see, "Just the Slew of Us."

His pulse picks up as he waits for his name as composer. But below the title, all it states is that Motown Records produced the song. That is it; the next song title appears. There is no mention of the Clevelands or Doorway Enterprises. Al's mouth gapes open in disbelief. His chest feels constricted, while confusion fills his head. It feels as if someone's hands are squeezing his neck, and he can't breath.

"They cut us out," he whispers, in the loudest voice he can muster up.

"There is nothing about us on the album," Daryl says, showing him the back of the cover. "It's like we didn't do a thing, and Motown is taking all the credit."

Al bends over and rubs the bridge of his nose, hoping to ease the massive headache that is already forming. He slowly looks at the back of his album cover. Everything Daryl said is true. There is no mention of them anywhere. Even Doorway Enterprises has been cut out of the deal.

"Why does that little bastard continuously do this to me?" he asks in an amazingly calm voice, as he buries the anger deep inside. The anger is there, but he wants to save it for Berry, and Berry only.

"I don't know, but we're sure to find out when we ask him." Daryl points to his wristwatch. "Our plane leaves here shortly."

Disgusted, they stand and march up the aisle. Now it makes perfect sense why no one from Motown is present, and why Berry insisted on handling the album cover. He didn't want anyone to see it until it was too late to do anything about it.

As soon as they make it out to the lobby, they spot Bill Cosby standing off to the side, saying good-bye to guests as they leave.

"Did you two enjoy the show?" he asks Al and Daryl, obviously happy with the turnout.

Al's anger begins to surface. "Why were we cut out of all the credits from the movie and the album? There is no mention of us anywhere, and you know I contacted you first! We—" He motions to Daryl and himself. "—did the song. We recorded it."

Bill's hands shoot up into the air. "Hey, hey. I have nothing to do with that. You need to speak directly to Motown Records."

He walks away before Al has a chance to reply, and resumes saying good-bye to the others. Al doesn't bother pursuing him. He is right; they will have to speak with Berry directly to find out what happened.

With their stomachs churning, they walk back across the street to retrieve their garment bag. All the excitement that they had has been replaced by anger and frustration. They get their belongings, and Al tips the waitress a few bucks as Daryl flags down a taxi.

The ride back to the airport is a long and quiet one. Their heads sway back and forth with each bump, as they stare straight ahead at nothing. Daryl looks at the album over and over, hoping he missed something. Al doesn't bother to look at it anymore; he knows he has been ripped off once again. He is beginning to wonder it this is his fate—to work hard, and to have everything taken away in the end.

CHAPTER 24

Back in Los Angeles, they walk across the long-term parking lot to their old car. It is a foggy morning, and the large car looks like a forgotten ghost. Their faces are still tight with anger as they open the doors, toss their garment bag in the backseat, and take off.

At the gate Al pays the bill. It is the last of his money, leaving him with just a few small coins, barely enough to buy a cup of coffee. They leave, and the large, eight-cylinder car roars down the road towards the Motown building.

The sun is just beginning to rise, so they will have several more hours to stew in their anger before Berry will be arrive at work—a lot of time to think about what they want to say, and what they are going to do.

Al flies down the freeway with a white-knuckled grip on the steering wheel. Daryl knows he is driving way too fast, but doesn't say a thing to him. It wouldn't do any good; his dad is too upset. He takes the exit, and heads straight for the Motown building.

The tires squeal as he pulls around back. Al comes to an abrupt stop in the back of the parking lot. He doesn't want to be too close, or Berry might see them and just drive away. He sits there for a second, and then gets out of the car.

"Where are you going?" Daryl asks."

"There's a pay phone over there." He points to the other end of the parking lot. "I'm going to call Ron, and tell him what happened."

Daryl figures he wants a moment alone, so he stays put as he dad slowly walks away.

Al makes it to the graffiti-covered pay phone, and picks it up. As he listens to the dial tone, he realizes that he has only sixty-five cents to his name. By no means is it enough to make a long-distance phone call. He dials the operator.

"Yes, I need to make a collect call to Las Vegas, Nevada." He gives the operator the number through gritted teeth, trying his best not to take out his frustrations on her. "It's from Al Cleveland."

He waits to hear the sound of a ringing phone, but instead the operator comes back on.

"I'm sorry, sir, but that number has been disconnected."

Al's mind goes completely blank, as he feels boiling anger surface again. "There must be some mistake." He pauses for a second. "Maybe I gave you the wrong number." He looks in his wallet, and reads off the number once again.

"That is the same number, and I am showing it was once registered to a Ron Jolley, but the phone has been disconnected. Thank you," she says, and hangs up.

Al stays by the phone. He puts his forehead against the cool metal frame, and wishes the pounding pain in his head would go away. He can already feel his heart working overtime; he pauses in an attempt to calm down. He stands there for a moment, realizing that the business must have gone bankrupt, just as Ron warned him it would. The phone begins to beep; he has it in his hand. Mindlessly, he hangs it up, and walks back to the car.

"What did Ron say?" Daryl asks, as he sits on the hood of the car.

Al shakes his head. "The phone is disconnected. We'll have to get in touch with him some other way. For now we are on our own."

He joins his son on the hood; the car sinks down with their combined weight. A few other early arrivers begin to show up. The two sit still, and watch them enter the tall building through the employee entrance. There is no sense in going in this early; the upper floors will be completely locked up.

* * *

The sun rises high into the air, and it heats up the California ground. The two men, who have had only a few catnaps in the last two days, doze off in the front seat. A dog barking wakes Daryl up. He sits up, rubs the sleep out of his eyes, and checks the time. It is nine thirty; Berry is surely in by now. They've been asleep for about three hours.

"Dad, Dad, wake up."

Al sits up like a bolt of lightning. "Is he here?"

"He should be; it's late enough."

Al looks at his watch to reassure himself of the time. He gets out of the car, and slams the door shut. Instantly, he is transformed from a sleeping giant into a raging bull. Marching steadily, he beats a path towards the tall building. Daryl follows in his footsteps, as anger drives them both to their destination.

High above the smog-covered city, the elevator doors open, and the two men immediately step off and onto Berry's floor. Both have fire in their eyes, and it is obvious, as people practically jump out of their way.

They step right into the first office. Berry's secretary shoots out of her chair. A worried look comes over her face. Her mind scrambles for something to say.

"Do you have an appointment?" she blurts out.

Neither of them bother answering her. Al grabs hold of Berry's closed doors, and flings them open. The heavy wood doors slam against the walls. Berry spins around in his chair; he is on the phone. His eyebrows cross with anger.

"Gotta go," he says, and hangs up.

The two angry men stride right up to his desk. The secretary runs back towards her desk and picks up the phone.

"Well, if it ain't the Clevelands. How was New York?" Berry asks, in a cocky tone.

Al's index finger begins to slam into the desk with each word he says. "Don't give me your crap, Berry! We have a contract, and you went completely around it! We want full compensation for what we've done."

"What *we've* done?" Berry repeats. Suddenly he stands and yells, "What *we've* done? The thieves come here, and make their demands. Where were those songs recorded? Where?"

Al doesn't answer; he can't come up with a good lie that quickly. Berry continues, his face filled with rage. "They were recorded here. Here! In *my* building, the one I own! It was done with *my* employees at the helm, and musicians that have contracts with Motown! Which, you might have forgotten, *I* own! And your little friend Eugene has been reprimanded for letting you hooligans in." He sits back down, and quickly adjusts his jacket. "I built Motown on trust and this is how you repay me?" Berry stops, and looks past them. "If you have any other questions, I suggest you address the gentlemen behind you. Good day."

Al and Daryl turn around. There are six very large security guards standing in the doorway. All of them look like bodybuilders on a steroid rage. The meeting is over before it has even started; Berry was expecting them, and had everything prepared. Al grabs Daryl's arm to get him to leave. His son resists; he wants to fight.

"Once he asks us to leave and we don't, he can have us arrested for trespassing. We can't fight this from jail. It will only make matters worse," Al whispers in his ear.

The guards begin to come in, and Daryl slowly turns around. He swears that if he had a gun, he would shoot Berry right there. The two men are escorted out of the building. As if they were a serious threat, the guards stay by the door, and watch them drive off.

Daryl stares at them and suddenly hits the dashboard.

"Just like that we give up?" he asks.

Al turns the corner, and heads down a different street. "We have contracts, son. This is a matter for the lawyers to handle. Physical confrontations are not going to solve anything."

Again his father buries his anger deep inside. It will lay there, waiting for the next chance to surface. It's something that Daryl cannot and will not do. He will always let his anger show.

Al pulls into a gas station and stops by a pay phone. He gets out, grabs the phone book, and looks up his old lawyer, Jack Ginsberg. Jack was the one who handled all the original, disastrous contract affairs. He almost smiles when he spots his name. The thought of revenge is already making him feel better. Now he can sue for his money, and maybe add pain and suffering to it. Quickly he jots down the new address, and then thinks it would be best to call him first.

He sticks his hand into his pocket for his spare change. His fingers tumble over the last few coins, and he looks at the old car. He knows it will need gas soon.

"Daryl, how much money do you have?"

His son's answer causes his knees to go weak. "Three bucks."

"Grab the garment bag and the suitcase."

"What are we doing?"

"There is a twenty-dollar deposit on each of the tuxedos; right now every penny counts." They change their clothes, and take the black tuxedos back to retrieve their deposit. Al pushes the thought of being homeless as far back into his head as he possibly can, but it is still there. He knows if things don't work out really soon, the thought will eventually turn into reality.

It is early in the afternoon as they approach Jack's offices. Anywhere else in the world, the building would be considered very modest, but in California, just a half block from the beach on West Hollywood Boulevard, the location is downright amazing.

The two men walk into the converted house. Daryl has blue jeans and a T-shirt on. Al also has blue jeans on, and a button-up shirt. Although he has some wealthy clients, Jack manages to keep things small. This is the way he likes it, and so do most of his clients. Al walks up to the receptionist, and leans on the desk. His face is swollen and sweaty.

"Are you all right, sir?" the lady asks cautiously.

"I'll make it," Al says with a deep breath. "I don't have an appointment, but could I please see Jack as soon as possible? It's an emergency."

"Well." She looks over the schedule, and wonders if Al should be seeing a doctor rather than a lawyer. "He's booked solid today, but if you hang around, maybe he can fit you in."

Al and Daryl sit down in the small waiting room. They stare at the coffee table that is covered with half a dozen old, well-read magazines. Neither bothers to move. They just sit and stare at nothing. Al feels horrible, and just wants to lie down, but he knows he can't stop yet. Jack's office door opens, and he walks out, with his hand on another man's shoulder. Jack is in his mid-forties, and has done well for himself. He has bleach-blonde hair, and just enough wrinkles to show his age. His blue eyes always twinkle with his perfect smile. He is wearing a light-blue sports coat with white slacks, comfortable while still looking professional.

The Clevelands stay in their seats as he says good-bye to his other client. He closes the door and turns to face them. Oddly, he doesn't seem to be overly surprised about them showing up unannounced.

"Al Cleveland, it's been a few years."

Al stands, and towers over Jack. "Yes, it has. You remember my son Daryl?"

"Yes, I do. Daryl, good to see you again."

He shakes their hands, and motions for them to follow him into his office. Like his suit, the office is done in blue and white. There are plenty of certificates and awards on the wall, along with a few family photos. There are also a lot of pictures from years ago of Jack participating in local surfing competitions. It looks more like a beach cottage than a lawyer's office, but Jack likes it that way. He's been a surfer all his life, and he always says, "You can take a surfer out of the ocean, but you can't take the ocean out of the surfer."

"Take a seat; tell me what's on your mind."

"It's Motown," Al moans, as he sits down in front of the desk on a white wicker chair that creaks and cracks with every movement.

"Again? Are you still having problems with them?"

"Oh, yes. Well, actually, it never stopped. We did the soundtrack for the new movie, *Bill Cosby Himself*—"

"I hear that movie is hilarious," Jack cuts in, upsetting Al, as if this were a joke.

"It is, but they ripped us off."

Jack leans back in his chair and nods, with a smug look. "I know exactly where you are coming from, Al. After all, you still owe me two hundred dollars."

The last statement catches Al off guard. Hoping to get things back on track, he retrieves the signed contract from his briefcase. He places it on Jack's desk, hoping to get him to be a little more serious.

"They owe us at least a quarter million."

Jack doesn't even look at the contract. His eyes stay on Al's sweaty face, wondering if he should call an ambulance. "Do you have the two hundred dollars that you owe me?"

Al's eyebrows cross in disbelief.

"No. Hell, no. Come on, you mean to tell me that you are not going to help me over a lousy two hundred dollars? You stand to make a lot more off of this if you handle it."

Jack folds his hand across his stomach, and shrugs. "You mean to tell me that I am supposed to forget about what you owe me?"

Al is dumbfounded. He can't believe what he is hearing. "Come on, Jack. You and I go way back. Don't you care about the little guy at all? Or is all that matters to you the big corporations, with the bank in their hip pockets?"

"I'm sorry you see it that way, but I could charge you another two hundred for this visit, Mister Cleveland. By the way, there's not a *pro bono* attorney around who would take this case. Money is the tool that gets things done in California."

Al's mouth falls open. He stares into Jack's eyes, looking for the friend he once had. "If you have a spark of decency left in you, you will help us. My son and I are stone broke, with no place to live. We're going to have to sleep in our car tonight. We need your help, man. Have a heart and please help us out."

Jack closes his eyes, and lets out a long, heavy sigh. "All right, Al. I'll look at your contract with Motown. Just to avoid a malfeasance lawsuit, which you can ill afford right now."

"Thank you so much," Daryl says.

Jack picks up the contract, and begins to look it over. "Have a good day; my secretary will show you out."

The men sit there for another second. They both want things done right now, but it will take time. Reluctantly, they stand and start to leave. The secretary greets them at the office door.

Suddenly the phone rings. Jack can see that his assistant is busy, so he answers it.

"Ginsberg law office, this is Jack speaking. Oh, hey... Yes, all is well. You have nothing to worry about. We can work it out."

Al spins around, his eyes wide open. The secretary closes the office door, and continues to show them the way out. Al walks backwards out of the office, waiting for Jack to come out and explain what has just happened, but he never does. It feels as if the room is closing in on him.

"You'd better drive, son," Al says, as he plops down on the passenger side.

Daryl looks at his dad's swollen and sweaty face. "Are you OK? Do you need one of your pills?"

"This ain't the same." He stops talking for a moment, as he struggles to breathe. "I'm hurting . . . take me to the hospital."

Daryl runs around the car and jumps in. Quickly he speeds off down the street to the nearest county hospital. Al seems barely alive as the car pulls up to the emergency-room entrance. Daryl shoves the car into park, and runs inside.

"Could someone please help me, my dad is having a heart attack!" he shouts out.

Several people come running out with a gurney. It is brought right up next to the running car. They find Al collapsed in the front seat, his motionless hand over his chest. His head hangs downward.

"Dad?" Daryl calls out. "Dad, can you hear me?"

Daryl is gently escorted out of the way. The gurney is lowered to the same level as the car, and the men groan and strain as they lift the six-foot-three-inch man out of the car, and place him on the gurney.

They raise him to waist level, and run inside. Daryl follows right behind them as they pass through the electric sliding doors, and right past the crowded waiting room. They barge their way through another set of doors, and then a nurse holds her hand up at Daryl.

"Sir, you can't go in there."

Daryl stops. His eyes stay on his father as they take him around the corner to another room.

"Sir, you might want to move your car before they tow it."

Quickly he looks at his car, and then back towards the spot where he last saw his dad.

"There is nothing more you can do. He's in good hands," she explains, walking back to her station behind the desk.

Daryl nods, and slowly turns around. He wonders if that was the last time he will get to see his dad alive. He parks the car in a space where it won't be towed, and then returns to the ER. It takes him almost an hour to fill out all the paperwork. He wracks his brain trying to give all the information he can about his father's heart condition, and the medications he is on. But he also knows that they have no money or insurance, so the care will be short and sweet.

"Are you Mister Cleveland's son?" a very tired doctor in a green smock asks.

Daryl's mouth falls open. Will the news be good or bad? "Yeah, that's me."

The doctor sits on the edge of the blue, hard-plastic chair in front of him. He doesn't want to sit all the way back for fear of falling asleep on the spot. He rubs his hands together and offers a compassionate look.

"Your dad is in stable condition. We have him in a room upstairs."

Daryl's eyebrows shoot up with happiness. "Can I see him?"

"Sure, you can," the doctor says with a tired smile. They stand and begin walking together towards the elevators. "He had a heart attack. It wasn't a massive one, but it wasn't a mild one either. What I'm trying to say is, he needs a lot of rest and relaxation. We're going to keep him overnight, and monitor him. And then—"

Daryl is surprised about the short stay. "One night. That's it?"

The doctor slowly nods, avoiding Daryl's eyes. "County's rule. There is nothing I can do about it."

"County's rules for people without money?"

Although he agrees, the doctor chooses not to reply to Daryl's comment. They stop in front of the elevator. The doctor pushes the call button, and they both stand there without talking for a moment. Then a loud voice comes over the PA system.

"Code blue in ER. Code blue in ER."

The doctor's shoulders slump as the vision of taking a fifteen-minute break slips away. "That's me. Your dad is in room 525. Good luck."

He runs off before Daryl has a chance to thank him. The doors to the elevator creak as they slowly open, with a warped-sounding chime ringing above. He rides up to the fifth floor, and walks to his father's room.

"Hey, there," Al says, in a soft, slightly sedated voice. His eyes are half shut, and he looks as if he has been up for a week straight. "You like our new place?"

Daryl takes his hand, and squeezes it. Al returns the touch, but his grip is very weak, and his hands are cold.

"Yeah, it's nice. But it's only ours for a night, and after that they are going to kick you to the curb."

Al adjusts the oxygen tube running into his nose. "I'm getting used to it. Did you see if there are any cute nurses yet?"

Daryl laughs, amazed at his father's playfulness. "No, not yet. I'll go check in a minute."

Al may be acting cool and calm, but the truth is that he is scared to death about dying. He doesn't know what to expect, and doesn't know how to handle it. In the past, he was always able to brush off his heart condition, but now it's catching up to him. It's right at his heels, and he can feel it. Worst of all, he would be leaving his son while he is down and out.

Daryl's growling stomach breaks the silence in the room. Neither one of them has eaten since they were at the restaurant in New York. Al turns and looks at him.

"My lunch should be here soon. I ordered the biggest plate they have, so we can share it."

Daryl shakes his head, and pats his father's arm. "You need your nutrition."

Al coughs, and grimaces as his chest screams again. "So do you; now don't argue."

A few minutes later, just as Al stated, lunch is brought to them. The man serving it must know they are hungry, because he brought extra, so they both could eat. They inhale the food like two half-starved wolves.

Daryl stays by his dad's side until visiting hours come to an end. The nurses come in and explain that he has to leave. He says good-bye, and heads down to the car. He sits in the driver's seat for a while, trying to think of someplace to go. Nothing comes to mind, so he climbs in the backseat to spend the night.

CHAPTER 25

The sound of a street sweeper running nearby wakes Daryl up. He is curled up in the backseat. Sweat drips off his face as the morning sun floods the closed-up car with its heat. He sits up and watches the street sweeper go by, raising a cloud of dust. It takes a few moments for his mind to unclog from the night's rest.

"We're homeless," he mumbles, as reality finally sinks in.

It's a horrible feeling, one that starts in the stomach, then envelops the mind. He stares at the traffic going by, and scratches his head. They have nowhere to go, and forever to get there. How will he feed himself and his father? How is he going to find a job, with no address? He could go back to live with his mom, but where would that leave his dad?

"If we have to, we can eat in soup kitchens," he whispers to himself.

He says it aloud for his own ears to hear—some type of reassurance that everything can still work out, if they just don't give up.

He grabs a change of clothes and his overnight bag. He glances over to the hospital entrance; things appear to be pretty slow. He climbs out of the car, and heads back into the hospital, hoping that he can at least shave and brush his teeth.

"What are you doing out of bed?" Daryl asks as he sees his dad standing by the window.

Al turns around. Although his mind is still just as sharp, his movements are extremely slow.

"They tell me that I'm OK to leave." He gives a small nervous smile. The thought of death is still on his mind, and it is scaring him.

Daryl tosses his stuff on a chair, and helps Al sit down on the edge of the bed.

"I can't believe that they're saying you're good to go."

"They have bills to pay, son. So they don't care about some old, washed-up black man. Why don't you hurry up and get in the bathroom, so you can wash and change."

Forty-five minutes later, Al is signed out of the hospital. They do a slow walk out to the car, with Al holding onto his son's arm to help steady him. Al sighs at the sight of his old car. It is nothing more than a reminder of the way things are going for them.

"Well, you're the brains in the family, so what do you think we should do?" Al asks.

Daryl opens the car door for his dad. "I was thinking we could go down and talk to Smokey. After all, he is my godfather."

Al almost smiles, and nods. It has been a long time since the two have talked to one another. "That's a good idea. It is definitely worth a try."

Daryl starts up the "green beast," as he likes to call it, and drives off. Problems aside, it is a perfect day, weather-wise. The temperature is a refreshing 73 degrees, and the blue sky only has a few small white clouds in it. If it wasn't for the fact that they are homeless, they would be able to enjoy it.

The drive to Daryl's godfather's house isn't far, but traffic slows them down to a crawl on the freeway. Al dozes on and off as they inch along the concrete slabs. Daryl keeps a close eye on him, watching for any sign of weakness or distress. His breaths change in their pattern—some long and deep, others short and choppy. It only makes Daryl worry more.

Finally, they are able to get off the highway, and head to Smokey's house. It is a modest home in a nice neighborhood. Midsized homes line the street, all of them with green grass and large trees in their front yards. It seems picture perfect, Al decides, as he watches some kids playing tag down the street, and a man pushing his lawnmower around.

They pull up and stop. Silently, they stare at the light-gray house with white trim, and wonder what is the best way to bring up their situation.

"The place hasn't changed much at all," Daryl says, as he opens his door. "Does he have the same problems with Motown as you do?"

Al stands up and stops as the blood rushes to his head, giving him a dizzy feeling. "I think so, but he never really talked about it."

They walk through the wrought-iron gate, and stroll up the narrow sidewalk. Al notices that the lawn and bushes are well taken care of. That's a good sign; it means things should be going well for Smokey and his wife.

Daryl rings the doorbell. It is only a few seconds before the door opens. Smokey's wife, Claudette, is there. Instantly, her face lights up as she sees the two of them. Her mouth falls open; she seems overtaken by joy.

"It's Al and my favorite godson! How are you two doing?"

She reaches out and gives them both a long, hard hug.

"We're doing all right," Daryl says. "Last I remember, I was your only godson."

"No time to be picky," she explains. "Come in, come in. I'll tell Smokey that you're here."

Claudette is the type of person who always stays in a good mood. She has a heart of gold that outweighs her five-foot-two frame. Her hair has wide curls and is streaked with gray; her eyes seem to always be looking towards heaven, and there's a constant smile on her face.

The two men walk into the living room. The aroma of fresh baked goods fills the room, causing their stomachs to growl. Just as Daryl noted outside, nothing much has changed. The house is decorated with a style that suits Claudette's personality—bright and cheery, with lots of flowers and plants. The midsized house feels cozy and clean.

Al, tired from the short stroll up the sidewalk, sits down on the couch to relax. He sinks into the soft cushions, thinking he could fall asleep in a few seconds.

Smokey walks out, wearing a navy-blue, nylon sweat suit. Patches of unfamiliar gray hairs dot his head, along with wrinkles brought on by Father Time. Daryl tries to remember the last time he saw him; it was years ago.

"My oh my, look who dropped in," he says, with a warm but rather cautious smile. "What brings you two all the way over here?"

They give each other a very brief hug, and sit down around the coffee table. Claudette comes out with a tray that has four cups of steaming coffee on it, and some freshly baked cake. She sets it down and joins them as Al explains the entire situation.

But even after Al pours his heart out, Smokey shows no emotion whatsoever. "So, all that drug use has finally caught up with you."

Al's jaw drops; this isn't supposed to be a lecture. His hands clench his knees, in an effort to suppress his anger. "We all fooled around in the past, Smokey."

"Yeah, but like everything else, you took it to new heights."

"OK, I did. But my health is not what brings me here. It's my financial problems. We are broke and homeless, with no one to turn to."

Smokey turns and points to a large golden crucifix hanging over the fireplace. "You need someone to turn to? Turn to Jesus. Go to Jesus, Al, He will help you."

This only upsets Al; his tone changes. "Tell me what bank He's at, and I'll personally go there and meet the man."

Smokey's wife doesn't like confrontations, but their hearts go out to the two men. She takes hold of the empty tray and stands.

"Daryl, could you help me in the kitchen?" She pauses and waits for him to stand, but he doesn't move. "Please?"

Daryl looks at her, and then back at his dad. He wants to stay there and help him, but reluctantly goes along. "Sure, I'll be glad to help you," he replies, in the same nice tone she offered to him.

He follows her into the kitchen. The living room falls silent, and they are within earshot of the two men. She sets the tray down on the counter, and walks over to a large, ceramic cookie jar that Daryl can easily remember dipping into when he was a kid back in Detroit.

"Would you like a cookie? I just made them."

Daryl rubs his stomach. "Oh, no, thank you. That cake you made was delicious. I had four pieces, and now I'm stuffed."

She opens the cookie jar, and sticks her hand all the way to the bottom. Then she pulls her hand back out, and shoves it into his hand.

"I really think you should have one," she insists.

She squeezes it into his hand. It's not a cookie, but something else . . . paper. He glances down at the four one hundred-dollar bills that she slipped him. She puts her finger against her mouth for him to be quiet.

He places the money in his pocket, and mouths, "Thank you."

With a tender touch, she takes his face, and makes sure their eyes meet. "Listen to what your godfather said, turn your life over to Jesus. Trust me, Daryl, it's the best thing you can do for yourself and your father."

He doesn't give it much thought, but nods anyway. They walk back out to the living room, where the two men are close to having a full-blown argument. Daryl stays on his feet with his hands in his pockets. His fingers play with the hundred-dollar bills that she gave him.

"Dad, we should go," he says.

Al looks at him; his brow is crossed with frustration. "Do you have anywhere in mind? Because last I remembered, we don't have anywhere to go."

"No, I don't. But we've obviously worn out our welcome here, so we should leave."

Daryl starts to walk towards the door. Oddly, Al follows. It's out of character for him, but he leaves without saying the last word. Daryl hugs his godmother one more time, waves good-bye to Smokey, and then closes the door behind his father.

"Well, that was pleasant," Al says as he gets into the car. "I can't believe that man. I write him a best-selling album, and he can't toss me a dime."

Daryl starts the car and drives away. He wants to tell his dad about the money, but decides not to. He is afraid his father will give it to Jack to help with the new case, and Daryl knows they need the money to survive. With it they can find someplace to live, and buy some food. And if it's a cheap place, they can stay for a while, and work things out.

Al's head lowers with shame. "I never thought I would see the day that I would actually have to beg for money. And even worse, I dragged my son into this mess."

"You didn't drag me into anything; I made my own decision," he quietly replies, as he pulls onto the highway again.

"Where are you going?"

Daryl is in a rather somber mood. His eyes gaze far down the road, wishing he were somewhere else, somewhere far away. "While you were in the hospital, I slept in the car. Someone saw me, and gave me some information on a low-income shelter that's across the street from a soup kitchen. We can check into it, and have a place to sleep and something to eat."

Neither one ever foresaw it coming to this. Al had all the fame he wanted. People knew him and recognized his work and achievements, but unfortunately he had none of the fortune. Silence fills the car for the next few miles. They exit the highway and begin a long journey to the roughest part of town. All the nice buildings fade into the distance, and are replaced by ones covered with bars and graffiti. They drive past gangs that have nothing better to do than hang out on the street corner. Al watches as they drive past several abandoned and stripped cars. *I don't think anyone would want to steal my old clunker,* he thinks.

"We'll have a roof over our heads, as long as we don't get shot in the process."

Daryl smiles; that's the dad he wants to hear. "Remember we were talking about buying a nice big house?" His dad nods. "Well, this place is big; we just have a lot of houseguests."

Al chuckles, and shakes his head. "This is the pits."

"Yeah, but on the bright side, it can only get better, because we've already hit rock bottom."

They check into a very old hotel that seems to have been built before Al was born. To say it's run down would be a compliment. The building is in horrible shape. A fresh coat of paint was placed on its old boards sometime during the fifties. Dirty, open windows with bars on them face the street. Clothes that were washed in the sink hang on the bars to dry.

The cinder-block walls all around are covered in multicolored paint. It is the best attempt people can make to keep the gangs from marking their territory.

They stop in the dirty parking lot, and stare at the front office. Both contemplate sleeping inside the car instead. But they need an address and a phone to conduct business. Without those, Jack will never be able to find them, if he's able to make a settlement at all.

They get out of the car, and walk into the front office. A bell over the door rings as soon as they open it. The lobby consists of one stained, plastic chair and a half-dead plant. Dirt and pieces of paper lay in every corner. Smudges from a thousand dirty hands are everywhere.

It is so bad that neither man wants to touch anything. Instead, they feel as if they should don full chemical suits, and spray the entire building down.

"What ya need?" an overweight white man in a dirty tan tank top asks.

The man is grossly obese, and has a greasy, unshaven face. His balding head sports a slicked-back brown hairdo that ends in a ponytail. He chomps on a cigar that is covered in slobber. Al is still looking around. His stomach is turning at the sight of all the filth. Daryl steps forward, being careful not to touch anything.

"We need a room, please."

The heavy man moans as he stands up. The fat from his belly juts out from under his tank top. He looks them up and down twice, and then a third time. "You two sure are dressed nicely. I don't want any drugs in here."

Daryl shakes his head. "We don't have any drugs; we just need a room."

The man looks them up and down again, as if he were a drug-sniffing dog. "Right. Forty bucks for the week, cash. And I don't want any trouble. Clear?"

"Crystal." Al isn't looking, so he pulls out one of the hundred-dollar bills, and slaps it on the counter.

The man looks at the bill, and shakes his head. "You have a lot of cash for someone who doesn't deal drugs. I bet you both are wanted by the police." He pauses as his eyes narrow. "I watch *The FBI Files*. If they show either of you on the screen, I'm calling you both in."

Daryl's shoulders slump; he has had enough of the games. "Fine, you can go ahead and call them now. But in the meantime, can we have a room or not?"

The man slides out the hundred, and takes a closer look at it. "Sure thing, big money."

He gives Daryl back his change, and slides him an old key attached to a chunk of wood the size of a man's hand.

"Now don't ya go losing that key. You're in room thirty-four. That's on the third floor, Money. I don't want any trouble in here. The maximum amount of time anyone can stay here without kids is one month. Clear?"

"Crystal," he replies again, with a sigh.

They take the wooden plank with the key on it, and head upstairs via a narrow and dirty stairway. Al's steps are slow as he struggles to make it up the three flights of stairs. *As usual we have a place on the upper floor,* he tells himself, as he struggles to climb the stairs.

They climb up to the third floor, trying not to notice the cockroach scurrying to get out of the way. The hallway, which used to be white, has turned yellow over the years. Broken and chipped off-white tiles line the floor. Two screaming kids dart pass them, playing, as a third one chases them on a Big Wheel. They walk down a couple of doors. A hostile argument between a man and a woman comes up the hall from a closed door further down. The kids keep playing, as if nothing is wrong.

Daryl feels like he has just made a mistake by coming here; maybe they should have gotten a regular room at a regular motel.

"Sorry about this," he says to his dad, as if there was need to apologize.

"Don't be. This is the right thing to do. We have access to a phone, and we have an address—things we will need to settle this case. I am sure it will only take a few days to get some type of settlement." He keeps a positive attitude about it; he feels he has to—that way it will keep his son encouraged to carry on.

Daryl wiggles the key into the sticky lock and opens the heavy, steel, fireproof door, which is filled with gashes and nicks. Daryl lightly raps his knuckles on the metal door, and wonders if it is bulletproof too.

The room is a reflection of what is outside. It is small, very small, with one window. The room can barely hold the two twin beds and one nightstand. The beds are made of iron, and have army surplus blankets on them. The nightstand doesn't match anything in the room, and somehow manages to stand on three legs. A two-person kitchen table sits in the corner, with an eight-inch, black-and-white TV on it. In what they mistook at first for a closet is the kitchen. It has its own smaller window, which they didn't see before, and below that is a half-sized refrigerator. A single sink sits in the middle, with chunks of porcelain missing. It's just big enough for one person, and a thin one at that.

Al walks over to the bed by the window and opens it, hoping that the fresh air will overpower the musky, stale air inside.

"It will do." He says it more for himself than Daryl.

Daryl tosses the key on the other bed, and notices how the mattress is sunken in the middle. "I'll go down and get our luggage; you take it easy and rest."

That night they walk across the street to the soup kitchen. The food is prepared by a Baptist church a few blocks away. Homeless people from all around gather here to eat. Volunteers form a line behind the food tables, and fill up everyone's tray with turkey, gravy, and mashed potatoes. It's not a meal fit for a king, but for the starving, it's just as good.

Daryl quickly notices the volunteers; they all seem so happy. He can't help but smile back and say "hi" to a few who greet him. He wonders what keeps them going, time and time again, as they feed the masses.

The two men don't speak much at dinner; they are both busy watching the others move around. They keep trying to smell the food, and not the constant stench of body odor that someone is giving off in ample amounts.

Daryl's eyes shoot across the room as a clean-cut, well-dressed black man stands up on a crate to address everyone.

"Can I have your attention, please?" he says, in a loud booming voice. "I want to thank all of you for coming here. And praise the Lord for letting us have the food to serve all of you. As you know, we are having a service right in there." He points to a large room to his left. "It starts in fifteen minutes, and all of you are welcome to come and worship the Lord with us. Hope to see you there," he says, with one last smile before stepping down.

Let Jesus into your life. His godmother's words shoot into Daryl's head like a bullet.

His eyes suddenly open wide. "We should go," he whispers. "We should go, Dad," he says louder, making sure he heard it. "It will be fun."

Al looks at him as if a marble just fell out of his ear. "Daryl, I am exhausted; we've hardly slept in three days."

"Well." His dad was right, but he felt something—a calling, maybe. "I'm going to go, anyways."

"That's fine with me . . . Money. But just remember, when they pass the basket, just keep passing it, because we can't afford to give away any of that cash that was given to you."

Daryl's eyes narrow. "How did you know about that?" Al slowly stands and picks up his tray. A knowing smile that only a knowing father comes his face. "Please, son, I used to wipe your butt; there isn't anything I don't know about you."

They stack their dirty trays with all the others. Al heads back towards the small apartment, and Daryl walks over to the room for the service.

The room is a simple addition that was built a few years before. Up front, there is a small, two-foot-tall stage built out of untreated plywood, and one podium. There are no pews, just several rows of folding metal chairs. Daryl walks to the back. Although he can't explain why, he just doesn't want to sit too close to the front. He'll save those seats for the serious believers, he tells himself.

The service gets under way right on time. The pastor is obviously a good speaker, Daryl notes right from the beginning. He talks about love and forgiveness. His stories are full of life, and are sometimes quite humorous.

Halfway through the service, helpers begin to pass something out. Daryl figures it is the basket, and prepares himself to just let it pass, without putting anything in it. After all, his dad is right, they are down and out. But when it comes to him, he realized it isn't a basket; they are passing out small songbooks. Blood rushes to his cheeks; he feels embarrassed that he thought it was a collection basket.

They stand and begin to sing, as a woman gracefully plays a piano. Before Daryl has a chance to think about it, he finds himself singing the words aloud. It feels so good, as if a heavy weight is slowly being lifted off his chest.

After the service, he rushes back to the tiny apartment to tell his dad all about it. But Al is already fast asleep by the time he gets there. Daryl changes as quietly as possible, and makes sure his dad is covered up.

He is about to shut off the light when he notices a slender drawer in the three-legged nightstand. He hadn't seen the drawer before, and it seems to be calling him. The table wobbles as he pulls it open. There, hidden from sight, is a worn-out Bible, with several whole chapters missing. Although very tired, he pulls it out and reads some of it before going to sleep.

* * *

Day after day, Daryl repeats the same process. He looks for work all day long, but the country is in a recession, so jobs are very hard to come by. He does manage to line up a few day jobs that pay cash. They help, but they don't do much for getting them out of the bind that they are in.

"Dad, last night I accepted Jesus Christ as my savior," Daryl says. As much as he tries not to, his voice is still filled with excitement.

He stares at his dad as they eat another meal at the soup kitchen. He has been waiting all day to tell him about it. He felt it would need the proper moment, and this is a close as it would likely get.

"Did you hear me?" he asks, after not receiving any response.

Al takes a healthy bite of his sandwich, and chomps on it briefly. "Yeah. That's great, son. Do you get a medal or a certificate with that?"

The comment is odd, and out of character for his father. Daryl's lips become tight with anger.

"No, but—"

"I know, maybe the Almighty could give us a job. Or, better yet, some money, so we can get out of this stinking hellhole."

Al tosses his sandwich down, and walks away. Daryl's head lowers in disappointment. He prays that, somehow, his father will grow to accept Jesus too.

"At least he gave you a healthy son that cares," he whispers.

Guilty feelings find their way into Al's heart before he makes it to the stairs that go up their apartment. It's not that he's mad at his son; in fact, he is very proud of him. It's just that he knows that their one-month time limit is running out. Al has made several dozen calls to his lawyer, with no luck at all. The same goes for finding Ron. If they thought it was the end of the road last time, what's in store for them now?

Out of breath and shaking, he makes it to their tiny room. The heart condition is becoming worse with each passing day, although some days are worse than others. This is a bad day. He glances in the mirror at his own reflection. He still considers the inevitability of death, and it continues to scare him. He imagines himself cold and stiff, laying in a coffin, with his son staring at him. *Will Daryl be sad? Will he miss me? Will anyone miss me?* he asks himself.

In an attempt to push these thoughts from his mind, he looks over to the nightstand. There on top lies Daryl's new Bible. Al hadn't bothered to argue about the money he spent on it. It was so important to his son to have one of his own. Now he reads it every night. Somehow the sight of the Holy Book calms him.

As the days continue to go by, Al's worries begin to turn into fear. And what makes matters worse, in his eyes, is the fact that Daryl doesn't seem to be worrying at all. He has this look as if everything is going to work out. It appears that Daryl has a magical umbrella that every care and worry bounce off of, and provides hope for better days down the road. It is obviously ridiculous.

They are down to two days left. The once-disgusting apartment that they didn't want to touch is now home, and they don't want to give it up. They walk over to the soup kitchen for another dinner, as Al envisions them sleeping under a bridge next week. He forges a smile as he thinks about gathering cardboard boxes to build their next home.

After they eat, Daryl goes to the service, and Al heads back home, telling his son that he and Jesus haven't walked down the same road in years. He is running out of excuses for not going, but still sticks to his guns, and stays clear of anything remotely religious.

As Al walks out into the parking lot, he notices a group of people standing around a man. Most of the people he knows are regulars at the soup kitchen. But the man in the center is someone new. Curiosity gets the best of him, so he goes over to investigate.

The man stands five foot eight, and that is with his black cowboy boots on. His curly brown hair is in desperate need of a cut, and he hasn't shaved in several days. He is wearing a gray, wrinkled suit that looks as if it's been slept in. As Al gets closer, he can smell alcohol on the man's breath. Others turn and start walking away. Al figures there is nothing to see, so he turns around as well.

"What's your story?" the man asks.

Al turns around and points to his chest. "Me?"

"Yeah, you. What's your story?" The man walks over, takes a silver flask out of his gray coat pocket, and drinks whatever whiskey he poured into it last. "You have a story, don't you?"

Al stands there with his eyebrows crossed, not too sure of how to handle this strange man. Without warning, the man suddenly sticks out his hand. Al resists the urge to jump back.

"R. J. Stewart." He said it loud and clear, as if everyone should know him.

"Al Cleveland."

He offers a cautious handshake, but R. J. grabs it with both of his, and gives a friendly squeeze. As they shake hands, Al can hear the whiskey slosh around in the flask. His stubble-covered face smiles broadly, as if they are long lost friends.

"I run the R. J. Stewart Traveling Sideshow. You know, kind of a mini-circus, with a few animals, jugglers, that kind of thing."

"That's nice," Al replies, gently pulling his hand back, and wiping it on his pants. "My son and I are songwriters."

R. J.'s eyebrows raise, as if Al's words are magic. He pulls the cap off the flask for another drink, and points at Al as he eagerly gulps down another mouthful. "I bet you two know how to set up a stage, don't you?"

Al nods, wondering where this is going. "We've done a few in our time."

"That's great; I need a pair of stagehands for my show. The pay is crap," he says, slightly slurring his words. He is obviously more intoxicated that Al had previously thought. "In fact, there is no pay. But there is free room and board wherever we go."

Al leans forward a bit, and tilts his head towards R. J. "Did you say free room and board?"

"Yes. And no pay. I said that too, right?"

"Yes, you stated that; your pay is crap."

R. J. glances at his wrist for a wristwatch that must have been there sometime before. "So, does that mean you want the job? Because we leave tomorrow morning." He stops, and stumbles slightly. "You got a car?"

Visions of a drunken man riding in the backseat and puking everywhere quickly develop in Al's mind. "Yes, we do," he replies, unsure what the outcome of his answer will be.

"Great, you're hired; follow me."

He waves him with his hand, stumbles again, and walks away. Al follows R. J. to the back of the large parking lot. There Al finds the rest of the circus performers, practicing and goofing off. He is introduced to all of them. And, just as R. J. told him, they are in need of a couple of stagehands. It's not much of an opportunity, but it will provide them with a roof over their heads, and food in their stomachs.

CHAPTER 26

Months later, the Clevelands are still homeless and working for R. J. Their new place to call home is the eastern part of Washington, near Spokane. They've been on the road ever since, living out of their suitcases and motel rooms. It is by no means an extravagant life. But it is one step above the homeless shelter they were in.

Just as R. J. told them, there is no pay. But the room and board are free. If they are in one spot for longer than a day, Daryl goes out looking for odd jobs that pay cash. That way, they still have some type of money coming in. Daryl continues going to church whenever he can. His faith grows stronger, as do his prayers for his father to see the light.

Al manages to receive a few small royalty checks here and there. But what is left over after the IRS garnishes it is hardly worth seeing. The stress he feels about it causes his heart condition to worsen. He can no longer stand for any longer than ten minutes without his head spinning. His legs and face are always swollen. Daryl does most of the work, just so his dad can rest.

"The bastard who runs the spotlight quit on me," R. J. states one day, as he plops down next to Al on a set of bleachers.

The traveling road show is in a small auditorium. It's their third night here. They had decided to stay longer because the crowds have been a reasonably good size. R. J. takes another drink, as he does on a continuous basis.

Daryl comes over, and sits down with them. He is in a good mood. He just finished working in a garage all day, sweeping floors and changing oil. The owner of the garage was generous, and paid him a hundred bucks. Daryl has almost a thousand stashed away in his suitcase. He knows one of these cities is going to catch his attention, that he and his dad are going to get a real life, and a place of their own.

"That bastard who runs the spotlight quit on me," R. J. states again, as if the others should be in shock.

Neither of the Clevelands bothers to say anything. Workers and performers quit all the time. Some get other jobs; others become fed up when they find out that R. J. drinks away the money.

"Bastard," he mumbles, while looking at his silver flask. He begins to pout. "The show starts in ten minutes too."

Even though he doesn't have a watch, R. J. always seemed to know when the show is supposed to start and stop. It might just depend on how sober he is at the moment. But nonetheless, it works.

"Daryl," he shouts, as if he was across the way.

Daryl sits up, and looks at him oddly. "I'm right here, R. J."

"Congratulations, you are my new spotlight man."

He waves his hand for his new man to get to work. Quickly Daryl looks over to the spotlight perched up on the balcony. He has never run one before.

"I don't know what to do."

R. J. seems unaffected by the comment. "You just turn it on and shoot. You'd better hurry up and get there; the show starts in eight minutes."

The gates open; a small stream of people come in and begin to take their seats. It's not a sell-out show, but enough to pay the bills. Daryl jogs up to the spotlight, and prepares to turn it on. The opening act comes onstage; several clowns are running around in a comical act, chasing a pink poodle.

Daryl flicks the switch for the powerful light, but nothing happens. The act continues as a juggler comes out and starts tossing bowling pins into the air with ease. Daryl flicks the switch two more times, and then realizes that it isn't plugged in yet. He jumps down, and dashes over to the wall. He plugs it in. Zap. The light comes on, blinding the juggler. The pins come streaking down, crashing on top of the juggler's head. The audience breaks out in hysterical laughter as the juggler stumbles around, seeing stars.

R. J. can't help but laugh too, as he slaps his knee several times. He leans over to Al. "I'm going to double your son's pay. I have always hated that juggler."

* * *

Almost two full years go by. Life on the road is getting old for Al and Daryl. They have stopped in Reno, Nevada, and their next stop will be Las Vegas. Both of them are wondering if they will ever see or hear from Ron again.

Daryl's pleas for his dad to turn to Jesus have had an effect on Al, although his son doesn't know it. While Daryl is out doing side jobs, he secretly reads his son's Bible. He finds himself drawing closer, but pride gets in the way of his talking to Daryl about it.

Then one lonely night it happens. Al feels something in his chest; it's not pain, but an empty hole slowly being filled, filled with love. It's nothing anyone can explain; it can only be felt. He reads the Book of John in the Bible, and suddenly his breaths become short and choppy. His lips quiver with buried, forgotten emotions. He tries to stifle his tears, but he can't; they just keep rolling down his cheeks.

"Forgive me, Jesus, for you are my savior," he whispers, in a shaky voice. He has known it all along, but has never said it.

The door to their small room opens, and Daryl walks in. Al quickly puts the Bible to the side, and attempts to wipe the tears away.

"Dad?" Daryl's mouth gapes open, as confusion fills his mind. What could possibly be so wrong? "Dad, are you all right?"

Al sits up, sniffles, and wipes away the last tear that escaped. He tries to talk, but he is still too choked up. Daryl comes over, and kneels in front of Al, placing his hand on his dad's swollen legs.

"Do you need a doctor?"

Al smiles and laughs. Without warning, he reaches out and gives his son a long and hard hug. "I love you, Daryl, and I am so proud of you."

Daryl hugs him back, and then pulls away. "I love you too." His voice is small, distant, and confused. Suddenly his eyebrows go up. "Have you been reading my Bible?"

Although there is no reason to be embarrassed, Al smiles, and looks away. "He is my savior too," he whispers.

Daryl jumps up, his hands held high enough to touch the ceiling. "Praise the Lord, praise the Lord!" he shouts. "This is what I've been praying for, Dad. Trust Him; everything is going to work out."

Al nods, although he doesn't quite have the faith that Daryl has.

Daryl claps his hands as he grins. "I made a few extra bucks today. What do you say we go out to eat tonight and celebrate?"

"That sounds great."

Daryl darts off to the bathroom to freshen up. Al moans as he bends over to put his shoes on. The loud ringer on their phone causes him to jump into the air. He sits up again, and stares at the phone as it rings once more. Daryl walks out and looks at it too. There is only one person that he gave their number to—their lawyer, Jack.

"Pick it up, Dad."

Al reaches over and grabs the phone as it rings again.

"Hello? Hey, Jack, it's me, Al. I'm doing fine, how are you?" Suddenly he stops; his body stiffens with excitement. "Sure, sure, I can give you the address here."

He snaps his fingers, and Daryl runs around the room until he finds a business card with the motel's address on it. Al reads it off to him.

"Can you overnight that to me?" Al asks. He pauses for a moment. "That's great; thanks a lot. I owe you."

He slowly hangs up the phone, and sits on the edge of the bed, his heart racing with the news.

"Well?" Daryl blurts out.

Al stands; a smile is waiting to explode onto his face. "He got us a partial settlement. It's not much, but—"

"But what; how much is it?" Daryl asks, the anticipation killing him.

"It's ten thousand bucks, and it will be here tomorrow!"

"Yeah!" Daryl hollers, as he jumps up and down. "Yeah! We can leave for Vegas tomorrow. We can stop doing this, settle down, get a place to live, and have a real life."

* * *

The next day the check arrives, just like Jack said. The two rejoice with the good news as they pack for the eight-hour drive to Las Vegas. They tell R. J. that they are quitting. Neither one of them are sure he understands; he is extremely intoxicated, as usual.

Daryl helps his father walk to the car. Al's steps are slow and cautious. It's only about twenty yards, but it might as well be twenty miles for him. Over the last few months, his condition has gotten worse, and walking is becoming a bigger chore. Daryl helps him sit down, and closes the door. They are about to leave, when one of the clowns comes over. His name is Mark, and he is a short, round little man with a bursting laugh and a balding head. In front of him, he pushes a folded-up wheelchair.

"Why don't you guys take this? It'll help your dad get around. No one here has used it in years."

"Thank you."

Daryl smiles and hugs the short man; they have been friends for some time. He takes the wheelchair, and slips it into the trunk of the car. It was kind of sad to receive it; it means that the reality of his father's deteriorating condition is obvious to everyone.

The miles pass quickly under the old car, and they make it to Las Vegas late that day. As with most days in the dusty valley, the sky is bright blue. It is in the spring, so the temperatures are still reasonable, even in the midafternoon. The first thing they do is look up their friend Ron Jolley, but he no longer lives here; he has moved on. To where, they don't know.

With growling stomachs, they stop in a fast-food restaurant for a bite to eat, and to get the local paper. Daryl gets out of the car, and looks at all the cars passing by. Once again, they see that Las Vegas is a city that is growing by leaps and bounds.

"There's a big mall right across the street," Daryl says, as he gets the wheelchair out.

"That could be a place for you to hang out, and look at the girls going by."

Al laughs and then stops, as the blood rushes to his head from a simple movement. "You think we can find a place around here?"

"I'm sure we can. The whole other side of the street is filled with apartments."

They eat their late dinner, and begin looking in the paper. As luck would have it, there are available apartments directly across the street. The rent is within their price range, so they decide to take a drive over.

The office is about to close when they walk in. Daryl quickly gets out of the car, and grabs the wheelchair again. He pushes his dad up the ramp and into the door as the landlord is about to flip the sign from open to closed.

"Hi. I saw an ad in the paper about an apartment for rent," Daryl explains, holding out the paper. "I was wondering if maybe we could see it?"

The hardened, weatherworn man with thinning gray hair and steely blue eyes looks them up and down. He can spot trouble from a mile away, and he can also see honest folks. A warm smile forms on his face.

"Where are you two from?"

"Pittsburgh, originally." It took a second for Daryl to answer, as lately they are from everywhere.

The landlord steps outside and takes a breath of fresh air before lighting up a cigarette. "We do have one place with wheelchair access. It's the old pool house. We converted it a while back. But the lady who had it passed away."

"I'm sorry to hear that," Al says.

The landlord shrugs. "It's all right. She was ninety-eight years old; we can't live forever." They walk down the sidewalk towards the pool. The smell of chlorine and other chemicals makes its way into their noses. The older landlord retrieves a ring filled with keys from his pocket, and begins to thumb through them as they come closer to the front door.

The outside appears promising. Nice trees and shrubs dot a freshly cut lawn. Kids can be heard playing in the background. All the buildings are covered in stucco and painted light brown, and the steel doors are a dark red. It's nothing too flashy, but it will definitely do.

The door swings wide open, and they stare into a rather spacious living room. The carpet is new, and the paint is so fresh that the plug and light switch covers are still off. Daryl pushes his father up the small ramp, and into the fresh-smelling apartment.

The kitchen is just off to the left, with the usual small dining room. In the back are two fairly large bedrooms and two bathrooms. Both men approve, looking forward to having a place of their own again.

"I like it," Al says. "This place is very nice."

The landlord smiles with pride; he is the one who fixed it up.

"Thank you. My wife and I have worked hard to keep it up. No one has made an offer yet, so if you want it, it's yours. But I will need first and last months' rent, and a security deposit. Of course we have to do a background check first.

Both know that they don't do well with background checks—they've been on the road for so long, it looks like a questionable background. Daryl speaks up. "What if we pay all those, plus the first three months in cash? Would that be a problem?"

The landlord's eyes light up with dollar signs. "Oh, no, no problem. We do cash just fine around here.

"Good, then we'll take it," Al replies.

* * *

Six months later, Daryl comes home from his job at the airport. Things have been working out well for them, and they are finally on their feet again. The apartment is now fully furnished, and has everything they could want.

Al's heath is still fading. The only way he can get around is in the wheelchair. Al's doctor gives Daryl a bottle of liquid morphine for the bad days, when and if they come. Daryl hopes it won't ever come to that.

"Hey, Dad, what ya doing?" he asks, as he sticks his head in the door to check up on him. It's nine at night, and Daryl has just gotten off of work.

Al is lying in his bed, already under the covers. The clothes that he wore are folded neatly on the side, indicating that he must have gone to the mall while his son was at work. His own Bible is resting on his chest, slowly going up and down with his deep breaths, as he stares out at the wall.

"Nothing," he says with a smile, feeling peace in his heart. His voice is soft and soothing. "Just sitting here, relaxing."

Daryl comes in the room, and heads for the TV. "Do you want me to put on M*A*S*H for you?"

"No, not tonight."

This strikes Daryl as odd; his father loves his sitcoms. He loves watching funny shows. "You feeling all right?"

"Have I ever told you that I love you, son?"

He smiles, and sits down next to him on the bed. "Yeah, but I never get tired of hearing it."

"I was thinking back about all the crap Motown put me through. All that stress putting me into an early grave. And none of it really matters. All that really matters is this," he says, patting the Bible. "Right there in front of me, and I choose to close my eyes and walk away."

"Well, I'm glad you made the right choice now."

His voice becomes softer, and more distant. "I'm telling you this because it's my last day here on Earth."

Daryl's heart sinks for a brief moment, and then he smiles. "Knock it off, Dad," he says, nudging him. His digital watch beeps, and he glances at it. "Oh, it's time for your medication. I'll go get it."

"Could you please get me the phone first?"

"Sure." Daryl picks up the phone and hands it to him. "Who are you going to call?" he asks on the way out.

"Your mom."

Daryl stops in his tracks. His voice shoots up several octaves. "Mom? Why are you calling her?"

"Because I want to. Now, if you'll excuse me."

Daryl continues to look at him oddly, and then walks out of the room. Al picks up the phone and begins dialing. He listens to it ring several times, until a tired voice comes over.

"Hello?"

"Hello, Ella; it's me, Al."

There is silence for a few seconds as Ella wakes up. Her head, clogged with dreams, slowly turns back to the real world. "Al, do you have any idea what time it is?" She isn't too upset, as she begins to worry that something might be wrong.

"I know exactly what time it is. I just wanted to talk to you."

Ella slowly sits up in her dark room. Al's voice sounds so different, so caring and nice. She turns on a lamp on her nightstand, as if the light will help her hear better. She squints from the bright light, and tries to think of the last time they spoke; it was almost a year ago. Maybe longer.

"What did you want to talk about?" she asks.

"Mistakes. I have made a lot of mistakes in my life. And now I am sure that number one on that list was leaving you."

Ella is about to stand and stretch, but instead she falls back down onto the bed. She can't believe he just said that. Never in a million years would she have ever guessed that he would admit it. Her eyes search the room, as if the reason for him calling would be written on one of the walls.

He takes a deep breath, and speaks again. "I want you to know something. You're a beautiful woman, and I have and always will love you. No matter what, Ella, I will love you with all my heart."

He wasn't expecting any big fanfare or a parade, but the silence on the phone is extreme. Then he hears her sniffle.

"Are you crying?" he asks, with a slight smile.

"Yes," she replies softly, with a trembling voice. "I love you too, Al, and I miss you so much. I just wish things could have worked out better for us."

"Maybe we can be together in heaven. I know a good woman like yourself is going to be there. And I'm going to sneak in by the skin of my teeth."

She laughs, and wipes away a few tears. "Thank you, Al."

They talk for a few more minutes, then Al says good-bye and hangs up the phone.

Daryl comes back into the room with a glass of water and a handful of pills. He takes the phone away, and gives him the pills. Al yawns, and doesn't try to hide it.

"Do you want me to turn the TV on?" Daryl asks. Every night, Al sleeps with the TV on.

He shakes his head. "Not tonight, son. I want to listen to some Nat King Cole on my headphones."

He takes his medicine as Daryl sits down by his side again. His dad is acting unusually calm. Al takes his Walkman and sets it on his chest. With a tender touch, he takes his son's hand.

"I'm real proud of you, son. You've done a fine job on growing up." He pauses for a moment, and stares deeply into his eyes. "You're safe now."

Daryl's brow crunches down. "What do you mean, safe?"

"You have a decent job, a roof over your head, and food on the table. You don't need me anymore."

"I will always need you." Daryl kisses him on the forehead. "I love you. See you in the morning."

Al puts on his headset and turns on the tape, as Daryl shuts the light off. "Thank you for all you've done for me, Lord," he whispers.

*   *   *

The next morning, Daryl's alarm clock goes off, sending soft, musical tones into the air. He can't help but smile as an oldies station plays "I Second That Emotion." He figures it is a great way to wake up.

The first order of business is to get his dad his medicine; it's the same every morning. With his eyes still half shut, and humming his dad's song, he walks out into the kitchen for a glass of water. The apartment is silent. He listens closer for his dad's TV, which is usually on. But this time, it's not.

"Good morning, Dad," he says in a cheerful voice, as he walks into his dad's bedroom.

Al is lying there with his eyes closed, and a small smile on his face. It appears that he is thinking about something good. Daryl sets the glass of water down, and opens the drapes just a little. The room suddenly looks very bright, as a single ray of sunlight streaks in.

Daryl looks at Al. It's odd that his dad didn't wake up; he is a very light sleeper.

"Dad?"

He stands there for a moment and waits, but there is no movement. Cautiously he reaches out and takes his dad's hand. It's still warm, but it does not move. Daryl's heart begins to feel lonely. His fingers search down his dad's wrist for a pulse, but there isn't any. His mouth drops open, as if all words have been stolen from him. There is no need to do anything else; he knows what has happened.

Daryl's eyes instantly well up with tears. His knees give way, and he collapses to the ground next to the bed.

"Oh, Dad."

He stays by his side for ten more minutes, just staring at him and hoping that he will wake up and take a bath. But he doesn't; he doesn't move at all.

Slowly Daryl stands again, and walks out into the living room. His mind is a blur as he considers what he now needs to do. He leans on the counter, feeling lost and lonely. The warm, loving apartment now feels cold and empty. He glances at the phone, and then calls the mortuary.

A half hour later, two men in a white van pull up. They are older, clean-cut, and quiet. They ask Daryl to leave the room as they put Al into a black body bag. It's hard for Daryl to walk out, to leave his dad there alone. But he does it anyway.

He stays out in the living room, staring at the TV that isn't on. The men open the bedroom door and pull the gurney out, with Al in the body bag. Tears begin to flow down Daryl's cheeks at the sight of the black bag. He doesn't try to stop crying as he follows them outside.

"Wait," he says as they make it out the front door.

Daryl stops them. He places his hand on the bag; he feels like he has already forgotten what his dad looks like. He looks at the two older men for guidance. Only one is watching him; the other respectfully has his head down. "It's OK if you want to look again," the man says softly.

Daryl unzips the bag, and looks at his father's lifeless face. He seems so peaceful, as if he is just resting. Slowly he bends over, and kisses Al on the forehead one last time. A single tear drips off, and lands on Al's cheek. This is the moment he has been preparing himself for all along. But as it turns out, he isn't nearly as ready as he thought he would be. He tries to zip up the bag, but can't bring himself to do it. One of the men gently zips it up for him. Then he walks out the rest of the way to the van with them, and watches them load Al up. Daryl gently taps the van twice, and they leave.

Greed killed my father, he thinks. *All he wanted to do was write and sing songs. Although that dream came true, he was never allowed to enjoy the full appreciation of his work. But I am still grateful that we were the best of friends, through the good times and the bad, the laughter and the tears. I love him so much, and I will deeply miss him.*

THE END

For sales, editorial information, subsidiary rights information
or a catalog, please write or phone or e-mail
Brick Tower Press
1230 Park Avenue, 9a
New York, NY 10128, US
Sales: 1-800-68-BRICK
Tel: 212-427-7139
www.BrickTowerPress.com
email: bricktower@aol.com

www.Ingram.com

For sales in the UK and Europe please contact our distributor,
Gazelle Book Services
Falcon House, Queens Square
Lancaster, LA1 1RN, UK
Tel: (01524) 68765 Fax: (01524) 63232
stef@gazellebooks.co.uk

Lightning Source UK Ltd.
Milton Keynes UK
UKOW05f1804061116

287002UK00023B/442/P